W9-BTP-861

Sexuality
and
Catholicism

SEXUALITY AND CATHOLICISM

by Thomas C. Fox

❖ ❖ ❖

GEORGE BRAZILLER
New York

First published in the United States in 1995 by George Braziller, Inc.

For further information, please address the publisher:

GEORGE BRAZILLER, INC.
60 Madison Avenue
New York, New York 10010

Library of Congress Cataloging-in-Publication Data:
Fox, Thomas C. (Thomas Charles), 1944-
Sexuality and Catholicism / Thomas C. Fox.
p. cm.
Includes bibliographical references and index.
ISBN 0-8076-1396-7
1. Sex—Religious aspects—Catholic Church. 2. Catholic Church—Doctrines. I. Title.
BX1795.S48F7 1995 95-6367
241'.66'08822--dc20 CIP

Book design by RITA LASCARO
Printed and bound in the United States

Second printing, 1995

Contents

In gratitude
for many blessings,
to Hoa,
in this, our twenty-fifth year
of marriage.

Acknowledgments

Some years back two newspaper editors, Neal Shine and William Serrin, encouraged me to write about the Catholic Church when I was a reporter at the *Detroit Free Press*. They said it was a good story. I followed their advice and am grateful to them for putting me on the course that led to this book. Adrienne Baxter of George Braziller, Inc., Publishers had the idea for this book. For her encouragement I owe her gratitude. My colleague Arthur Jones has been especially encouraging, even long before I sat down to write the manuscript. This book would not have taken shape without the helpful feedback of other colleagues at the *National Catholic Reporter*, including Michael Farrell, Nancy Vaught, Leslie Wirpsa, Tom Roberts, Chris Curry, Robin Edwards, Robert Folsom, Demetria Martinez, Dorothy Vidulich, Toni Ortiz, and our company's publisher, William McSweeney. Jean Blake, my assistant, was enormously helpful, especially in her reference research and for maintaining a first-rate library. I owe special gratitude to Patty McCarty and Richard G. Gallin for their copyediting and fact-checking assistance. Others who provided encouragement and assistance included Charles Curran, Jeannine Gramick, Robert Nugent, Madonna Kolbenschlag, Thomas A. Shannon, Rosemary Radford Ruether, Joan Carlton, Ken Briggs, Joan Chittister, Carol Meyer, Clarence Thomson, Jim Conlon, and Dan Grippo. My children, Daniel, Christine, and Catherine, endured more conversation about the book than they deserved. They are always inspirations. Finally, I would never have been able to take on the project without the spiritual, emotional, and physical support of my wife, Hoa.

Preface

On the eve of its third millennium, Catholicism seems unsure of its identity. An uncertainty affects many of the nearly 1 billion people who call themselves Catholic and who look to the church for guidance. Discontent festers; Catholics are divided. Meanwhile, in the past quarter century a rift has grown between official church pronouncements and the practices of tens of millions of Catholics. Many have simply stopped listening to their bishops.

At the heart of this malaise and division rests the Catholic Church's teachings on sexuality. Unlike any other time in Catholic memory, the response of the faithful to these issues has become in some quarters of the church a measure of orthodoxy. It is deeply ironic that this should happen. Jesus said almost nothing about sexuality. His message focused on compassion and forgiveness. It is that very message that many Catholics, including priests, nuns, and even bishops, fear is getting lost as the Vatican focuses on sex and gender issues. These are serious charges and represent widespread feelings within the church.

The times call for dialogue, for creative responses to a host of global problems—rapidly expanding populations in less developed nations, the prevalence of sexually transmitted diseases, the sanctioned abuse of women in many societies, to name just a few. Religion needs to play a key role in the quest for harmony. However, the all too frequent impression is that the Catholic hierarchy, which should be in the forefront of these crises, stays apart from the real world, issuing absolutist statements. The result has been to lessen church influence by keeping it out of broader moral conversations. Instead of reasoned persuasion, the Vatican appears to utter unequivocal condemnations. It prohibits all forms of artificial birth control, rejects sterilization and abortion in every circumstance, and condemns in vitro fertilization and reproductive technologies that replace sexual intercourse. And to the women who feel marginalized, entirely out of the church's authority structure and decision-making process, the Vatican says never to women's ordination.

And yet the church, as always, has much to offer. Pope John Paul II's March 1995 encyclical, *Evangelium Vitae* ("The Gospel of Life"), addressing a growing "Culture of Death," reaffirms the sacredness of life. It is a message the world desperately needs to hear. The Vatican's approach and the method of theology that drives that approach, however, force absolute teachings and rigid moral condemnations that mix birth control with abortion, sterilization with euthanasia; in the end, benefits from the Vatican's approach are greatly diminished. Many Catholics and others who have found the Vatican's proclamations too sweeping and unyielding have abandoned the church; others who stay find it difficult to engage their children and pass on their religious beliefs. The pronouncements don't make sense in their lives.

In addition, all too frequent reports of priests molesting children have driven laypeople even further away. Church leaders downplay the importance of these reports, saying all organizations have "a few bad apples." Others, however, see in these reports pervasive illness within the institution of the male, celibate priesthood. Despite dwindling numbers in seminaries and a widely perceived drop in the quality of young men willing to enter the priesthood, church leaders adamantly resist studying the problem. They will not allow discussion of optional celibacy.

For the past fifteen years as editor of the *National Catholic Reporter*, I have witnessed these complex issues unfold. I have seen their often harmful effects on the lives of countless Catholics and on the policies of governments worldwide. *Sexuality and Catholicism* looks at the critical sexuality questions facing the Catholic Church as it enters the twenty-first century. This book presents the histories, backgrounds, people, and theologies that have brought Catholicism to this juncture. It attempts to tell the Catholic sexuality story in a straightforward, comprehensible way. It is my hope that a better understanding of the issues will assist Catholics and members of the broader community in a healing process and will help them move past a point of polarization to an acceptance of sexuality and faith as gifts of a loving Creator.

Thomas C. Fox
Roeland Park, Kansas
May 1, 1995

I

❖ ❖ ❖

Sexuality and the Christian Tradition

The story of the Catholic Church and human sexuality begins with Genesis and the Adam and Eve narrative. For twenty centuries, it has been a tale of virtuous faith, hope, and love. It has also been one of ignorance, fear, corruption, and abusive power. More than any other institution, Roman Catholicism has molded Western values and morality. Catholics and non-Catholics alike have been shaped by the religion. Now approaching 1 billion members, the church is vibrant and expanding rapidly in many parts of Latin America, Africa, and Asia. For the first time in its history, Catholicism is no longer merely Western; it has truly become a global religion. Meanwhile, its influence extends well beyond church limits. Today, Catholic leaders shape the policies and politics of nations throughout the world.

As Catholicism faces its third millennium of belief, its

endurance hardly needs to be questioned. The church ought to have much reason for optimism and hope. Yet the contrary appears to be the case. Evidence mounts that the religion is ill, even seriously so. In Europe many churches are empty. Throughout the West, church teachings fail to hold the young. They alienate women by the millions. Priests are overworked, and many demoralized. Church pronouncements frequently go unheeded. The faithful are divided, seemingly as never before. Why so much pain in a religion that ultimately professes hope?

The good news is that the illness does not appear to stem from basic doctrine: faith in a Trinitarian Deity, a loving Creator, compassionate Redeemer, and guiding Spirit remains very much alive. The bad news is that the illness appears to be woven into a Catholic fabric that makes up much of twenty centuries of sexual teachings supported by a moral theology that for now appears intractable. It is the hope of this book that the telling of the Catholic Church's story of sexuality will lead to greater understanding and perhaps even to healing. There is enormous pain here. So too is there much energy. Catholic attitudes toward sexual matters are changing, in some cases rapidly. This is happening even as official teachings stand firm, adding again to anxieties and church tensions. Hearing the story that has knotted a religion might in itself have a salutary effect. Once described, sized up, and assessed, Catholic sexuality might better find its proper proportion and place. Empowered by such knowledge, it could even free Catholics and others, often confused or immobilized by church teachings on these matters, to get on with their lives and the works of mercy the Catholic religion is intended to preach.

The word *Catholic* comes from the Greek adjective *katho-*

likos, meaning "universal," the goal of the faith. The term was first used to describe the church by St. Ignatius of Antioch near the end of the first century.[1] Catholicism involves many things: personal faith, a sense of community, culture, a way of life. It also involves spiritualities, theologies, and doctrines. It shapes the moral outlook of believers—but not precisely for each person in the same way. Catholics share much but are a diverse lot. This is especially so as ancient tradition increasingly mixes with indigenous cultures.

The Catholic faith is grounded in core beliefs: Life is a gift of the Creator. It is sacred. The entire human family has been mysteriously created in God's image, that is, it shares a divine spirit. Each person, therefore, possesses human dignity—and this must not be violated. Sin, meanwhile, has cast a veil over existence; the human story is full of failed, sinful efforts.

Jesus, possessing both a divine and human nature, came into the world to redeem it and to set example. His was a life of compassion and forgiveness. In the end, the church's mission is simple, or is supposed to be: Catholics are called to be faithful to the words and life of Jesus the Nazorean.

Further, the church teaches that divine Revelation—God's communication to humanity—lives on within it. The faith holds that from generation to generation the church is guided by the Holy Spirit and is, therefore, both a human and divine creation; it is subject to human failings but guards and articulates essential Christian truths.

Catholicism also holds that Revelation ended with the death of the last apostle. New insights and clarifications, however, shape the faith as they are proclaimed, increasingly understood in the light of the different historical and cultural circumstances of the faithful. This is why the church has strongly disagreed with a sole emphasis on Scripture alone. This is why most Catholics do not get swept into fundamentalism. Speaking of Catholicism, the word *Scripture,* goes hand in hand with *tradition.* The two are inseparable. Together, they constitute the faith. It is in this light that Catholicism remains a "living religion." The manner in which Catholicism maintains this life can be a hotly debated matter among the Catholic faithful. This is especially so when it involves the most personal of moral matters, human sexuality.

Today's experience is tomorrow's tradition—or can be. What becomes tradition—what gets clarified from experience—is the work of the teaching church, or the teaching magisterium, the bishops who work with theologians. The church teaches that Scripture must always be understood in light of the ideas of the time. For Catholics to better understand their faith, church leaders gather from time to time to proclaim new truths or denounce heresy. They do this at ecumenical councils. Only twenty-one have taken place through twenty centuries of Catholic history, the most recent having been the Second Vatican Council, or Vatican II, in Rome (1962–65).

Scripture is the starting point of faithful reflection. However, it does not concern itself much with sex. Efforts to find a systematic presentation of a moral sexual ethic will be found wanting. Neither the Old nor the New Testament offers much specific guidance. (The same, of course, is true of peace or social or political ethics.) While the Bible contains many references to sex and some concrete demands, it offers only a few general directions such as "Be fertile and multiply" (Genesis 1:28 NAB) or "You shall not commit adultery" (Exodus 20:14).[2] The Catholic tradition looks to Scripture for guidance but views it only as the starting point. Additionally, many advances in Scripture scholarship have taken place in recent decades, with a focus toward a keener understanding of historical and cultural contexts. Scripture scholars no longer want to know only what a word says, but what it *meant* at the time it was written.

Catholic Scripture scholarship, meanwhile, has made revolutionary advances as scholars have begun to apply developing insights from the social sciences. Increasingly, scholars now want to know who wrote the words of Scripture, when, and what their intentions where at the time. Also considered to be of importance is the access an author had to the events about which he wrote. Much contemporary Catholic biblical scholarship, then, delves into textual, literary, and historical sources to cast new light on long-held beliefs and moral interpretations.

Catholic theologians speak of attempting to formulate a "reasoned faith," one that employs human intelligence to gain understanding of God's will for humanity. Of course, people in different places and in different times reason differently and come to different conclusions after they do. So there are many Catholic theologies. The Jesuits, for example, and the Dominicans have frequently not seen eye to eye, although both are religious orders and both have placed much emphasis on teaching theology. Being Catholic means being part of a church that seems forever to be discussing and debating moral matters, often heatedly. This is not to say Catholics disagree on basic doctrine. Virtually all Catholics cite without reservation the Nicene Creed, which dates back to the fourth century and contains the basics of the Catholic faith. This creed begins with the words, "We believe in one God, the Father, the Almighty, maker of heaven and earth . . ." and ends with the words, "We look for the resurrection of the dead, and the life of the world to come, Amen." Other than the words "he was born of the Virgin Mary, and became man" and references to God as "Father," the creed makes no sexual references. The point is that while there has been much public attention on the Catholic Church's dealings with sexual matters, these matters have relatively little to do with basic faith.

Much is frequently made about the emphasis Catholics place on tradition, and with reason. Catholics hold it as important. A good portion of the debate in the church today, given the fast pace of change, and given the hunger for authentic spirituality, involves efforts to sort out tradition, separating the accidental belief (that which may have been held in faith by groups of Catholics at given times) from that which is essential belief (that proclaimed by the official church to be held by all the faithful). On matters of morality, especially personal morality, this has not always been as clear as some in the church would like. At one level, then, Catholic theology is always developing, always unfolding as the human story progresses. There is another side. Throughout Catholic history, church leaders have preached what they have proclaimed to be immutable truths, especially in matters of sexual morality and ethics. Some of these seeming "absolutes," however, have at times come under attack and have even been modified or changed. At one point the church taught that usury, the practice of charging interest to a borrower of money, was sinful. That teaching went out in the early stages of capitalism. The church used to teach that slavery was morally permissible. That belief was abandoned in the nineteenth century. Today, the most controversial church teaching among Catholics surrounds its opposition to all forms of artificial birth control. Will the church eventually change here, too? It is never easy for a church with a twenty-century history and tradition to shift teachings. The birth control debate, meanwhile, is just one of many involving human sexuality to have rocked the Catholic Church in recent decades. Why this has happened and how it will eventually turn out not only personally affects the nearly 1 billion Roman Catholics but also, because of the vast social implications involved, has far wider consequences. To better grasp the dimensions of what is involved, it is best to go back to the beginning of the story.

Scripture

The Old Testament, the Hebrew Bible, contains a variety of references to sexual matters, revealing different theologies and attitudes regarding sexuality. Generally, the Jewish people viewed the Creation as the handiwork of God. They saw it as good, sex included. Sexual matters were not something to be ashamed of or embarrassed about. The Creation accounts in Genesis reveal Yahweh's love for his people, hardly a contempt of nature or sexuality. Nor alternatively does the Old Testament celebrate the pursuit of sexual pleasure, which characterized some of antiquity's thought. The Jewish people viewed sex simply as a given, as an aspect of life, associating it with human relationships and the need to overcome loneliness. "It is not good for the man to be alone; I will make a suitable partner for him" (Genesis 2:18). In this light, sex was viewed as enhancing companionship. It was a gift from the Creator.[3]

Old Testament attitudes toward sex were influenced by

important notions involving genealogy, marriage, and family. Whereas women were included in some genealogies, descent was generally taken from the father's line. Women were viewed as inferior, of lesser value, and they held lesser legal and social positions. Since marriage was the means of perpetuating lineage, women were called upon to produce children, preferably sons. Such was the pressure on a wife to provide her husband with a child that if barren, she would allow him a consort to continue the genealogy (Genesis 30:1–13). Sexuality in the Old Testament was seen as part of nature and also as the means for continuing the sacred story. Monogamous, lifelong marriage was the ideal. As the centuries passed, this ideal became more emphasized. It solidified social patterns. Sexual prescriptions in the Old Testament were not legislated as much as they grew out of social conditions and needs of the times.

Jesus in the New Testament said very little about sex. He was more concerned with teaching compassion and forgiveness, defending the downtrodden, and siding with the oppressed. He spoke about repentance. He lashed out against overbearing laws. Some Catholic theologians maintain the key to understanding Jesus' attitude toward marriage and the family is to understand his uncommon concern for the dignity of women.[4] His attitude toward women was especially remarkable given their socially inferior positions in society at the time. "You have heard that it was said, 'You shall not commit adultery,'" Jesus said. "But I say to you, everyone who looks at a woman with lust has already committed adultery with her in his heart" (Matthew 5:27–28). Jesus goes on: "But I say to you, whoever divorces his wife (unless the marriage is unlawful) causes her to commit adultery, and whoever marries a divorced woman commits adultery" (Matthew 5:32). Some have said that in this context Jesus' strong affirming attitude toward women can best be understood. He associated with them publicly and allowed himself to be touched by an "unclean" woman. He took compassion on them, counted them among his close friends, and welcomed them among his disciples. After his Resurrection, the glorified Christ appeared first to women to announce the good news (Matthew 28:9–10). He showed little trace of the common assumption of his times—that women were inferior. A Christian ethics of sexuality needs to consider Jesus' prohibition of divorce, his affirmation of fidelity within marriage for both sexes, his emphasis on the equality of men and women, and his giving primacy to the law of love. He affirmed human dignity, and this moved him at times to stand up against the lawmakers of his day.

In the New Testament, Paul made repeated references to matters of sexuality.[5] This may be because of the conditions in which he found himself. Prostitution was rampant. Men, married and unmarried, commonly had sex with slaves and prostitutes. He protested it, warned against it. Further, he believed the world would soon be ending and the risen Christ would return. To Paul this was no far-off future event; it was closer to a compelling reality soon to be fulfilled. The result was that he encouraged the unmarried to prepare for Christ's impending return by avoiding marriage (1 Corinthians 7:26–27). He thought such a spirit of detachment would better prepare the Christian for Christ's return. In the tradition of the then contemporary Greek Stoics, Paul warned against the passions of desire, associating them with impurity. Contrary to some of the exaggerated asceticism within cults of his time, however, he affirmed the goodness of sex, as long as it occurred within marriage. Nevertheless, believing Christ's return was imminent, Paul made his personal preference for celibacy clear.

The biblical authors consistently viewed God as loving and gracious. They stressed the ideal of fidelity in marriage. This loyalty was viewed as a loving response to God. As for absolute dictates regarding sexual morality, they provided few. To the degree that sexual morality was taught, it was done so within the larger context of what was good or useful in preserving relationships and fostering the general health of the community.

Early Christians

Many commonly believe that Christianity brought some form of sexual self-restraint to a largely pagan world, one that delighted in pleasures of the flesh. This does not seem to have been the case.[6] Many first- and second-century Mideast communities were heavily influenced by Greek culture and thought. Among the Greeks, the Stoics and other ascetics exhibited much hostility to bodily pleasure, and their influence was widely felt. Elements of this legacy and ethic eventually managed to enter Christian thought where they became enshrined and where they have remained to modern times. Like other religious and cultural traditions, the thoughts and teachings of early Christian communities regarding sexuality were complex and subject to many outside influences. To single out any one is to oversimplify history. Nevertheless, to sense the development of life in the early Christian communities it is helpful to consider the sexual attitudes among the Greeks and Romans of that time—as theirs were the dominant cultures. Both helped shape early Christian sexual beliefs and practices. Both, for example, believed in monogamous marriage. In ancient Greece, however, sex was not confined to marriage. Human nature was viewed by many as bisexual. Homosexual relationships were commonly accepted. Meanwhile, both Greek and Roman civilizations were heavily male dominated. Double standards were common. What was allowed for men was not necessarily allowed for women. Among the Greeks, both sexual license and asceticism were ways of life, depending on the particular community and time. The earliest Christians, still very much a subculture and vulnerable to persecution, had formulated no single systematic code of sexual ethics. As recorded in the New Testament, their central focus was summed up in the simple command: love one another. Survival, however, was at times an even greater concern.

How Christians during the first several centuries A.D. approached sex and sexual morality cannot be divorced from the varied cultural influences of the time. While early Greek philosophers wrote lofty treatises on the importance of seeking pleasure for its own sake, this emphasis slowly changed as the influence of the Greek Stoics emerged, especially during the first two centuries of the Christian era. The Stoics rejected the quest for pleasure. One effect of their influence was the reinforcement of the ideal of keeping sexual activity confined to marriage; another was that all carnal pleasure became suspect—so much so that even marriage was called into question. This reinforced the notion that celibacy should be valued as a noble ideal. Later, Christians and others began to view marriage as a concession to those who simply could not achieve the celibate ideal. This attitude toward marriage among Christians, once it took hold, would not let go in the Catholic Church. Even today many Catholics continue to view celibacy and the commitment to priestly life, with which it has primarily become associated, as a special gift, a response to the highest of all callings to serve God. An examination of the New Testament offers grounds for a sexual ethic that values marriage and procreation; it also provides for an ethic that celebrates celibacy. A study of early Christian communities reveals this curiously ambivalent attitude toward sexuality. The early Christians viewed sex as good and as a means of fulfilling Jesus' command. However, they also esteemed sexual abstinence as a means of freeing themselves in preparation of Christ's return. Both seemingly contradictory values have played themselves out among Christians throughout much of church history.

Of all the Greek philosophies, Stoicism had the greatest impact on early Christianity.[7] Greek philosophers such as Seneca (c. 55 B.C.–c. A.D. 39), Epictetus (A.D. 55–c. 135), and Roman emperor Marcus Aurelius (A.D. 121–180) taught that willpower should regulate emotion and that this discipline would lead to inner peace. Sexual desires along with the passions of fear and anger were viewed as irrational and in need of control, if not elimination. Along with the Stoics, the Gnostics also had an impact on some Christian thinking. While the Stoics were philosophers, the Gnostics were members of religious movements, and they deeply affected the formation of Christian sexual ethics during the first three centuries. The Gnostics combined Eastern mysticism, Greek philosophy, and Christian belief. They taught among other things that marriage was evil. They went so far as to teach that the procreation of children was the vehicle for evil forces. The Gnostics were a pessimistic lot. Their thinking went in two directions, one opposing all sexual intercourse; the other embracing every possible sexual experience as long as it was not procreative. Under the influence of the Gnostics and seeking to combat their extremes, Christians sought the middle path. They affirmed sexuality as good. However, they subjected it to strict moral limits. In effect, they latched onto the Stoic idea that sexual intercourse could be justified only by its procreative function.[8] Christians adopted the restrictive notion of marriage as intended solely for the purpose of procreation. The idea shaped Christian thinking on marriage until well into the twentieth century. To view marriage in this light led to other logical conclusions: Sexual intercourse within marriage, Christians believed, was morally acceptable only when a woman could become pregnant. If she was already pregnant, sex was no longer allowed. It was sinful. The Christian Church during the second and third centuries affirmed that the central purpose of sexual union was procreation and procreation alone. Along with this negative and limited view of sexual intercourse came its positive counterpart, abstinence as a virtue.

The Christian tradition in sexual ethics, nearly from its earliest origins, became influenced by a pervasive dualism of both a philosophical and theological nature. Platonic philosophy in the early church looked upon matter in general and sexuality in particular as inferior to spirit and soul. This dualism, once formulated, had far-reaching consequences on the way Christianity—and, indeed, Western thought—would evolve throughout the centuries.

Meanwhile, celibacy as an ideal was beginning to take hold; among Christian women, virginity began to be seen as a response to a higher calling.[9] The early classless church of the followers of Jesus slowly began to separate into different roles. For the weaker "ordinary" Christians, there was married life; for others, there was the "gift" of celibacy and virginity.[10] A Stoic-Gnostic legacy had successfully been implanted, if not imposed, upon the carriers of the "good news." Celibacy grew after the early Christian martyrdom era ended. This occurred as Christianity became established as an accepted religion and monasticism with its vows of poverty and celibacy became a significant witness of the faith.

Augustinian Pessimism

Christians generally view St. Augustine (354–430), bishop of Hippo in Roman North Africa, as the greatest thinker of Christian antiquity. He is credited with fusing the religion of the New Testament with the Platonic tradition of Greek philosophy. At the age of about forty-five, he wrote the *Confessions,* the story of his own sensual youth, which ended in his conversion to Christianity a dozen years earlier. Augustine showed promise from an early age of being a bright student. By age nineteen, he traveled to study at Carthage where he was influenced by Manichaeans who viewed existence in starkly dualistic terms, as a conflict between light and dark substances with the human soul caught up in the struggle. The Manichaeans claimed to be the true Christians. Some practiced deep asceticism, preaching that the Redeemed Christ enabled imprisoned particles of light to escape from darkness. The philosophy influenced but did not satisfy Augustine's spiritual quest. At about age twenty-eight he moved to Milan, Italy, where he heard Ambrose, the bishop of Milan, and the most eminent Christian churchman of his day, preach. This was Augustine's first intellectual exposure to Christianity. In the seventh book of the *Confessions,* Augustine describes how he finally found God—the "changeless light," at once imminent and transcendent. The discovery was more than the conclusion of a reasoning process, he wrote. It was a mystical experience. For Augustine, God came to be light, and evil to be darkness. The Manichaean influence remained, and the dualism continued; but in Augustine's emerging formulation, God was pure spirit and evil became non-existence. To reach pure spirit, however, it would be necessary to escape the from the prison of bodily limitations, most especially those involving sexual urges.

It was largely in response to the Manichaeans that Augustine reaffirmed a belief in the general goodness of marriage and procreation. Sexual intercourse without procreative purpose, however, was a serious sin, he thought. The only sinless sexual union he could imagine was one intended for procreation. Augustine's writings were extensive and many focused on human sexuality. He devoted a chapter in *The City of God* to attempting to show that before the Fall in the Garden of Eden, Adam was fully able to control his sexual urges. With the Fall, that ability ended. Augustine could not fathom the notion of sexual pleasure in Eden, not when Adam and Eve were in their pre-Fall state.

Pondering sexuality, Augustine once considered its various degrees of sinfulness. There needed to be degrees, he reasoned. Why? Since it takes two to have intercourse, one might engage in it out of lust while the other merely obliged. Augustine was convinced that the person who demanded sex from a spouse (except for procreation) committed sin. Certainly, he reasoned, the partner who agrees to sex simply to please—but who does not seek pleasure—commits the lesser sin. And since procreation was the only moral reason for sex, did it not follow that to have sex with a women who could no longer bear children was a sin?

These were just some of the considerations Augustine addressed in his writings. They help throw light upon how early Christian attitudes toward sex later, under the scrutiny of theological consideration, began to work their ways into church laws. The basic consideration was, What was to God a morally pleasing act? The corollary was, What was not pleasing, what was sinful, and what, therefore, required confession and forgiveness by church authorities?

While Catholics view Augustine as one of the greatest of all church teachers, he has come under increasing criticism in recent times for his excessive sexual pessimism. Augustine eventually came to see human nature as corrupted and totally dependent upon the grace of Christ. In effect, Augustine had taken the dark sexual pessimism of the Greek philosophers and formulated it into what was seen as foundational Christian theology. He did this by arriving at an explanation of the fallen state of human nature and linking it with the sexual act. The sin of Adam and Eve, he came to believe, was passed down through the generations by the very act of sexual intercourse. Thus, all humans carried Adam and Eve's *original sin,* a term he is widely viewed as having coined. This linkage further enshrined in Christian thought the duality of the goodness of spirit and the evil of the corporal world.

All religious belief systems, of course, at some point are forced to cope with the existence of evil and its baffling origins, given the almighty goodness of the Creator. Religions respond with myth and storytelling. Augustine was no exception. Christianity has traditionally explained the existence of evil through the Genesis story, the original innocence of Adam and Eve, their temptation in Eden, their fall from grace, their banishment. Augustine, however, had an enormous impact upon Christian thought because he wedded original sin to the sin of the flesh. He wrote that after Adam and Eve's sin "they were ashamed and covered their sexual parts with fig leaves."[11] Augustine taught that since some concupiscence, or sensual appetite, is involved in virtually every human sexual act, all sexual acts are in some sense sinful. He taught that it took Jesus' birth, death, and Resurrection to rescue sinners. According to Augustine, although God desires salvation for all in Christ, only those justified by faith and baptism are saved and can share eternal bliss with God. Without Redemption, there is only darkness, only eternal damnation. To the degree these ideas sound familiar to the Christian, one begins to understand the central influence of Augustine's thought in Christian history. In Augustine, Manichean sexual pessimism and early Christian skepticism toward sex were, in effect, raised to the level of a systematic theology. This theology has permeated Christian thinking to this very day.

PENITENTIALS

During the early Middle Ages, the sixth through the tenth centuries, sexuality was viewed as basically good but only if procreation was the conscious intent.[12] Many related questions, however, needed to be answered. Under what precise circumstances was intercourse sinful? And what about other marital sexual acts? Handbooks called penitentials, catalogs of sins with corresponding lists of penances, or acts of amends for sins, were provided by the theologians to local confessors. The oldest known penitentials came from monasteries in Ireland where they were composed by abbots. The penitentials, though elementary in their approach to morality, were not simplistic. They reflected at times a rather sophisticated appreciation of the varieties human experience. Confessors, priests to whom people confessed their sins, were called upon not only to consider the gravity of a particular sexual offense but also the degree of its malicious intent as well as its frequency. All this had to be properly weighed for before absolution, the words and the blessing of a priest by which sins are forgiven, could take place. The penitentials provide interesting insights into church thinking on sexual matters. Contraception, in the form of *coitus interruptus,* withdrawal of the penis before ejaculation to avoid the deposit of the semen into the vagina, was a most serious sin because it stood in the way of procreative intent. To obtain priestly absolution a sinner was required to do penance, such as fasting on bread and water—often for years. In the case of contraception, a penance could last up to ten years. Anal sex, oral sex, and even certain positions of sexual intercourse were also viewed as gravely sinful acts. The penances for these sexual offenses might extend from seven to fifteen years, in some cases. Because they were considered "unnatural" acts, they drew more severe penances than other sins, including abortion or murder.[13]

Women, meanwhile, continued to be viewed as especially fallen. The idea of Eve, the temptress, found its way into Judaism and developed in early Christian history. One sign of the fallen state was the notion of "impurity" associated with periodic menstruation. To have sex with a menstruating women was an especially grave sin. It was further believed that having sex during such a time could result in a malformed child. As was often the case in the Jewish tradition, when women were "impure," there would be rituals to purify them so that they would not contaminate the rest of the believing community. These occurred, for example, after childbirth and before the new mother could reenter the local place of worship. Additionally, the requirements of ritual purity led to prohibitions against sexual relations during various sacred times, including Sundays, holy days, and other sacred seasons of the year. Married couples were told they could not have relations before receiving the Eucharist.

Marriage and sexuality began to figure prominently in church law. The golden era of church or canon law began with the Italian monk Gratian who about 1140 compiled all the laws of the church. The twelfth and thirteenth centuries witnessed a remarkable growth and systematization of church laws in all areas—but especially with regard to sexuality and marriage. At that time marriage was viewed as a contract that stemmed from the free consent of the spouses but only became fully indissoluble when consummated through sexual intercourse.

Scholasticism

Scholasticism was a system of thought and an intellectual approach associated with the scholars of the medieval universities. With antecedents going back to Augustine, it sought a better understanding of revealed truth by using disciplined philosophical methods. The *Summa Theologica,* a work of Dominican St. Thomas Aquinas (1225–74), was considered the greatest achievement of Scholastic theology. He bridged Aristotle's thought with Augustine's, attempting to show how reason and revelation enhanced each other. Aquinas began to look at marriage as both a civil and a sacramental institution. He departed from the Augustinian tendency to be suspect of all pleasure, viewing it as natural insofar as it was governed by reason.[14] Aquinas was more optimistic than Augustine (classical Protestants were more attracted to Augustine), but Aquinas used reason to accept the "procreative rule" for sexuality. Roman Catholic thought was for centuries very heavily influenced by Thomism and Scholasticism. By the early nineteenth century many Catholic scholars were abandoning this approach to moral reasoning, but Pope Leo XIII in 1879 installed Thomism as *the* Catholic philosophy and theology.

Scholastic thought considers human reason as the key to unraveling the mystery of the divine. It paints orderly relationships between the supernatural and the natural worlds, showing how they relate to each other and interact. Closely associated with this approach to theological pursuit has been the natural law theory. It has heavily influenced Catholic moral theology.[15] The Catholic tradition has insisted that its moral teaching is based primarily on natural law and not primarily on faith or Scripture. The natural law is understood "to be human reason reflecting on human nature." Even those teachings that have some basis in Scripture (e.g., the indissolubility of marriage, the sinfulness of homosexuality) were also said to be based on natural law. This emphasis on the rational recognizes such teaching can and should be shared by all human beings of all faiths and no faith. For natural law is that law that governs all of nature, including human beings and the animal world. It asks, What does nature require? How does it act out? What are the norms? Knowing these laws and following them, this thinking holds, allows human beings to live in accord with the will of the Creator, the source of all life. In general, natural law argues that human reason reflecting on human nature can arrive at moral wisdom. The importance of natural law theology in Catholic thought, while disregarded by other Christians who emphasize the importance of Scripture alone, has shaped Catholic moral theology to this day. Some contemporary Catholic theologians point to two questionable characteristics of the scholastic natural law theory—classicism and physicalism—which have become embedded in official church teaching. Classicism sees reality in terms of the eternal, the immutable, and the unchanging. The universal essence of human nature, it holds, is everywhere the same. This approach insists there are immutable absolute norms, always and everywhere true, that they can be known and, indeed, are known and proclaimed, guided by the Holy Spirit, by the Catholic Church. Physicalism, meanwhile, refers to the identification of the human and moral reality with the physical and biological aspects of human acts. With this in mind, sexuality becomes understood in light of those acts common to human beings and to other animals. Thus, the human can never morally interfere with the physical act of sexual intercourse. It is unnatural, wrong, and sinful to do so. It follows that any form of artificial contraception is always wrong.

The church's continued emphasis on the procreative aspect of marriage coupled with its emerging emphasis on reason led to the appearance of moral manuals written by theologians and intended to train priests. These manuals divided sexual sins into those "in accord with nature" and those "contrary to nature." The former (fornication, adultery, incest, rape, and abduction) preserved procreative possibility and were consequently regarded, apart from other considerations, as lesser violations of the moral order. The latter (masturbation, sodomy, homosexuality, and bestiality) violated procreative purpose and therefore were seen as more serious abuses of human sexuality.[16] Today many look upon this approach as a highly negative, juridical, and act-centered morality that proclaims moral absolutes with little regard to person-oriented values. The Scholastics continued to teach that sex was permitted only within marriage and for the sake of procreation. Based on what was understood from the sciences of the times, they viewed the male seed as the active principle. Women were viewed as having little value except as receptacles for the seed. Further, Scholastics held that the pleasure derived from sexual acts was associated with sinful concupiscence.

Most theology during that time was developed and studied by celibate monks and priests. This seems to have been one more factor that worked against the enhancement of a notion of marriage as sustaining and supporting the love of two persons. Sexual intercourse as an expression of love and mutual sharing was an idea quite foreign to the celibate monastics of the time. In the eleventh century the early Scholastics fixed the number of church sacraments at seven. While marriage was one of them, they viewed it as a lesser sacrament, not as grace giving, but as a necessary remedy against sin. By the thirteenth century, the later Scholastics begrudgingly conceded that God's grace could come from marriage. But that was still because it suppressed lust.[17]

Reformation

Catholic teachings on human sexuality and marriage played a role in the sixteenth-century Protestant Reformation. Anglicanism began when England's Henry VIII (1491–1547) led the Church of England out of the Roman communion, placing it under his own leadership. Though the direct issue leading to the separation dealt with papal authority, Henry's desire to divorce and remarry played a part in his decision to split from Rome. From that time to the present, Anglicans and Catholics have expressed different moral teachings on sexual matters. Catholics and Protestant reformers also diverged on these issues, especially clerical celibacy, which the Catholic Church had insisted on for its clergy beginning in the eleventh century.

Martin Luther and John Calvin accepted most of the existing Christian sexual morality. Both were deeply influenced by the Augustinian tradition regarding original sin and its consequences.[18] Both shared Augustine's pessimistic view of fallen human nature, and both believed this fall meant that sexual desires could no longer be fully controlled. Unlike Augustine, however, who argued for celibacy as a response to sinful nature, Luther's remedy was marriage. He believed that virtually all Christians needed to live in a married state. To do otherwise would be to expose them to excessive temptation. Calvin, too, saw marriage as a needed corrective to otherwise disordered desires. Following the Protestant Reformation, the Council of Trent (1545–63) became the first ecumenical council to actually consider the role of mutual love within marriage. It ended up, however, reaffirming the primacy of the long-held Catholic procreative ethic in marriage. It also reemphasized the superiority of the celibate state.

The belief remained dominant throughout the Middle Ages that the sole justification for sexual intercourse in marriage was procreation. However, in the fifteenth century the first faint efforts emerged within Catholic theological circles to reconsider this teaching. Catholic writers such as Denis the Carthusian and Martin Le Maistre, teaching at the University of Paris, argued that sexual intercourse in marriage could be justified for its own sake. The later maintained that "not every copulation of spouses not performed to generate offspring is an act opposed to conjugal chastity." Another Catholic writer, Thomas Sanchez, a marriage specialist, also asserted, contrary to prevailing opinion, "there is no sin in spouses who intend to have intercourse simply as spouses." These represented revolutionary ideas in their times. They stirred much heated controversy and church reaction.[19]

Part of the reaction to what was viewed by some as an unreasonable loosening of marriage ideals was the growth of the Jansenist movement with its claim to be following Augustine. The views of the Dutch theologian Cornelius Jansen (1585–1638) regarding sexuality were rooted in dark pessimism and the notion of original sin. Only through Christ's grace did the Christian have any hope whatsoever to live a moral life, he taught. His teachings, austere and in some ways akin to Calvin's doctrine of predestination, were eventually condemned by Pope Innocent X (papacy 1644–55) in 1653 and again by Pope Clement XI (papacy 1700–21) in 1713. These condemnations led to Jansenist persecution, especially in France. The movement, however, lingered on. Both the Jansenists and the Puritans, who broke from the Church of England in the sixteenth century, saw themselves as reformers, and both reasserted harsh views on sexual matters. While the Jansenists influenced Catholics in northern Europe, the Puritans were later to settle in New England in the early seventeenth century and help shape a relatively strict North American attitude toward sexual matters. Although Jansenism had been condemned by the church, its influence was still felt well into the twentieth century in both Europe and the United States. Consider, for example, the writing of Henry Davis in 1936:

> *It is grievously sinful in the unmarried deliberately to procure or to accept even the smallest degree of true venereal pleasure; secondly, that it is equally sinful to think, say or do anything with the intention of arousing even the smallest degree of this pleasure. . . . [T]he smallest amount of this pleasure is an inducement to indulgence in the fullest amount of it.*[20]

By such a standard it would not take much to be accused of sexual license. The sexual mores characteristic of the twentieth century, set in contrast to such Puritan thought, can be seen not only as an outgrowth of modern culture, but as a stormy reaction to repressive and constrictive beliefs.

The Jansenists' influence reached Catholics in the Americas, principally through Ireland, the Irish clergy, and other clergy who had been heavily influenced by the Jansenists. The Irish during the mid-nineteenth century made up the first major Catholic immigrant group to migrate to the United States. Many priests traveled with them and brought a Catholic theology steeped in legalisms and rigid sexual mores. This Catholicism, by contrast, was unlike that of the more relaxed Catholics of southern Europe who for centuries have viewed church laws as guides or ideals rather than as absolutes. The influence of an Irish-flavored Catholicism in the United States became even more pronounced during the early- and mid-twentieth century as these priests became the nation's first generation of Catholic bishops. Irish theology in the United States, at least until shortly after Vatican Council II (1962–65) when Catholicism worldwide undertook major reforms, was the theology for mainstream Roman Catholics living in the United States.[21]

The twentieth-century sexual revolution, which gained

momentum in the 1960s with the introduction of "the pill" as a new contraceptive, marked a shift in Western cultural attitudes. Understandably, the sexual revolution presented a challenge to the Catholic Church, which for twenty centuries had been the chief enforcer of traditional sexual ethics.

ENTERING THE MODERN ERA

Throughout most of its history, the Catholic Church shared the belief with most of the rest of the Western world that each conjugal act was by its nature procreative—and could only accidentally fail to be so. In the nineteenth century, however, scientists began to better understand human biology and its relationship to procreation. Research revealed that a certain rhythm in nature, a woman's monthly cycle, played a role in fertility. Indeed, scientists learned that a woman was fertile only for a few days each month. This knowledge would eventually send Catholic moralists scrambling to reexamine marital guidelines. Considering sex in marriage, they now had to consider *intent* as well as the actual act. Was it moral, for example, to have intercourse but consistently time it to infertile periods? Never before had this precise moral question arisen. After all, for centuries the church had taught that sexual intercourse during pregnancy was immoral because it could not lead to the birth of a child. The church had generally tolerated marital sex for sterile persons, assuming their intention would be to have children if they could. Where there was neither hope nor desire for pregnancy, however, the church discouraged intercourse.

Among the abandoned agenda items of the abbreviated First Vatican Council, or Vatican I (1869–70), was the call for the codification of all church law. By that time, extensive legislation had grown within the church, and church laws were often difficult to locate, contradictory, and difficult to understand. Work on putting together an official Code of Canon Law began in 1904 and was completed in 1917. This provided greater simplification and clarification, but it also did much to solidify church teaching on sex at the very time the world was beginning to experience change in the ways it looked at sexual intimacy and reproduction. As it pertained to marriage, the codification, perhaps understandably, emphasized marriage as a contract. Marriage was described in the new canons functionally, as having a primary and a secondary end: the procreation and education of children being primary, with other marital aspects, including mutual support and intimacy, as secondary. Missing in the codification was an understanding of the free giving of one another that couples find in healthy marriages. The codification of church law also had the effect of making any discussion of ethics more rigid and difficult. The answers, as it were, were already in writing and set in law.

A little more than a decade later, the Catholic Church was to face a serious crisis. In 1930 the bishops of the Church of England adopted a statement giving a conditional approval to birth control. The vote at the Lambeth Conference was 193 to 67. The resolution in part read:

> *Where there is clearly felt moral obligations to limit or avoid parenthood, the method must be decided on Christian principles. The primary and obvious method is complete abstinence from intercourse (as far as may be necessary) in a life of discipline and self-control lived in the power of the Holy Spirit. Nevertheless, in those cases where there is such a clearly felt moral obligation to limit or avoid parenthood, and where there is a morally sound rea-*

son for avoiding complete abstinence, the Conference agrees that other methods may be used, provided that this is done in the light of the same Christian principles. The Conference records its strong condemnation of the use of any methods of conception-control from motives of selfishness, luxury or mere convenience.[22]

The bishops passed the statement, having failed to do so in two earlier attempts in 1908 and 1920. The resolution was historic in that it marked the first time a major Christian group had publicly gone on record in support of the separation of the procreative (birth-giving) and unitive (mutual enhancement) ends of marriage. Lambeth sent tremors through the Roman Catholic hierarchy. Before 1930 ended, Pope Pius XI (papacy 1922–39) reacted by issuing a rebuttal encyclical, *Casti Connubii,* referred to in English as "On Christian Marriage."[23] The encyclical, in part, reads as follows:

Our voice promulgates anew: any use of marriage whatever, in the exercise of which the act is deprived of its natural power of procreating life, violates the law of God and nature, and those who commit anything of this kind are marked with the stain of grave sin.[24]

The encyclical, however, did make one important concession to the times. It affirmed church support of the use of the rhythm method of birth control as a means to regulate births.

Stated *Casti Connubii:*

Nor are those considered as acting against nature who in the married state use their right in the proper manner, although on account of natural reasons either of time or of certain defects, new life cannot be brought forth. For in matrimony as well as in the use

> *of matrimonial rights there are also secondary ends, such as mutual aid, the cultivating of mutual love, and the quieting of concupiscence which husband and wife are not forbidden to consider as long as they are subordinated to the primary end and so long as the intrinsic nature of the act is preserved.*[25]

As a result of this paragraph the encyclical represented a historic shift toward what in theological circles are termed the "personalist" ends of human sexuality. The concession is even more dramatically seen in the following paragraph from *Casti Connubii:*

> *This mutual inward molding of a husband and a wife, this determined effort to perfect each other, can in a very real sense, be said to be the chief reason and purpose of matrimony, provided matrimony be looked at not in the restricted sense as instituted for the proper conception and education of the child, but more widely as the blending of life as a whole and the mutual interchange and sharing thereof.*[26]

Taken together, these paragraphs represented a giant step forward in Catholic thinking. On the issue of artificial contraception, however, the official church stood firm. It was viewed as immoral and received an unqualified condemnation.

Why the sudden changes of church outlook toward marriage after so many centuries of having held to the status quo? It appears the change resulted from a partial acceptance of the growing public writings of prominent Catholic theologians who were disagreeing with the Vatican on marriage matters. With the onset of the twentieth century, prominent Catholic theologians had begun to write more frequently about marriage and its purposes and they began to articulate personalist values in Christian sexuality. Marriage, they argued, had not been properly understood by the church and had more in it than a couple's desire and responsibility to continue the human race. It was also about the love of a couple and their desire to serve and please and sustain each other. These ideas were gaining in popularity even as they countered official teachings.

The 1930s, meanwhile, witnessed the continuation of a lively controversy regarding marriage in the Catholic Church. In 1935 Herbert Doms, a German diocesan priest, published a book that appeared in a 1939 English translation as *The Meaning of Marriage.* Doms objected that the recently proclaimed church canons seemed to say the meaning in marriage comes only from its primary end, the procreation and education of children, and not from any secondary end. Doms did not deny that marriage has these primary ends, but he insisted that it also has important meaning apart from these ends, the drawing together of the two persons in marriage. His views stirred considerable reaction in Rome, so much so that the Vatican issued a decree in 1944 responding to his arguments, though not specifically referring to him. It insisted that procreation and education of children were the primary ends of marriage—and no other ends would be considered as equals. These were arguments with weighty theological and moral implications. Less than a decade later, in his "Address to the Italian Catholic Society of Midwives," Pius XII (papacy 1939–58) reiterated the church's unyielding rejection of artificial contraception but in the process addressed the question of periodic continence to intentionally avoid procreation. He characterized procreation as a positive duty from which couples could be excused because of "serious reasons." In so doing, he shifted the question away from the meaning or purpose of the marital act and onto a couple's "duty" to contribute to the propagation of the human race. This shift would later cause a good number of Catholic theologians to question the logic of the church's stance against birth control. Pius XII viewed his objection to contraception as binding for all times, drawing on an earlier papal statement to bolster his authority:

> *Our predecessor, Pius XI, of happy memory, in his encyclical Casti Connubii, December 31, 1930, solemnly proclaimed anew the fundamental law governing the marital act and conjugal relations: [T]hat any attempt on the part of married people to deprive this act of its inherent force and to impede the procreation of new life either in the performance of the act itself or in the course of the development of its natural consequence, is immoral. . . . This principle is as valid today as it was yesterday; and it will be the same tomorrow and always, because it does not imply a precept of the human law but is the expression of a law which is natural and divine.*[27]

This unequivocal statement was of such strength that it led some theologians to conclude that for all practical purposes it was "irrevocable" and nothing more could be discussed. Little did they know the birth control debate was just beginning.

How then might one summarize the outlines of official Catholic teaching on sexuality after twenty centuries—and as the assault against them became intense? First, genital sexuality can be expressed only within the context of an indissoluble and permanent marriage of male and female. Second, every sexual act must be open to procreation. Third, the natural law theory supporting such an understanding results in an absolute prohibition of artificial contraception and other acts deemed as "unnatural," such as masturbation, homosexual genital relations, and all premarital and extramarital sexual relationships. And fourth, virginity and celibacy are generally looked upon as higher states of life than marriage.[28]

The church was headed for a serious clash with the modern world. Some Catholics sensed it and desperately wanted to avoid the conflict.

II

Church Reform

For Roman Catholics, the 1960s began on October 28, 1958. That was the day a rotund Italian named Angelo Giuseppi Roncalli, patriarch of Venice and a cardinal of the church, at age seventy-six was elected pope. He took the name John XXIII. The new and short-lived pontificate would end four centuries of Catholic defensiveness to the world, the lingering aftermath of the Reformation.

Pope Pius XI's pontificate (1922–39) had lasted almost until the outbreak of World War II in Europe. A conservative man, he was impulsive and autocratic. Upon his death, the church's cardinals gathered at the Vatican and, as the Sacred College of Cardinals, elected an accomplished diplomat to be the next pope. An Italian, Cardinal Eugenio Pacelli had been papal secretary of state since 1930. He took the name Pope Pius XII. Pacelli was a thin, ascetic-looking man. His pontificate lasted nearly twenty years. By its end, he had been ill for some time—and Catholics waited.

As word of his death October 9, 1958, spread around the world, Catholics were relieved, feeling both uncertainty and anticipation. A new pope is always a major event in the Catholic Church. Again the church's cardinals, fifty-three in all this time, came to Rome to elect a new pontiff. They were an aging group. Before they could even enter the secret conclave where they would cut themselves off from the world until emerging with a new pontiff, two died. Only fifty-one eventually sealed themselves off within the Vatican.[1] In the 1950s instant global communications were still a dream. Satellite linkups did not arrive until nearly ten years later. Information went by telex or simply by mail, taking weeks. It was not surprising then that when the cardinals gathered in Rome they lacked a consensus on where the church should be headed or what kind of leadership was required. Vatican bureaucrats, generally conservatives, were comfortable with the state of the church. They did not look kindly to "outsiders" coming in to tell them things needed to change. Other cardinals wanted new ecclesial life but were unsure what form it might take. Throughout most of Catholic history the "princes," or cardinals, of the church elected the pope. In the Middle Ages only a handful were involved. As the church grew and the religion spread, however, the number of cardinals expanded. (The title *cardinal,* is largely honorary; bestowed on a bishop, it allows him only one additional function—the election of a pope.) The traditional signal a new pope has been elected comes in the form of white smoke above a small chimney on top of the Sistine Chapel where this most exclusive men's club in the world gathers. Black smoke indicates a failed vote. A majority of two-thirds plus is required in a vote to elect a pope. It took eleven ballots to elect John XXIII. At seventy-six, Roncalli was chosen to be a "transitional" pope; the cardinals did not expect him to have a long pontificate. His papacy, they thought, would be an interim one, setting the stage for a longer one the next time around. His pontificate would provide breathing space, they felt. At least, that was the expectation.

As Europe's last absolute monarch, a pope has considerable ecclesial power, albeit control over a state of only 108.7 acres. Roncalli would wield his power, confounding his electors. He was a maverick from the start. Asked by what name he would be known, he answered in Latin, "*Vocabor Joannes*"—I will be called John. No pope had used that name in 540 years. The last John XXIII was considered an antipope, meaning he claimed the papal title but was not recognized by the official church. From the moment John XXIII stood on the balcony overlooking St. Peter's Square, he was a stark contrast to his predecessor. Pudgy and easy mannered, John XXIII was affectionately described by one U.S. bishop as looking more like a pizza maker than a pope. His warmth and simplicity captured world attention. The timing of his election was also significant.

Throughout the West, the 1960s ushered in a period of optimism, idealism, and hope. A young U.S. president, also named John and also Catholic, John F. Kennedy, came to epitomize that promise. In his way, John XXIII brought similar optimism to the Catholic Church. It was an exciting time to be a Catholic. Yet, despite the hope, despite the new energies, despite the fresh enthusiasm, before the 1960s gave way to the 1970s, there would be conflict, revolution, and disillusionment—both inside and outside the church.

John XXIII was a pivotal figure in Catholic church history, the first Catholic shepherd of the modern world. A conservative by instinct, he showed the unusual ability to grow and to change. He was elected pope as the world and church were changing. It was also a time when the balance of Catholicism was shifting, and for the first time in history there were more Catholics living in Africa, Asia, and Latin America than in the church's traditional population centers of Europe and North America. By the early 1960s, Roman Catholicism was truly becoming a world church, and with recognition of that emerging reality came a sense that the church needed to deal more directly with the global issues of the day. Population growth was certainly one of them.

If John XXIII's election was not shock enough—virtually no one had ever heard of him—more tremors were felt when on January 25, 1959, just months after becoming pope, he announced he planned to hold an ecumenical council. Through all Catholic history there had been only twenty earlier ecumenical councils. Called to determine new doctrine or protest against heresy, councils are solemn occasions, gatherings of prominent church prelates and theologians during which they give more definitive shape to Catholic belief. John's idea was different. He wanted this council to be "pastoral" not "doctrinal" in nature. He felt it was time to update Catholic belief and practice to make it more understandable to the modern world. He wanted to reformulate church thinking and practice to make it more relevant, more vibrant. Most simply, he wanted to modernize the Catholic Church. At the time, the church was seen as so set in its ways that the very notion of modernizing seemed impossible, a contradiction of words. How, indeed, does one go about the task? It is said—although some call it church lore—that John, speaking of the church, remarked he wanted to "throw open the doors and windows and let a little light in."

Controversy surrounds his inspiration to call the council. Some reports say a number of cardinals suggested the idea to him while still in the conclave; others say the idea came to him within days of his election. That, at least, is how he recalled it in his personal diary.[2] On September 16, 1962 he wrote:

> *To have been able to accept as simple and capable of being immediately put into effect certain ideas which were not in the least complex in themselves, indeed perfectly simple, but far-reaching in their effects and full of responsibilities for the future. I was immediately successful in this, which goes to show that one must accept the good inspirations that come from the Lord, simply and confidently. Without any forethought, I put forward, in one of my first talks with my Secretary of State, on 20 January, 1959, the idea of an Ecumenical Council, A Diocesan Synod and the revision of the Code of Canon Law, all this being quite contrary to any previous supposition or idea of my own on this subject. I was the first to be surprised at my proposal, which was entirely my own idea.*

Rome's cardinal bureaucrats did not want to be bothered. Many were cool to the idea. Undaunted, John persisted, sending out word to Catholic leaders to start planning for the gathering. His popularity, meanwhile, mushroomed. Within weeks, during the very infancy of his pontificate, Catholics were calling him "the good Pope John."

The Second Vatican Council, or Vatican II, opened on October 11, 1962. A total of 2,860 prelates attended the first session; between 2,000 and 2,500 participated in each of the last three sessions. Each day for several months, the world's bishops gathered inside St. Peter's Basilica to discuss, debate, and vote. The atmosphere was highly politicized with sharp differences among the prelates. The last session's last day was December 8, 1965. Before it was all over, the council had promulgated sixteen documents, all aimed at forcing change, or church renewal, as it was called. Vatican II was the most stunning facelift in all of Catholic history. Pope John XXIII, the father of the event, however, did not live to see it all happen. And he knew early on he would not. During the council's first session he told his fellow bishops, "The council is like a big ship. I got it out to sea, but someone else will have to maneuver it into port." On June 3, 1963, six months after the close of that first session Pope John XXIII died of cancer. Condolences arrived from throughout the world, from rich and poor, from black, yellow, and white, from individuals and governments alike. Soviet Premier Nikita Khrushchev sent his; so, too, did Orthodox Patriarch Athenagoras I in Istanbul. Pope John had touched millions of souls.

John XXIII was succeeded on June 21, 1963, by Giovanni Battista Montini, the archbishop of Milan, who was elected pope on the fifth ballot. Montini took the name Pope Paul VI and immediately said he would carry through with the work of the council. He, too, wanted to update the church. Speaking in his first radio address the day after his election, Montini said: "The main duty of our pontificate will be the continuation of the Second Vatican Council." He had been involved in the council's preparation and had been elected as a council supporter. A man of similar pastoral outlook as John, Paul, however, had an opposite temperament. He was not as jovial and optimistic as John had been. He was rather a deliberate thinker, wanting to weigh matters carefully.

Decisions did not come easy to him. He simply foresaw too many long-term potentially painful consequences.

The council's second session began on September 29, 1963, just over three months after Montini had became pope. That session had more energy and direction than the first. The council fathers were settled in, and debates were growing in intensity. It was by no means clear where the council was going. Renewal and reform were by no means certainties. The bishops dealt with almost the full panoply of church issues, considering changes in church liturgy, communications, missionary life, religious freedom, evangelization, and ecumenical ties, to name a few. The prelates touched on human sexuality issues in a serious way only once, in a chapter on marriage in a document entitled *The Pastoral Constitution on the Church in the Modern World.* At long last, the bishops who studied marriage and its place in the church began to view it as something more than a "contract," as something other than a hierarchical arrangement of primary and secondary purposes. In fact, the bishops decided to put an end altogether to the long-standing ordering of the purposes of marriage, the first and foremost having been the intention of have children and educate them. Instead, they now recommended a new approach, an integrated principle to harmonize both ends of marriage—"the nature of the human person and his acts." They acknowledged the conjugal act as having two natural purposes, as having both procreative and unitive values. Not only was marriage concerned with having and educating children, it was also about drawing two people together in mutual love and support. This opened the door to seeing sexuality much more in relation to the interpersonal qualities of the relationship of wife and husband and to interpreting the morality of sex in this light. It meant that the goal of procreation was no longer the dominant moral standard in Catholic sexual ethics.[3] For the church, this was a revolutionary step. But would it open the door to seeing marriage as fulfilling even without children? Would it possibly lead to the notion that not every marriage absolutely required children? And would it just possibly provide a justification for using contraceptives to avoid having children? Implicit in the new document were a host of unanswered questions begging for further clarification.

Why weren't these questions addressed at the council? Certainly a good number of bishops wanted to do just that. Many thought a thorough reexamination of the entire birth control topic was called for—and demanded it be placed on the council's agenda. However, it was not to be. With pressure growing on Pope Paul VI to address the burgeoning issues of birth control, he declined and reserved the final decision to himself with advice from a special commission. Thus, the specific conclusions regarding the implications of the new principle for artificial contraception were not permitted to be drawn. Likewise, Paul VI took the issue of priestly celibacy out of the hands of the council. And for those two decisions, some began to see in him the tendency toward autocracy. Some began to compare him with his twentieth-century predecessors. Whether those judgments were fair or not, they would, it turned out, have significant implications for the church. His decisions meant artificial birth control and priestly celibacy would not get the thorough, *public* examination other church matters did. The bishops were not be able to express their opinions and hear the voices of other prelates who were obviously being called upon in their dioceses to deal with these delicate matters.

Keeping the issues at arm's length from the atmosphere of change that swept through the council protected the controversial issues from fresh scrutiny. They were, contrarily, dealt with in private ways.

One of Vatican II's most important accomplishments was the development of the idea of collegiality among bishops. Catholic tradition holds that each bishop is ultimately responsible for running his diocese. This is the church comprised of thousands of dioceses around the world, each independent and each coming together to make up the universal church. Each bishop is viewed as a descendent of one of the apostles. Together the bishops recognize the bishop of Rome as the sign of their unity. This is the decentralized model of church. A contrary view sees power and authority as trickling down from the pope through the Vatican and other bishops and to the clergy and laity around the world. This view, carried to its extreme, sees the local bishops as little more than papal delegates, or representatives. The centralized model throughout most of Catholic history has been in competition with the decentralized one. Vatican II represented an effort to reconfigure the church after it appeared to reach a new and unprecedented stage of centralization during Vatican I (1869–70) when the doctrine of papal infallibility was first officially proclaimed.

Etymologically, *infallibility* means inability to err. It does not mean freedom from sin or moral perfection. The doctrine is widely misunderstood both inside and outside the church. In theological terms it means the Holy Spirit protects the church from error when it solemnly defines a matter of faith or morals. Infallibility, as defined by the Vatican I, states that the pope possesses "the infallibility with which the divine Redeemer willed his church to be endowed in defining the doctrine concerning faith and morals."[4] When does the pope speak infallibly? According to the doctrine, he speaks infallibly when he officially speaks *ex cathedra* (from the chair of Peter) on a matter of church doctrine or morality. While this doctrine of papal infallibility has never been officially used in relation to any teaching on sexual morality, in recent years it has entered into church discussions concerning papal intentions on statements dealing with sex matters. Papal infallibility has had the affect of giving popes more authority. It has also raised other church authority questions. What if a pope was wrong on a moral matter? If he was—and many Catholics believe this an impossibility—how could the church reverse itself without damaging institutional credibility? Papal infallibility has had the effect of making official church teachings on matters of sexual morality, even those contested among Catholics and not officially declared infallible, more intractable.

Vatican II represented a significant movement back toward shared episcopal authority. Decisions came after much discussion, much give-and-take, and only after votes were taken. The decision by Pope Paul VI to remove birth control and priestly celibacy from council scrutiny seemed definitely out of step with the collective episcopal will of the time. The decision was not without its serious critics.

One such voice was that of Belgian Cardinal Leo-Jozef Suenens, who for years had been particularly concerned about birth control and the population issues. He worried about exploding world population and felt the church had to face up to the issue. There could be no denial, he thought. It was a grave concern to the church. With this in mind, he had for months gathered European scientists to discuss the issues and determine how they related to the church. Suenens asked them to keep him informed about what scientists and demographers were saying. Finally, with the world's bishops gathered in Rome, he felt it was an ideal time to speak up. During the council's first session, in one of its more closely watched episcopal interventions, he told the assembled bishops that birth control was a critical issue and that the church had to address it. He further warned that any renewed condemnation of artificial contraception could become another Galileo affair.

In 1633 the Italian mathematician, physicist, and astronomer, Galileo Galilei had been summoned to Rome for supporting the then hundred-year-old notion of the Copernican universe, which placed the earth in rotation around the sun. For his bold advocacy and defense of the Copernican system, Galileo was charged with heresy. Until the seventeenth century, Europeans believed the earth was the center of God's creative design. A lesser place was simply not conceivable. After a trial by the church Galileo was ordered to recant and was sentenced to house arrest where he stayed until his death in 1642.

Suenens could see the same embarrassment if the church did not find a way to incorporate scientific research and collective wisdom and apply it to the population issue. This was more than just a family-planning issue; it related to development, justice, and even world peace. He argued that the council had no choice but to broaden its scope to deal with the peace and justice issues of the day if it wanted to have a positive moral voice in such discussions. Further, Cardinal Suenens wanted Catholics to begin working seriously with other Christians to attack the perplexing problems facing the human family. His was a forceful voice at the council:

> *We must say something about the very life of the human person, the inviolability of that life, its procreation, its extension in what is called the population explosion. The church must speak on social justice. What is the theological and practical duty of rich nations toward the Third World or the nations that suffer from hunger? The church must speak about bringing the Gospel to the poor and some of the conditions the church must meet to make that Gospel relevant to them. The church must speak about international peace and war in a way that can help enlighten the world.*[5]

Suenens's sentiment was shared by other progressive-minded bishops, and together they tried to shape an activist council agenda. Their intended purpose, they said, was to infuse the basic values of the Gospels into the lives of the human family.

The birth control issue was festering elsewhere as well. Only a few months later, on March 21, 1963, it burst forth in the media in the Netherlands as William Bekkers, bishop of 's Hertogenbosch, went on television and publicly questioned the church's traditional teaching.[6] This was the first public call for change by a Catholic theologian, an important moment in church history. The battle for public opinion had begun. Speaking of "birth regulation" rather than "birth control," he said couples alone had to decide the size of their families. Their "human love and the sense of responsibility may encourage them to create a large or small family," he said, calling for a discussion of this question. Bekkers said that the church had to interpret *Casti Connubii,* Pope Pius XI's 1930 birth control encyclical, within the context of the time it was written, adding that new church thinking was now leading to new dogma because the context of church life had changed.[7] Then on August 10, 1963, in part to deflect criticism from Rome, seven bishops from the Netherlands, speaking as a national hierarchy, suggested that in some instances couples might morally use the still relatively new contraceptive, "the pill." The bishops of the Netherlands throughout their history have prized their independence from Rome. The Dutch are noted for speaking their minds, and they do not like outsiders interfering with what they have to say. In Catholic history tensions between Rome and the Netherlands are nothing new. The Dutch statement represented a serious attack on the church's official birth control position, and the most serious to that time by a group of Catholic bishops. They joined others in asking that the birth control issue be taken up by the council.

The early 1960s were a time when many prominent world voices began to speak out about demographics and a world population that was "exploding" in the decades following the introduction of antibiotics and better infant-health care. Some were saying at the time that the world's population would double in thirty-five years. The church could not be disinterested.

The first step the church had taken to face up to the problem had occurred more than a decade earlier, when in October 1951, Pope Pius XII, in his "Address to Midwives," gave Catholics explicit permission to regulate the birth of their children by means of the rhythm method, that is, purposefully refraining from sexual activity during a woman's fertile periods. He challenged scientists to take a serious look at the rhythm method as a means of limiting expanding population. Later, in 1954, Pope Pius XII told delegates to the World Population Conference in Rome that the church was attempting to do something about the problem. But what he offered again was the rhythm method.

Pope John XXIII made further references to population problems in his papal encyclicals, or teaching documents, *Mater et Magistra* ("Mother and Teacher") in 1961 and *Pacem in Terris* ("Peace on Earth") in 1963. He insisted that there was not a single population problem but many varied population problems throughout the world and that there were no simple answers. Population problems were on people's minds during Vatican II, but the reason birth control was a hot issue was the recent development of the birth control pill.

In the spring of 1963, John Rock, a Harvard professor who was a Catholic and one of the developers of the birth control pill, challenged his church to reevaluate its position on birth control. He said flatly that the pill was a "morally permissible variant of the rhythm method."[8] The challenge to the church was clear. Bernard Häring, a German Redemptorist teaching in Rome who had preached a spiritual retreat for Pope Paul and his curia, told *Time* magazine correspondent Robert Blair Kaiser he was somewhat open to Rock's suggestion. "We have a right to help nature," he said. Kaiser recalls Häring as saying it was important to him that the church no longer take a "moralistic, sin-centered approach" to this question. He wanted to see couples give themselves to each other in meaningful acts of true love. Questions and demands for a thorough reevaluation of the issue could not be silenced.

The Birth Control Commission

Early in 1963 Pope John XXIII, increasingly concerned about world demographic projections and the pain the church's birth control stance was causing Catholic couples, had quietly appointed a six-man commission to advise him on birth control. He died before the group met but had established a precedent for his successor, Pope Paul VI. The group members were men who had been recommended to him by Cardinal Suenens, members of the group the cardinal had quietly called together to examine the issue. The prestigious group consisted of a French Jesuit specializing in the sociology of the family, a British physician who had pioneered the temperature rhythm method, a Belgian Jesuit and demographer, a Swiss Dominican who worked as a Vatican observer at the United Nations in Geneva, a Brussels physician, and a professor at Louvain in Belgium. The newly formed papal commission met for the first time in October 1963 in Louvain. Part of their intent was to determine what stance the Vatican should take at an upcoming United Nations conference on population scheduled to be held the next year in New Delhi, India. An additional intent was to offer the pope advice on how to respond to the birth control pill. Commission members deliberated but were not able to give him much help, at least as far as the pill was concerned. No one among them felt comfortable enough to speak about the pill from a scientific point of view. They simply did not know the full ramifications of the pill's interaction with the female anatomy. The pill itself, a synthetic form of progesterone that suppressed ovulation, was something entirely new. It had not been developed until 1953. It was not approved by the U.S. Federal Drug Administration until 1960.

Because the 1963 meeting of Paul VI's special commission had produced so little, the pope asked its members to meet again. They met in Rome for three days secretly in April 1964. By this time the group had grown. Seven new members had been added, among them theologians, and it was hoped this time the team would provide the pope with a more theological reflection. Pope Paul wanted the issues to be studied from various perspectives. An intellectual, he moved slowly. Earlier while working in the Vatican's secretariat of the state, Montini had developed the reputation of being a Hamlet figure, ponderous and slow to come to decisions.

During the April 1964 gathering, the group still had two items on its agenda, both suggested by the pope: the morality of birth control and world demographics. The thirteen-member commission came no closer to a solution on either item than did the group of six. The commission found itself wrestling with an assortment of questions and issues, among them the church's teachings on natural law, Scripture, and the sacramentality of marriage. Discussing the issues, they found themselves being drawn yet deeper into theological questions. For example, what was meant by "natural" in natural law theology? On this there was wide disagreement, especially when they introduced the concept to marriage. After all, some argued, famine and disease were also "natural," but science had done something about these—which was one reason for the world population crisis. At one point, one commission member suggested a reformulation in thinking, not a change as such. His thinking was based, perhaps, on Pope John's words at the opening of the council: "The substance of the ancient doctrine is one thing, the way in which it is presented is another." Peter Hebblethwaite, the late Vatican affairs writer for the *National Catholic Reporter*, once wrote that the church needed "a new theological genre that would combine observation of what was going on with theological reflection upon it; in this way, the theology springs from the event and constantly refers back to it."[9]

In a way, this was what the prelates who gathered at the

Second Vatican Council were attempting; it was what some commission members were attempting; it meant viewing the church as a living, breathing organism, always developing, always trying to understand God's will for humanity. At issue here is the meaning of Revelation in Catholic theology, commonly understood as the truths disclosed by God for human salvation. Traditionally the church has taught that these truths are all contained in Scripture and the lives of the earliest Christians, ending with the death of the last apostle. More recent theologies have spoken about the evolution of doctrine and have seen Revelation as a never-ending process.

Church credibility and authority were also at stake. This became clear to commission members discussing the birth control issue. After all, how could the church change its teachings without losing credibility? How could it admit it had been wrong for so many years on birth control? Wrong on this most intimate of issues? And if it had been wrong, what might be the implications for other church teachings? What if they were wrong, too? What could be believed? What was beginning to emerge was a greater appreciation of how the birth control issue was tied up with other church issues, each potentially with grave implications for the future of the institution.

There were deep divisions on the commission, but eventually the group was able to affirm one important point: Love was at the heart of marriage. A majority agreed that the love of husband and wife should not, in any way, be ranked as a matter of secondary importance, a secondary end of marriage. This was already progress and represented a complete break with Augustinian thought. This new line of thinking could, at least theoretically, justify artificial birth control. Meanwhile, the commission agreed that rhythm was a morally acceptable birth control technique. Further, many in the group were reluctant to condemn the pill.

The contraceptive pill, meanwhile, remained a hot topic in the press, and Catholics were getting into the discussion. Rumors grew that the church was in the process of reconsidering its position on birth control. The Vatican was mum. No confirmation; no denial. Catholic theologians began to appear on television. They were being quoted in newspapers and magazines. Everywhere, it seemed, people were talking, both pro and con, about the pill. No pope had ever faced a situation quite like it. Theological discussion had entered the mainstream. No other theological dispute had such popular interest, and never before had there been media so ready to participate in the discussion. Theological questions had spilled out of the monasteries and university theology departments into the kitchens and living rooms of the world. Further, now that some Catholic theologians had dared to disagree openly with the old teaching, others felt they could as well. Dissent had its own momentum. The University of Notre Dame held two conferences on the "Problem of Population." They featured leading U.S. Catholic philosophers, moral theologians, physicians, and social scientists. There was, as a result, much uncertainty—and much expectation. As for the Vatican, it sensed the debate was slipping out of its hands.

Commission members remained divided. None yet supported a papal statement giving church approval to the pill. The group, however, wanted the pope to speak out, to say something, even if it was to be an inconclusive statement. On June 23, 1964, Pope Paul VI finally went public, though obliquely, with the information that a church commission was studying the birth control issue. Meanwhile, he cautioned that the norms established by Pope Pius XII "must be considered valid, at least until we feel obliged in conscience to change them." He continued: "In matters of such gravity, it seems well that Catholics should wish to follow the law, that which the church authoritatively puts forward. And it therefore seems opportune to recommend that no one, for the present, take it upon himself (or herself) to make pronouncements in terms different from the prevailing norm." He went on to say that the church would have to "proclaim the law of God in light of the scientific, social and psychological truths, which in these times have undergone new and very ample study and documentation." Finally, Pope Paul VI concluded with the words that "the question is being subjected to study, as wide and profound as possible." The commission was no longer a closely guarded Vatican secret.[10]

By the end of 1964 the papal commission had again grown, this time from fifteen to fifty-eight members. Pope Paul had concluded that even wider input was needed, and this time he wanted the opinions of Catholic lay couples. The new makeup included thirty-four laypersons, five of whom were women; twenty-two were priests and two were bishops. The commission would now have thirteen medical doctors, including three gynecologists and two psychiatrists. Other professions included demographers, sociologists, and economists.[11] Among those invited to join was a Chicago Catholic couple, Patrick and Patty Crowley. They received the invitation the first week of December from Cardinal Albert Meyer, archbishop of Chicago. Patrick had gone to Notre Dame and was a lawyer. Patty was an activist Catholic, a mother who had had six pregnancies, four children. During the last birth, she almost died. They were told to report to Rome in March. The couple had been active in a national Catholic organization, the Christian Family Movement, an organization that attempted to respond to contemporary problems in light of Scripture. To better prepare themselves, they asked for and received permission to send a questionnaire to members of their organization to see how other Catholic couples felt about the church's birth control stance. They sent out the questionnaires in late January, and by the time they set off for Rome, they had a sheaf of surprising replies. They had found widespread disenchantment with church teaching.

The fourth commission meeting was held from March 25 through March 28, 1965. The Crowleys remember approaching the gathering in awe but were relieved to find there a familiar voice—a young professor from Notre Dame, John T. Noonan Jr., who had achieved notoriety for a study he had done on the church and usury. That study showed Catholic teaching could change and had; theologians who had once condemned the practice of the lending of money for a fee—usury—had changed their minds and church teaching when the practice became a part of sound economics. The lesson was obvious. If it could happen once or twice (the church had also changed its views on slavery in the nineteenth century), it could happen again.

Pat and Patty Crowley told commission members that many of the couples they had surveyed felt that the rhythm method hurt their married life. They viewed it as a "detraction" and not as a marriage enhancement. One couple with six children, married thirteen years, told this story, which they relayed to the commission. According to the husband:

> *Rhythm destroys the meaning of the sex act: it turns it from a*

spontaneous expression of spiritual and physical love into mere bodily sexual relief; it makes me obsessed with sex throughout the month; it seriously endangers my chastity; it has a noticeable effect upon my disposition toward my wife and children; it makes necessary my complete avoidance of all affection toward my wife for three weeks at a time. I have watched a magnificent spiritual and physical union dissipate and, due to rhythm, turn into a tense and mutually damaging relationship. Rhythm seems to be immoral and completely unnatural. It seems to me diabolical.[12]

His wife, writing independently, reported:

My doctor advised me, recommended the basal temperature combined with the calendar method, and was constantly consulted. The psychological problems worsened, however, as we had baby after baby. We eventually had to resort to a three-week abstinence and since then (three years) we have had no pregnancy. I find myself sullen and resentful of my husband when the time for sexual relations finally arrives. I resent his necessarily guarded affection during the month and I find I cannot respond suddenly. I find, also, that my subconscious dreams and unguarded thoughts are inevitably sexual and time-consuming. All this in spite of a great intellectual and emotional companionship and a generally beautiful marriage and home life.[13]

Some commission members pointed out that the official church had already abandoned its traditional teaching on birth control when Pope Pius XII in 1951 approved the rhythm method. If the intent was to avoid a pregnancy, it was asked, does the means to fulfill that intent really matter? Traditional Catholic theology has always taught that intent is one of the elements that must be weighed to determine the gravity of a sin. On the last day of their meetings that month, the commission members met with the pope who encouraged them to continue their deliberations. They in turn advised him, pending the final outcome of their work, not to reiterate past birth control condemnations.[14]

The Vatican Council ended on December 8, 1965, the Feast of the Immaculate Conception, the Catholic feast day that celebrates the conception of Mary without original sin. Pope Paul VI was eager to get direction from his commission. Previously, he had authorized three- and four-day meetings. Now he gave the commission two months and a budget. The final session of the pope's commission for the Study of Population and Family Life began on April 13, 1966. The theologians came first. The others arrived in May and stayed until late June. And now "the others" included fourteen new members, cardinals and bishops appointed by the pope, "to give the new pastoral emphasis to the deliberations." Among them was the archbishop of Kraków, Poland, Karol Wojtyla, the future Pope John Paul II. He attended no meetings, however. For unknown reasons he decided to stay in Poland.

Late May and early June were a particularly productive time for the commission. It was a time of bitter dispute as well as growing consensus. Two camps had formed. A solid majority, however, had emerged in favor of changing church teachings on birth control. On May 26, the theologians' committee turned in their paper titled "Responsible Parenthood." It was to become known in later years as the Commission's Majority Report. On his own, the Jesuit theologian John Ford, with the help of a young professor of philosophy at Georgetown University in Washington, D.C., then in Rome to provide assistance, wrote a treatise titled

"The State of the Question: The Doctrine of the Church and Its Authority." This paper defended the status quo and in the years that followed was to be called the Commission's Minority Report.

By late June, the work of the commission had come down to three questions, and the cardinals and bishops were to vote on them: (1) Whether all contraception was intrinsically evil. (2) Whether they could affirm that contraception could be affirmed in continuity with tradition and the declarations of the church. (3) Whether the church ought to speak as soon as possible. After the votes were counted, on the first question, nine bishops said contraception was not intrinsically evil; two said it was; one said it was, but with a reservation; three abstained. It was a clear victory for the forces of change. On the second question, nine said they could affirm change in continuity with tradition; five said they could not. Still a vote in favor of change, but with troubling reservations. On the third question, fourteen said the pope should speak as soon as possible; only one said no. Several published reports stated that the full commission voted before adjourning and that the result was 52 to 4 in favor of the Majority Report.[15] Its work completed, the commission handed over their work to the pope.

Paul VI's agonizing task, however, was not yet completed. He was to have assistance from the future Pope John Paul II. Not having participated in the commission's work, Wojtyla set up a commission of his own in Kraków, Poland, to help the pope formulate his encyclical. Wojtyla prepared materials and forwarded them directly to the pope. A Polish theologian who worked with Wojtyla on the matter later reported that "about sixty percent of our draft is contained in the encyclical."[16]

GOING PUBLIC

Time passed, and there was still no final decision from the pope. Public opinion among Catholics continued to shift perceptibly away from traditional rejection of "artificial contraception." On January 19, 1966, the *National Catholic Reporter (NCR)*, the independent Kansas City, Missouri, lay-edited weekly, published a paper with the headline: "Pill Ban Unenforceable Unless Pope Speaks Soon." The article quoted the Jesuit moral theologian Father Richard A. McCormick as saying that because of the long delay in a definitive pronouncement from the pope, a state of "practical doubt" would soon exist in the church that would allow freedom of choice of birth control.

On October 29, 1966, Pope Paul VI, obviously under pressure, stated that the official magisterium, the teaching body of the church, was in a state of "reflection" on the issue of birth control—but not in a state of "doubt." Appearing before members of the Italian Society of Obstetrics and Gynecology during a papal audience at St. Peter's, he admitted that the birth control issue was "a very delicate question." He said he knew they awaited his decisive pronouncement, but he could not make one at the time. His commission had given him its conclusions, he said, but he did not consider them "definitive."[17] In the meantime, what were Catholics to do? "Church teaching," he said, "demands faithful and generous observance."

In the early spring of 1967, *NCR* editor Robert Hoyt received a telephone call from France. It was from an American freelance journalist, Gary MacEoin, who asked Hoyt if the *NCR* would like to join *Le Monde*, the Paris daily newspaper, in publishing the texts of the previously secret reports of the papal birth control commission. Hoyt responded affirmatively. MacEoin had learned from sources in Paris that a member of the papal commission was releasing the documents to *Le Monde.* He inquired as to whether they would offer a simultaneous newsbreak in the United States. *Le Monde* and the commission member agreed. So MacEoin offered the documents to the *NCR* to assure that the entire texts, not just stories about them, would appear in print. *NCR* and *Le Monde* agreed to a simultaneous publication. The *NCR* came out with the story on April 15, 1967, but for some reason *Le Monde* held off one day and the *NCR* had a world exclusive. The front-page headline read: "Reveal Papal Birth Control Texts—Pill No Issue; Focus on Magisterium." *The New York Times* followed two days later with a front-page story with the headline, "Majority Report Seeks Papal Shift on Contraception."

The commission documents had come to light.[18] The Majority Report had been signed by nineteen of the theologians and by a number of the other experts on the commission. First, although it favored allowing artificial contraception in some cases, it insisted that sex and marriage are properly oriented toward the procreation and education of children. Second, it approached the issue from the viewpoint of what is good overall for a marriage and not by focusing on the sex act. Third, it did not see artificial contraception as intrinsically evil but approached the question of morality from a situational viewpoint. Fourth, it saw the church as being consistent, even as it changed its position on contraception, by arguing in both instances that the values of having and educating children were best being protected. It was the circumstances and not the values that had changed. Fifth, it condemned any "contraceptive mentality," that is, the attitude of entering marriage without any willingness to raise a family.

The Minority Report, meanwhile, argued against the various positions in the Majority Report. Its four authors maintained that questions of contraception could not be solved by reason alone and that church tradition needed to be upheld. It stated that "if we could bring forward arguments which are clear and cogent based on reason alone, it would not be necessary for our commission to exist, nor would the present state of affairs exist in the church as it is."[19] The authors went on to argue that the church could not possibly have erred on such a grave matter and, therefore, the church must be right on contraception. "If the church could err [on this issue], the authority of the ordinary magisterium in moral matters would be thrown into question," the report stated. "The faithful could not put their trust in the magisterium's presentation of moral teaching, especially in sexual matters." Further the authors argued that the church opposed contraception not because it interferes with human biology as such, but because it runs contrary to the "generative" orientation within marriage.

The news of the documents made headlines around the world, angering Vatican officials while further raising expectations the church would soon be changing its position on birth control, viewing the purpose of marriage in a different light and accepting a form of situational morality that it had steadfastly condemned for centuries. Like it or not, this would be the Catholic Church entering the modern world in a bold and brave new way.

His advisers had spoken. All that was left was to hear from Pope Paul VI. Catholics and others around the world awaited his words.

III

❖ ❖ ❖

Birth Control

The year 1968 was momentous in U.S. history. Many remember it for the Vietnam War's Tet Offensive, the raucous Democratic National Convention in Chicago, the assassinations of Robert F. Kennedy and Dr. Martin Luther King Jr. However, for U.S. Catholics it was also the year of *Humanae Vitae,* the controversial birth control encyclical. To understand fully its significance it is necessary to look back briefly to the mid-nineteenth century. Until then in some parts of western Europe (and until the early twentieth century in other parts of Europe), unlimited fertility was not viewed as a serious problem. To the contrary, it was considered a plus. Until then, infant mortality remained high. It took many pregnancies to assure the birth of enough children to replace and care for aging parents. A century ago it was still common for a woman to give birth to up to a dozen children, depending on her diet, health, and her age at the time of marriage. Most offspring died before reaching adulthood. Indeed, up until a century ago it took more than seven pregnancies to produce two adults. Further, having many children was considered an economic asset, a necessity in the largely agricultural society of the time.

Fundamental changes in living conditions began to occur after elementary health measures were introduced, reducing infant and maternal mortality rates. This change, which demographers call the demographic transition, happened almost overnight as human history goes. Meanwhile, large migrations to the cities were taking place for the first time, turning children from economic assets to economic liabilities.[1] Catholic France was among the first to face the revolution of a rapidly expanding population. The French, lacking the yet-to-be-developed twentieth-century contraceptives, responded by practicing *coitus interruptus,* or withdrawal, and by using crude condoms. This presented a new moral dilemma for the Catholic hierarchy, who were not quite certain how to respond.[2] Pope Leo XIII (papacy 1878–1903), in his 1880 encyclical on marriage, *Arcanum Divinae Sapientiae,* written when contraception was widespread in France—and he knew it to be so because of his contacts with the French bishops—said nothing on the subject. His encyclical focused on what he saw as the largest problem in society at the time, civil divorce. It is not clear what precisely changed Rome's thinking between the late nineteenth century and early twentieth century, but clearly there was an about-face at the Vatican. Some speculate that it took a few decades from the perception of the problem to clerical reaction against it. In any case, Pope Pius XI's 1930 encyclical, *Casti Connubii,* saw contraceptive practices as grievously sinful. In turn, by the mid-1930s, priests in the United States, Ireland, England, and Canada had also changed their views, moving from not troubling lay consciences to troubling them very much.

Father Arthur Veermersch, a Jesuit, drafted *Casti Connubii* for Pius XI. Veermersch insisted on dealing with the issue of contraception not only because the Anglican bishops earlier in the year at the Lambeth Conference had offered their reluctant tolerance to contraception, but also because he feared many priests were not enforcing the doctrine in the confessional.[3] Perhaps the reason for the reversal was that a third of the way into the twentieth century the demographic transition had begun to affect so many countries that contraception was becoming a universal practice. Nearly four decades later, by the time Pope Paul VI was thinking through all the implications of birth control for a possible change in church teaching, ecclesial concern had reached a feverish pitch. After the Second Vatican Council had concluded and after the papal birth control commission had offered its reports, it was now up to Pope Paul to make the final decision and either free Catholics from the heavy weight of church teaching or to continue to uphold traditional teachings. Either way, it would be the most important decision of his pontificate—perhaps, the most important moral decision of any pontificate in modern times. The decision did not come easily, especially for this pope. The Italian Cardinal Achille Silvestrini was one of many who saw Pope Paul as a kind of Hamlet figure. Silvestrini remarked once that Montini, the intellectual, saw all too clearly "the infinite complexity of situations." Adding to the pope's problems were the already vastly raised expectations of the world's Catholics.

Since the close of the council in December 1965 expectations continued to rise within the church. This was especially so after April 1967 when the leaked commission reports hit the newsstands. Months passed. The year 1967 passed and no word from Rome. The next year brought even higher expectations. During the summer of 1968, rumors spread throughout the church that the Vatican was about to release the long-awaited birth control statement. The Vatican press office called these reports absolutely false. Then on July 29, word finally came. It was the encyclical entitled *Humanae Vitae,* literally "Of Human Life." The encyclical was a sensitively written expression about the sanctity of marital love and the need to nurture life in marriage. Some said the encyclical was almost poetic and came as a much-needed statement concerning human dignity. Maybe so, but whatever else it stated, it has been remembered for only one thing: upholding of the Catholic Church's ban on artificial birth control. Pope Paul VI rejected the findings of the Majority Report of the commission and reaffirmed the position of Pope Pius XI and Pope Pius XII. It was an unambiguous reiteration of the church's traditional act-centered morality: "The Church, calling human beings back to the observance of the norms of the natural law, as interpreted by her constant doctrine, teaches that each and every marriage act must remain open to the transmission of life."[4]

However, *Humanae Vitae* reiterated Catholic moral ideas first found in the Vatican II document *Pastoral Constitution on the Church in the Modern World* in saying there is an inseparable connection, willed by God, between the two meanings of the sex act: the procreative and the unitive. Pope Paul wrote the following:

The teaching, often set forth by the magisterium, is founded upon the inseparable connection willed by God and unable to be broken by the human person on his [or her] own initiative, between the two meanings of the conjugal act: the unitive meaning and the procreative meaning. Indeed, by its intimate structure, the conjugal act, while most closely uniting husband and wife, capacitates them for the generation of new lives, according to laws inscribed in the very being of man and of woman. By safeguarding both of these essential aspects, the unitive and the procreative, the conjugal act preserves in its fullness the sense of true mutual love and its ordination towards humanity's most high calling to parenthood. We believe that the men and women of our day are particularly capable of seizing the deeply reasonable and human character of this fundamental principle.[5]

The encyclical upheld Pope Pius XII's support of the rhythm method (now called natural family planning) and in doing so, revealed its particular understanding of natural law. By using artificial birth control techniques, a couple "impedes the development of natural processes"; using planned abstinence, a couple makes "legitimate use of a natural disposition." The pope wrote the following:

If therefore there are reasonable grounds for spacing births, arising from the physical or psychological condition of husband or wife, or from external circumstances, the Church teaches that then married people may take advantage of the natural cycles immanent in the reproductive system and use their marriage at precisely those times that are infertile, and in this way control birth, a way which does not in the least offend the moral principles which we have just explained.[6]

The encyclical, therefore, rested its case on the physiological structure of the act of intercourse, while dissenting theologians insisted the conjugal act itself must be viewed not as an isolated reality but in the larger context of human love and family life. This is called the principle of totality and was specifically rejected in the encyclical. Many in the church were deeply disappointed by the encyclical. Among them were Catholic theologians whose only consolation was the fact that the pope, in promulgating the encyclical, had not designated it to be an infallible teaching. These theologians pointed out that Paul VI purposefully refrained from designating it as such, noting that his spokesman, Monsignor Ferdinand Lambruschini, explicitly stated the encyclical was not irreformable.[7]

Clearly the 1960s marked a critical turning point in Catholic attitudes and practices regarding sexual matters. The changes were so remarkable that theologians examined the development and traced these changes to a confluence of factors that came together at the time. They were the following: (1) The development in biblical, historical, and systematic theology that had led to a more holistic and person-oriented approach to moral matters; (2) advances in the behavioral and social sciences that provided a new understanding of the purpose and meaning of human sexuality; (3) a deeper appreciation of the dignity, uniqueness, and freedom of each individual human being; (4) the personalist-oriented theology of marriage and sexuality as expressed in the papal commission's Majority Report and in the Vatican II document *Pastoral Constitution on the Church in the Modern World;* (5) an increased sense of personal freedom and responsibility in the determination of one's own life; (6) easy availability of sophisticated birth control means; and (7) a growing awareness of the world population problem and its potential threat to the overall quality of human life.[8] In the midst of these new trends, however, one determinant more than any other eventually stood out, and it came to symbolize the serious rift that began to grow between official church teaching and Catholic attitudes and practices regarding human sexuality: *Humanae Vitae,* the birth control issue.

Pope Paul later discussed with confidants his disappointment in the way his encyclical had been received. He said he had expected some opposition from the secular media but had not been prepared for the widespread opposition from priests and theologians. One of the most vocal U.S. critics has been the sociologist and author Father Andrew M. Greeley, whose studies in the years that followed traced the magnitude of the encyclical's rejection by the laity: "Church leaders," Greeley wrote, "have a lot to answer for, and their responsibility is all the more serious because so much of what they did and said was both arrogant and ignorant and done and said by men who had no personal involvement in the experiences about which they were making judgments."[9]

Many bishops were lukewarm to the encyclical. Although the Vatican asked all national episcopal conferences for statements in support of *Humanae Vitae,* many attempted to nuance that support without denying or directly challenging it. Some conferences of bishops explicitly recognized the possibility of dissent; others stressed its pastoral directives, pointing out that in some instances grave sin might not always be present among those who failed to uphold it. Among the encyclical's most prominent casualties was Bishop James P. Shannon, auxiliary bishop of St. Paul–Minneapolis, considered then to be one of the more articulate members of the U.S. Catholic hierarchy.[10] As president of St. Thomas College in St. Paul, Minnesota, Shannon had become prominent in educational circles as well. When he was appointed bishop in the mid-1960s, he quickly became a popular national speaker. By 1966, Shannon was made assistant episcopal moderator of the Catholic Press Association. A year later, he appeared on an NBC documentary called "The New American Catholic," commenting on the various trends and conflicts in the church at the time. His comments were low-key, but they disturbed Los Angeles Cardinal James F. McIntyre, one of the U.S. hierarchy's most conservative prelates. McIntyre issued a statement that accused Shannon of not "speaking for the people of God." He sent copies of his criticism to all the U.S. bishops, filing an official complaint with the administrative committee of the National Conference of Catholic Bishops, the official episcopal governing body.

At their late September 1968 meeting in Washington, D.C., the bishops heard McIntyre's charges and voted in agreement with him. Shannon was crushed. In the spring of 1969, he moved away from church work, assuming a teaching position at a nondenominational college in Santa Fe, New Mexico. That summer it became public that following the 1968 publication of *Humanae Vitae,* Shannon had written a formal letter to Pope Paul disagreeing with the encyclical and asking to be relieved of episcopal duties. In August 1969, he announced his resignation from the priesthood, married, and continued as a college administrator while he entered law school in New Mexico. He was not the only vocal episcopal critic. Denis Hurley, archbishop of Durban, South Africa, told his people in a front-page interview in the *Southern Cross,* a Catholic weekly in Capetown, that he believed the pope "had a right to make the decision. But I would be dishonest if I agreed with the method of consultation or the result."[11] He said the encyclical was "the most painful experience of my life as a bishop. I have never felt so torn in half." The bishops of Belgium, West Germany, and Canada also expressed their objections, though respectfully.[12] The Canadian Bishops Conference noted the birth control question must ultimately be left to individual conscience. (Catholic theology teaches that, in the final analysis, a person's conscience is the final moral arbitrator. Of course, the official church stresses a healthy conscience listens to and acts in accord with church teaching.) Thomas D'Esterre, the retired Archbishop of Bombay, India, was among those objecting Catholic voices coming from the Third World. He said the pope's natural law arguments simply did not convince him.

To fully comprehend the encyclical's impact on the church at the time it helps to recall the mood within the church. The Second Vatican Council appeared to be moving Catholicism toward a less hierarchical model of the church, one that paid greater attention to the *sensus fidelium,* literally "the sense of the faithful." (Catholic theology teaches this is an important measure of theological truth, passed down by Christians through the centuries.) As a result of the council, the idea of "episcopal collegiality" was a resurrected and intriguing notion in Catholic circles. This was the notion that the world's bishops, as successors of the apostles, all share—with the pope—the authority to govern the church. The Second Vatican Council's deliberations and votes were the most visible signs of this newly come-to-life collegial church. They were solid indications the church was truly getting a needed facelift, adopting modern governing techniques.

Many Catholics were optimistic about the future of their

church. In 1968, change was already occurring in the parish liturgies. Latin was out and use of the vernacular language was in for celebration of local masses. Religious orders were examining their "founding charisms," attempting to recapture and rekindle formative spirits. Religious women were updating their habits—or discarding traditional religious garments altogether. Vatican II had fired Catholic imagination. The church, it was said, was once again to become "Jesus-centered" and "gospel-based." Members of the Catholic laity were being challenged to "come alive" and take on greater responsibility for their faith. The church was no longer simply to be an organization of bishops, priests, and nuns with some laity at the bottom. It was, instead—as primarily defined during the council—"the people of God," inclusive, and without clerical-lay distinction. Catholics were energized and involved—and impatient to get on with breathing new life into their faith. There was much talk and many plans to build a church founded in gospel values and peace and justice work.

In Catholic universities students were enthusiastic; lectures were crowded; the laity was taking greater interest in theology and religious education; priests and religious were eager to find out about the work of the council. The optimism was infectious. Those were heady days. And while some cautioned against the dangers of over optimism, few listened. The tide of church reform, held back for centuries, finally was moving forward. The Roman Catholic Church, at long last, was on the move—entering the modern world.

And then came *Humanae Vitae.*

It differed in tone from *Casti Connubii,* the 1930 artificial contraception condemnation by Pope Pius XI—but that wasn't enough. *Humanae Vitae* included a section on pastoral directives. Pope Paul admitted to the difficulty he knew Catholics would have in living in accord with the teaching. He seemed to agonize writing that he knew many couples might fail to live up to the teachings. He told them not to become discouraged. He never spoke of moral sin. Instead, he reminded couples to have recourse to the mercy of God in the sacraments. Paul VI wrote: "We hold it as certain that while the Holy Spirit of God is present to the magisterium in propounding sound doctrine, he also illumines from within the hearts of the faithful and invites their assent." *Invites their assent!*[13] This was not the order of an authoritarian tyrant seeking to impose his will. It was, rather, the tortured, faith-filled response of a man who eventually came to believe he simply could not break with earlier church teachings. Not in good conscience.

It would be inaccurate to say that *Humanae Vitae* was without its strong supporters. When it finally came out, many Catholics were relieved. Many found in it the "proof" that the church was, indeed, guided by the Holy Spirit. The church, they argued, was not giving in to fashion. Instead, it was standing up for truth—and doing so was not an easy task. It was, on the contrary, an act of courage. Some Catholics lauded the encyclical's theology, saying it reaffirmed the sacred idea that sexual intercourse is a deeply human act, involving a union of body and spirit not found in any other human activity. They found in the encyclical the reminder that sexual intercourse demands freedom, respect, equality, and joyful playfulness and that only in such conditions could it be truly a language of love.[14] This is the solid foundation on which, they said, *Humanae Vitae* is built: Human sexual intercourse is an act of love that expresses the truth of a relationship that is permanent, enduring, and exclusive. It is, in the strict sense, lovemaking. This is the "unitive" meaning of marriage. But—and this is the heart of *Humanae Vitae,* they maintained—human sexual intercourse also has another meaning "in itself." The unitive meaning unfolds into the procreative meaning. It is natural, they argued, to want a child as a concrete expression of mutual love. *Humanae Vitae,* they said, does not teach that every act of intercourse should lead to a pregnancy and offspring. But, they said, it does say that if systematically and deliberately the possibility of ever having children is always excluded, then there is something wrong. Against a pragmatic view of life, *Humanae Vitae* proclaims a vision of human sexuality as participating in the creative act of God. Contraception, the encyclical maintains, drastically alters the sacred balance between the unitive and procreative in marriage.

Catholics have been on divergent paths at least since the Second Vatican Council. One of the first and most visible indicators of the rift came in reactions to *Humanae Vitae.* More than sexual morality, it turned out, was at stake. What soon became clear was that a deeper issue was involved, the credibility of church leaders, in this case, the pope himself. What happens when prominent Catholics simply believe, in good conscience, their pope is wrong. Do they remain silent? Are they obliged to say nothing? Or should they speak out? Indeed, does their faith require them to say what they believe to be true? Nothing like this had happened before. At least not in the modern era. Something new as a response was definitely called for—but what? The Catholic Church had arrived at a new moment. There needed to be a new way of looking at one's Catholicism, a way that combined a faith assent to fundamental belief but that also was willing to disagree with certain aspects of church teaching. Some in the church began to make the distinction between upholding infallibly declared doctrine while reserving the right to dissent from some specific noninfallibly proclaimed expressions by the official church. If there was room for this new type of Catholic, the space within the church was being carved out by a new wave of vocal critics; among the most prominent were a number of theologians connected to Catholic University in Washington, D.C.

Dissenting Voices

On the afternoon of July 29, 1968, a group of ten theologians met in a basement meeting at the Catholic University of America in Washington, D.C., to study the new document, *Humanae Vitae.*[15] One of the group's members was Father Charles Curran, a young moral theologian. "We concluded that the encyclical offered no new arguments and in our judgment would cause great problems for the church. In that situation, we felt a responsibility to make a public statement," he recalled years later.[16] Curran drafted a statement that was accepted by the group with some modifications. In the process, the theologians asserted the common (but not well-known) teaching that Catholics may dissent from authoritative, noninfallible church teachings. The theologians took exception to the implied "ecclesiology" and "methodology" used in the writing, saying they were "incompatible with the Church's authentic self-awareness as expressed in the acts of the Vatican Council." On ecclesiology, they wrote the following:

> *The encyclical consistently assumes that the church is identical with the hierarchical office. No real importance is afforded the wit-*

ness of the life of the church in its totality; the special witness of many Catholic couples is neglected; it fails to acknowledge the witness of the separated Christian churches and ecclesial communities; it is insensitive to the witness of many men and women of good will; it pays insufficient attention to the ethical import of modern science.[17]

On the encyclical's ethical conclusions and methodology, they wrote as follows:

They are based on an inadequate concept of natural law: the multiple forms of natural law theory are ignored and the fact that competent philosophers come to different conclusions on this very question are disregarded. . . . Other defects include: overemphasis on the biological aspects of conjugal relations as ethically normative; undue stress on sexual acts and on the faculty of sex viewed in itself apart from the person and the couple; a static world view which downplays the historical and evolutionary character of humanity in its finite existence. . . .

The theologians concluded that "spouses may responsibly decide according to their conscience that artificial contraception in some circumstances is permissible and indeed necessary to preserve and foster the values and sacredness of marriage."

The next day, the group held a news conference to announce that 87 scholars in the sacred sciences had signed their statement. The number subsequently grew to more than 600. What was unique about this reaction, recalls Curran, was the prompt, public, and organized manner of the dissent. Such an approach had never been tried before. The response of the Catholic University theologians constituted the first Catholic organized theological resistance in the mass media age. Life in the church would never again be the same.

Two days later, on August 1, two birth control commission members, Dr. Andre Hellegers and Thomas Burch, along with John T. Noonan Jr., who had been the commission's expert on the history of contraception, appeared at a news conference in Washington. Speaking for all three, Noonan said the encyclical suffers from "internal inconsistency" since the central teaching that every marriage act must remain "open to the transmission of life" contradicts the encyclical's parallel teaching that "the rhythm system of contraception may be used for appropriate reasons."[18]

Meanwhile, the dissenting faculty at Catholic University had become an informal coordinating center for pubic dissent on *Humanae Vitae.* Some bishop trustees threatened to remove them from their teaching posts, but a faculty investigating committee defended what they did as academically responsible. They were not the only protesting theologians. Twenty European theologians, including two of the most prominent theologians in the church, German Redemptorist Bernard Häring and Austrian Jesuit Karl Rahner, added to the voices of dissent shortly after the encyclical's release. Häring was one more to question the logic of condemning contraception while arguing the morality of family planning through periodic abstinence. He noted the tone of the new encyclical was milder than that of *Casti Cannubii,* expressing the hope the tone would help guide its teachings. Then came a "demand" in the official Vatican newspaper, *L'Osservatore Romano* that, according to Häring's account, "whoever does not accept the encyclical in obedience and in belief should leave the church. With that one blow my determination to be silent on the questions was set aside."[19] Häring issued a statement that was printed on the front page of major newspapers in several countries. Häring stated that Catholics who are convinced that *Humanae Vitae* correctly interprets divine law "must earnestly endeavor to live according to this conviction. Whoever, however, after serious reflection and prayer is convinced that in his or her case such a prohibition could not be the will of God should in inner peace follow his/her conscience and not thereby feel her/himself to be a second-class Catholic."[20]

Catholic reactions to *Humanae Vitae* were summed up by Jesuit moral theologian Father Richard A. McCormick, a vocal critic of the official church's birth control stance. There was, he said, "solace or shock, suspension or silence." The "solaced" were the few who had staked their marriages on *Casti Connubii* and had numerous children out of fidelity to what they thought was the church's teaching. The "shocked" were those who had been led to expect change as a result of the existence of the pontifical commission. The "suspended" were those priests who voiced public dissent from the encyclical. From the rest, he said, there was silence.

Pope Paul VI, seemingly beleaguered by the Catholic reaction, never wrote another encyclical after *Humanae Vitae;* he seemed to ossify in its wake and in advancing age. Meanwhile, the divisions between hierarchy and laity on birth control, serious from the start, grew more so. Less than a decade after the encyclical's promulgation, polls indicated more than eight out of ten adult U.S. Catholics simply disregarded it. But that was not all. It was eroding Catholic confidence in the institution. Father Andrew M. Greeley, sociologist and director of the Chicago-based National Opinion Research Center, reported that *Humanae Vitae* resulted in a dramatic decline in church credibility and Catholic contributions. He reported that one of his U.S. studies showed that shortly before *Humanae Vitae* 67 percent of responding priests said they would not refuse confessional absolution to lay people practicing birth control. Five years later, after *Humanae Vitae,* that number had risen to 87 percent. The encyclical had the result of increasing active dissent among parish priests. In fact, 60 percent of the U.S. priests queried said they rejected the church's birth control teaching.

Humanae Vitae was quite explicit in explaining why Pope Paul concluded he could not in the end accept the recommendations of his commission. He wrote the following:

> *The conclusions at which the commission arrived could not, nevertheless, be considered by us as definitive . . . above all because certain criteria of solutions had emerged which departed from the moral teaching on marriage proposed with constant firmness by the teaching authority of the church.*[21]

It was argued by some that in rejecting the advice of the broad-based commission, the pope had implicitly rejected any concept of the church as a community of participation and was returning to the crudest of appeals to papal power. The result of the conflict between the findings of personal conscience and what most saw as the unsupported decision of the pope was the loss of papal authority.

In summary, it appears that church hierarchy began a serious effort to talk the Catholic faithful out of birth control only early in this century (because only in this century was it perceived as a problem). The effort became official in the 1930s, but for practical purposes had concluded four decades later by which time Catholics had made up their minds by themselves. The vote, as it were, once taken, would unlikely occur again, much to the frustration and disappointment of those church officials who continue to view artificial contraception as a grave intrinsic evil.

It is easy, meanwhile, to forget that all other Christian religions along with most people in the Western world held that contraception was wrong up until the nineteenth century and in some cases well into the twentieth century. Why then could others change while official Catholic teachings held firm? Among the factors cited by a number of Catholic moral theologians for this unwillingness or inability to change include the following:

One, by the twentieth century the Catholic Church had developed a theological-ethical theory that explained in a systematic way its total teaching with regard to sexual morality. The purpose of sexuality is procreation (and later love union), which means that sexuality must be restricted to marriage and that every single act of sexuality must be open to procreation. This provides the rationale for the acceptance of the generally held Catholic moral beliefs that extramarital intercourse, homosexuality, masturbation, and artificial contraception are always wrong. This systematic theory thus provides a basis for the whole understanding of sexuality. Seen as a systematic whole, to change positions on any one of these beliefs might be viewed as potentially opening the church to changes in other teachings.

Two, the Catholic Church, with its great emphasis on tradition, always finds it difficult to go against what has been proposed in the past.

Three, the Catholic Church, coming out of the nineteenth century, often saw itself in opposition to the modern world and what was taking place there. As it rejected many modern developments, it found itself becoming increasingly defensive and even ghettoized. It was easy to cast contraception as simply one more evil creeping into modern society and its wayward morality.

Four, by the time *Humanae Vitae* became public it had become not just a morality question but also an essential authority question. The question would be asked in varied ways: How could the Holy Spirit allow the church to have been wrong?

With all the Second Vatican Council's deliberations, it never confronted the issue of how to change church teaching. Yet it has had to do it on several important issues—usury and slavery are two. More recently it has been instructive to see how the church changed its teachings on religious liberty. In the nineteenth century, it condemned religious liberty. By the end of the Second Vatican Council it had embraced the idea. Was the church being inconsistent? The council bishops at the council said, "no." It was correct, they said, to condemn religious liberty in the nineteenth century, and it was correct again to accept the idea in the twentieth century. They argued that the circumstances had changed requiring a change in church teaching. What some moral theologians lament is that the council bishops never got the chance to try the same logic on birth control and thereby head off the need for any pope to write an encyclical on this controversial subject.

IV

Abortion

In the summer of 1969, a single twenty-five-year-old woman told a frightful story. She was walking home from work one night when she was grabbed and gang-raped. Several weeks later she learned to her great dismay that she was pregnant. Abortion was illegal in Texas, where she lived at the time. Unable to terminate her unwanted pregnancy, she decided to challenge the state's abortion ban for the sake of other women. Her condition was that she remain anonymous. She became "Jane Roe" for the sake of the law suit. Henry Wade was the name of the Dallas county prosecutor. The suit became the momentous *Roe versus Wade* case, or simply *Roe v. Wade.*[1]

It took several years for the suit to work its way through the legal system to the Supreme Court of the United States. The mood of the country had been changing: abortion rights activists were gaining an upper hand, pointing to the fact that botched "back alley" abortions often resulted in serious illness and death. The scope of civil rights was expanding to include women. Interest was gaining in preventing unwanted pregnancies.

Then on January 22, 1973, a new era opened in the United States. The Supreme Court ruled in a landmark 7 to 2 decision to invalidate the Texas statute that made it a felony for anyone to destroy a fetus except on "medical advice for the purpose of saving the mother's life." The decision applied across the nation and had immediate repercussions, legalizing abortion and intensifying already fierce divisions in the country. *Roe* pitted against each other two prized U.S. values, life and freedom. It set a woman's ability to control her body above the life of the fetus—except in the third trimester of pregnancy. In effect, *Roe v. Wade* permitted legal abortion in all states of the United States during the first trimester of pregnancy, and it limited the states' regulatory powers over abortion in the second and third trimesters. Approximately 1.5 million abortions have been performed annually during the past two decades. For abortion foes and advocates of the right to choose, the stakes could hardly have been higher.

Abortion has been a Catholic issue—some say *the* Catholic issue. No other religion has been tied in the public eye to the abortion controversy as much the Catholic Church. The Catholic hierarchy, galvanized by *Roe,* took on abortion as a political cause. Acting on the uncompromised belief that unborn life is human life or at least life with human potential in need of protection, the Catholic bishops gathered their resources to stop what many called "the slaughter of the unborn."

Catholic opposition to abortion is deeply ingrained in the

Catholic psyche. The church has opposed it since the earliest times in its history. With an estimated 50 million abortions occurring worldwide each year, church leaders see the phenomenon as a callous and immoral betrayal of an inalienable right—the right to life. Nearly across the board, Catholics abhor the notion of abortion. Efforts to translate that abhorrence into civil laws, however, have divided many Catholics, just as it has divided many outside the church. Catholic political differences on abortion become more complex when women's issues and rights are considered. Even among those who agree that abortion involves the taking of a human life, divisive questions remain. Should abortion be outlawed? In all cases? Including rape and incest? How are Catholics to wield their moral convictions in a pluralistic society? Do these moral convictions necessarily require a political response? If so, what kind? Who, in the final analysis, should decide if an abortion is to occur? The mother? The state? If prenatal life has intrinsic value, can the state abandon its protective role? And if it has such a role, is it proper to force a woman to give birth against her will?

Practicing Catholics offer varied responses to these questions. This has not pleased the Catholic hierarchy, which has granted little room for Catholics to debate these questions. The U.S. bishops want Catholics to be unyielding in their opposition to abortion. In the eyes of most bishops, a Catholic's response to abortion is a measure of moral orthodoxy. In the political realm many bishops have shown little tolerance for Catholic politicians who say they personally oppose abortion but remain politically "pro-choice."

Catholics occupy at least three distinct camps on abortion: Progressives see abortion as at least partially rooted in poverty and the nation's social ills. They say abortion must remain a legal option for women. Conservatives see it a grave moral evil that must be outlawed. Then there are those who support a "consistent ethic of life," seeing abortion as one of many modern attacks on life. Their political agenda is progressive, but they also work to curtail abortion rights. Divisions can be deep. Less noticeable to many is that similar splits exist within the ranks of the U.S. bishops. More than twenty years of church abortion debate confirms a lesson that shared moral convictions don't always lead to shared political responses to those convictions.

Since *Roe v. Wade*, the National Conference of Catholic Bishops (NCCB), the official U.S. bishops' administrative structure, has been on record opposing legalized abortion. The NCCB sees it as a grave moral evil, working tirelessly to overturn *Roe v. Wade*. The U.S. bishops involvement in the abortion fight has given them high visibility. Fairly or unfairly, it has also branded them as a "one issue" lobby group and has at times made them bedfellows with some of the most staunchly conservative politicians in the land. Yet, after more than two decades the bishops have little to show for their hard-fought efforts. Legalized abortion, with some modest restrictions, remains the law of the land. The Democrat Party feels it owes the bishops few favors, and the Republican Party is apparently becoming increasingly lukewarm, or at least divided, on its anti-abortion stance. The bishops' political allies on abortion appear to be fewer with each passing year.

It was in the early 1970s that U.S. episcopal abortion politics first flared up and in the process began to draw the Catholic hierarchy away from its long-time affiliation with the Democratic Party, the party of immigrants, labor, and social reform. Before abortion became a major U.S. political issue, Catholic politics and Democratic Party politics were closely allied. Curiously, this Catholic shift toward the Republican Party accelerated in the wake of the 1960 election of the first U.S. Catholic president, John F. Kennedy, a Democrat. More than at any other time in U.S. history, that election signaled the "arrival" of Catholics as part of the U.S. establishment. Catholics during the 1960s and 1970s were among the many of the relatively new affluent to move from the cities to the suburbs. The grandchildren of immigrants, the sons and daughters of the working class, these Catholics were often business managers and corporate executives. Abortion may have pushed many Catholics out of the Democratic Party and into Republican ranks, but social and economic trends had a lot to do with it as well.

Curiously, charting the Catholic abortion story is to find diversity and not uniformity in thought. The bishops may issue marching orders but the rank and file—Catholics in the pews, as they are sometimes called—remain an independent-minded lot. This is especially the case when it comes to politics. Some may see in this the failings of a religious institution to convince its members to follow its teachings; others may see in it a healthy diversity within the family of believers. Surveys of Catholic attitudes and practices on abortion reinforce the notion that Catholics are not unlike other U.S. citizens. Repeated polls show that most Catholics, like most non-Catholics, say abortion should be available at least in some cases. Most Catholic women, meanwhile, have abortions with almost the same frequency as do non-Catholics.[2] This is not what the bishops have wanted to hear. Pope John Paul II more than any other twentieth-century pontiff has been adamant in his moral and political opposition to abortion. He has insisted

Catholics actively fight legalized abortion. He feels that there can be no wavering whatsoever on abortion. He sees it as an essential of Catholic morality, supporting life in its most vulnerable form. Those Catholics who have differed with him, including some theologians, have been labeled "dissenters." In some cases they have been pressured to leave their teaching posts in Catholic institutions.[3]

The issue has been further exacerbated by simmering tensions between Catholic women and the church hierarchy. Catholic women, some with degrees in philosophy and theology, have criticized the church for being an institution in which celibate males maintain all positions of authority. These women, including some Catholic theologians, have argued that the all-male clerical posture weakens the church's teachings on sexuality issues, even more so on abortion, a uniquely women's issue. They point out that it is women who are frequently abused and who become victims of violence, women who are dominated by men, women who become pregnant, women who carry the unborn, and women who give birth to children. When it comes to authoritative Catholic voices, however, it is the men's voices that are heard within the Catholic Church. The hierarchy's response to such charges has been to reiterate that abortion is not simply a women's concern, but one affecting the moral fabric of the entire society. The bishops see the abortion issue as above gender, a theological issue, one that speaks to the way the human family addresses and values life itself. Therefore, abortion, the bishops say, must be everybody's concern. Fetuses have inalienable rights—the first being the right to life.

The abortion issue reveals that science, philosophy, and theology have all played roles in helping shape the Catholic moral responses. Over the centuries the most basic questions have included the following: When does life begin? What determines when a being is human? When does "ensoulment" or "hominization" occur? And when, if ever, is it lawful to kill? Even now, official church teaching holds that there can be no certainty as to when human life first begins and that lacking such knowledge, the most prudent course is the most conservative course. Life, official Catholic teaching holds, must be preserved from the moment of conception. The 1994 *Catechism of the Catholic Church* reads:

> *Human life must be respected and protected absolutely from the moment of conception. From the first moment of his [her] existence, a human being must be recognized as having the rights of a person—among which is the inviolable right of every innocent being to life.*[4]

How the church got to this point reveals much about the divisions, frustrations, and complexities of modern Catholicism. The backdrop is a moral debate spanning centuries in which answers only seem to spawn new questions.

Abortion in Church History

The teaching of the moralists of the Catholic Church on abortion is rich in interaction between specifically supernatural themes—for example, the Nativity of the Lord and the Immaculate Conception of Mary—and principles of a general ethical applicability.[5] In the Mediterranean world in which Christianity first appeared, abortion was a familiar art. Abortifacient drugs were common and abortion was widely practiced. This did not necessarily mean there was widespread approval of abortion. The practice was debated by physicians. Some, influenced by the oath of Hippocrates, simply refused to prescribe abortifacients.[6] The law of the Roman Empire, meanwhile, punished abortions committed without the father's consent. It also punished those who gave drugs for abortions, although it was unlikely the law was enforced unless the recipient died.[7]

It was within a wider culture largely indifferent to fetal life that the first Christian teachings on abortion developed; it was in opposition and conflict with the values reflected in popular behavior that the Christian word was first enunciated.[8] Christian teaching on abortion developed in a theological context in which the commands of the Old Testament to love God with all your heart (Deuteronomy 6:5) and to love your neighbor as yourself (Leviticus 19:18) were singled out as the two great commandments on which depended the "whole law and the prophets" (Matthew 22:40). The Christian valuation of life was made in view of this commandment to love.[9] Meanwhile, the ethos of the Christian infancy narratives reflected a high interest in infant and fetal life. The infanticide practiced by Herod and its violent threat to the life of Jesus formed the introduction to the life of the Messiah (Matthew 2:1-18). Mary was described as "with child through the holy Spirit" (Matthew 1:18). That abortion could have been specifically in the mind of the authors of Galatians and the Book of Revelation and that it was specifically dealt with by the early Christian communities, is established by several writings, the most important of which is the *Didachē*, or *Teaching of the Twelve Apostles*, one of the earliest church documents.[10] Written about A.D. 100, it lists sins and expressly prohibits abortifacients. Abortion was ranked as a serious sin included with those expressly named by the Ten Commandments.

As the church emerged as a legal religion and a social force in the fourth century, the sentiments on abortion so uniformly expressed in the first two centuries of Christian life took the form of legislation. Women who conceived in fornication and committed an abortion were excluded from the church for life. The Council of Ancyra in 314 denounced such women, but "more humanely" the council reduced their penance to ten years.[11] It retained a life penance for voluntary homicide. The reduction appeared to mark a recognition of mitigating circumstances in the character of the crime. These laws, like earlier condemnations, made no distinctions between the formed and unformed fetus. It was in the fourth century this distinction became a focus for serious analysis among Christians. Theologians could not agree if early abortion was homicide because they could not agree when human life began. While they generally agreed that abortion was wrong, some argued it was not homicide in the earliest stages of pregnancy. Others said it was homicide at any point and that a woman who obtained an abortion should serve penance as if it were homicide. These theologians argued that hominization—the point at which a developing embryo becomes a human being, also known as "animation," or "ensoulment"—is immediate upon conception.[12]

One reason for the early disagreement was the church's decentralized nature; there was no single canon code. During this early church period, sins of fornication and adultery were viewed as gravely sinful; abortion was often viewed as a secondary sin, undertaken to cover up the other sex sins. By the mid-fifth century, most Christian writers saw abortion as a violation of the love owed to one's neighbor. They saw it as failure of maternal love. Some depicted it as a failure of reverence for the work of God. Whereas the wider culture had generally accepted abortion, Christians condemned it.[13]

Augustine of Hippo, the church father and bishop, writing in the early fifth century, condemned both birth control and abortion, saying they broke the necessary connection between sex and procreation. This upheld the teachings of the early church fathers on sexuality. On the other hand, Augustine wrote that abortion, in its early stages, did not involve the killing of a human life. He wrote the following:

> *The great question about the soul is not hastily decided by unargued and rash judgment; the law does not prove that the act [abortion] pertains to homicide, for there cannot yet be said to be a live soul in a body that lacks sensation when it is not formed in flesh, and so not yet endowed with sense.*[14]

From the fifth through the fourteenth century, penitential literature, generally the work of monks, grew and consistently treated abortion as a serious sin, needing grave penance. In the seventh century, in some parts of the church, a feast was established, marking the Annunciation of Mary or the Conception of Christ. This feast was set for March 25, with the understanding that nine months elapsed between conception and the birth of Jesus, December 25. The implication was that what had come from the Holy Spirit had been holy from the moment of conception. This gave momentum to viewing fetal life as sacred from the instant of conception.[15]

In about 1140, Gratian compiled the first collection of canons, or laws, accepted as authoritative by the official church. In one canon he concluded that abortion is homicide "only when a fetus was formed."[16] In another section of the canons abortion and contraception were condemned if they were done for "the sake of fulfilling lust or in meditated hatred." Penance for homicide was required in such cases. The theological debate over whether or not abortion is homicide, however, continued. The majority view still held to the delayed hominization theory. These theologians generally agreed that hominization took place forty days after conception for males and eighty days after conception for females, a distinction earlier made by Augustine.

The noted church teacher Thomas Aquinas, following Augustine on the common view at the time, wrote that abortion is not a sin of homicide unless the fetus is ensouled and, thus, fully a human being. He was sure this did not take place until some time after conception.[17] Borrowing from Aristotle, he taught that body and soul unite to make a human being and no soul exists until a fetal body forms. Aquinas accepted Aristotle's notion that the fetus is first endowed with a vegetative soul, then an animal soul, and then, when the body is developed, a rational soul. Each "soul" is subsumed by the succeeding one until final ensoulment takes place and the human is fully formed.

From the fifteenth through the eighteenth century, various theological opinions concerning the time of fetal hominization remained in circulation. Pope Sixtus V (papacy 1585–90) attempted to resolve these varying opinions in 1588, by issuing the papal bull *Effraenatum*. It stated that abortion at any stage of pregnancy and contraception constituted homicide, both as a mortal sin and as a secular crime. The prescribed penance, he said, was excommunication. No exceptions. This papal ruling stated that the abortion of a fetus "whether animated or not animated, formed or unformed" is homicide. He took the stand, however, not to protect fetal life but to confront the sin of prostitution, which was rampant in Rome at the time.[18] His bull, nevertheless, brought serious legislative problems. It became clear the penalties were too harsh and largely unenforceable. In 1591, not long after Sixtus's death, Pope Gregory XIV (papacy 1590–91) issued *Sedes apostolica* restricting the earlier bull, including all penalties except those applying to a fetus that had been ensouled. This was to be the last papal pronouncement on the theory of hominization for more than three hundred years, until 1869. The theory of delayed hominization remained a common philosophical assumption throughout that period.

In the seventeenth century, however, a trend took hold. In 1621, Paolo Zacchia, a Roman physician, published a treatise called *Medico-Legal Questions*, in which he argued the Aristotelian metamorphosis of souls was "an imaginary thing." He proposed, instead, that the rational soul is present from the moment of conception. From then on this viewpoint gained influence. In 1679, the Holy Office under Pope Innocent XI (papacy 1676–89) rejected the notion that abortion to conceal sin is permissible in situations in which the parents of a girl would murder her for becoming pregnant.

During the late seventeenth century, the church witnessed the growth in veneration of the Immaculate Conception of Mary, the belief that Mary was conceived without original sin, that is, her soul was sin-free from the moment of conception. When in 1701, Pope Clement XI (papacy 1700–21) declared the Immaculate Conception a feast of universal obligation, requiring church attendance, belief in immediate ensoulment at conception of all human beings received indirect support.[19] The doctrine holds that Mary, though the product of human parents, was bestowed with sanctifying grace in her soul at the moment of conception and was born without original sin. This implies that Mary had a soul when she was conceived. The doctrine of immediate hominization gained implicit support, although questions still lingered about the specific timing of conception and ensoulment.

The question of when a fetus became human continued to trouble the church into the eighteenth century as is seen in a 1713 statement by the Vatican dealing with the baptism of miscarried and aborted fetuses. It stated that "if there is a reasonable foundation for admitting that the fetus is animated by a rational soul, then it may and must be baptized conditionally. If however there is no reasonable foundation, it may by no means be baptized."[20] The decision on baptism still supports delayed hominization. The time of ensoulment is officially no longer certain to be forty days after conception, but appearing rather to depend on the human form of the fetus.

The question of the morality of abortion came up in other ways as well. Two issues dominated discussion of therapeutic abortions in the eighteenth and nineteenth centuries. First, physicians wanted to be certain that in performing these abortions they would not commit homicide. Second, they were asking whether or not abortion to save the life of the mother was permissible. What happened during this period was the gradual development of a "just in case" approach to abortion, a mentality that has helped shape church thinking on abortion to modern times. During this period, church writers agreed that it is not homicide to abort a fetus before ensoulment. They wrote, however, that abortion to save a woman's life is permissible only if there is no direct intent to harm the fetus.

Caution increasingly became the norm. St. Alphonsos Maria de' Liguori, for example, taught in the eighteenth century that it is safer to prohibit contraception and abortion altogether, just in case these practices would be truly homicidal. But this is a function of his general moral theory called tutiorism. It tried to solve moral problems by stating that when in doubt a law must always be obeyed unless the opinion favoring liberty be most certain. Tutiorism, however, along with rigorism was virtually condemned by Pope Alexander VIII (papacy 1689–91) in 1690.

During the nineteenth century, centralization of church authority grew and with it so did papal authority. In 1854, Pope Pius IX (papacy 1846–78) proclaimed as dogma that Mary, the Mother of Jesus, was free from sin "in the first instant of her conception." But he never specified exactly when conception occurred. The new dogma, however, appeared to deal a blow to the old formulation of delayed ensoulment. New biological understandings were making it difficult to support the earlier widespread notions that males received souls at forty days and females at eighty days. There was simply no plausible evidence to support such delineation and distinctions. In 1869, Pius IX published the *Apostolicace sedis,* which completely ignored the question of hominization and required excommunication for abortions at any stage of pregnancy. To Pius IX, all abortion was homicide. This view is especially important in the development of church thinking on abortion. Pius's statement represented a major step in the endorsement of immediate hominization by the church, and it came just years before scientists concluded in 1875 that the joint action of sperm and ovum generated fetal life. If a moment had to be chosen for ensoulment, no convincing argument appeared to support old Aristotelian ideas or to put ensoulment at a later stage of life.

In the early twentieth century, immediate hominization was implicitly supported in the 1917 revised Code of Canon Law, the first codification since Gratian in about 1140. The new code prescribed excommunication for both the pregnant mother and any others, such as physicians and nurses, who took part in an abortion.

In 1924, Arthur Vermeersch, the Belgian Jesuit, advanced the theory that therapeutic abortions should be prohibited in all but two circumstances, ectopic pregnancies (implantation of the egg in the fallopian tube) and cancerous wombs. In both cases, the fetus would die anyway. These then would be indirect and not direct abortions. This formulation reflected the principle of double effect. It states that medical procedures aimed directly at saving the life of the mother are permissible, even when they indirectly take the life of the fetus. No direct intent to abort is involved, and hence no blame for homicide could be assigned. However, the direct killing of a fetus to save the life of the mother was not allowed in any case. This theory was adopted by Pope Pius XI in his 1930 encyclical, *Casti Connubii,* which condemns abortion in general.

The most recent development in church thinking on abortion has been the theological concept of protecting the embryo from the moment of conception, whether the life is human or not, ensouled or not. This has been described by the phrase the "right to life." The unborn has the "right" to develop because it has the *potential* for human life at any moment after conception. The church has linked this with the need to defend the dignity of all life. This development is evident in at least five Vatican documents:

- Pope Pius XII's 1951 "Address to the Italian Catholic Society of Midwives," in which he declared there are no grounds for taking an innocent human life. "The baby," he said, "still not born, is a person in the same degree and for the same reason as the mother."[21]
- The 1965 Vatican II document, *Gaudium et Spes* (section 51), which declared: "Life must be protected with the utmost care from the moment of conception; abortion and infanticide are abominable crimes."[22]
- Paul VI's 1968 *Humanae Vitae,* which declared that all abortions, therapeutic or otherwise, be prohibited, as well as contraception.[23]
- The Sacred Congregation for the Doctrine of Faith, which, in the 1974 "Declaration on Procured Abortion," opposed abortion on the grounds that "one can never claim freedom of opinion as a pretext for attacking the rights of others, most especially the right to life." This declaration came as an apparent response to the Roe ruling, with its emphasis on privacy and a woman's freedom of choice.

The 1974 "Declaration on Procured Abortion" states the following:

> *In reality, respect for human life is called for from the time that the process of generation begins. From the time that the ovum is fertilized, a life is begun which is neither that of the father nor of the mother; it is rather the life of a new human being with his or her own growth. It would never be made human if it were not human already.*[24]

The 1974 declaration states that the fetus is human life, with the potential for becoming a full human being, from the moment of conception. This represents the completion of the shift away from viewing the ensoulment question as central and towards a teaching that favors protecting all fetal life while disregarding the ensoulment question altogether.

- *Donum Vitae,* the 1987 Vatican document that proclaims "the inalienable rights of the person must be recognized and respected by civil society and the political authority. . . . Among such fundamental rights one should mention in this regard every human being's right to life and physical integrity from the moment of conception until death." Here the church is taking the moral discussion into the political realm.

Donum Vitae also states that it "is immoral to produce human embryos intended for exploitation as disposable biological material."[25]

Has the debate ended? Try as it might, the Vatican has not been entirely successful in putting the lid on the discussion. Catholics, including theologians willing to accept public disfavor with Rome, continue to raise questions. Pointing to recent discoveries in reproductive biology, some ask, for example, whether individual human life is present during the first two or three weeks after fertilization.[26] These theologians argue that hominization cannot possibly take place before fourteen to twenty-two days after conception because of the radical and categorical changes that take place during that period. They point, for example, to twinning. Writes Father Charles Curran, a moral theologian:

> *My own particular opinion is that human life is not present until individuality is established. In this context we are talking*

> *about individual human life, but irreversible and differentiated individuality is not present from the time of fecundation. The single fertilized cell undergoes cell division, but in the process twinning may occur until the fourteenth day. This indicates that individual human life is not definitely established before this time.*[27]

Another perplexing question raised by the official church's current position that the fetus must be viewed as sacred from the moment of conception and protected as such asks what is to be thought of the large proportion of embryos lost before and during the process of implantation. Estimates of this loss vary widely, but more than 55 percent appears a reasonable approximation. Writes one of the leading twentieth-century European moral theologians, Jesuit Father Karl Rahner: "Will [today's moral theologians] be able to accept that fifty percent of all 'human beings'—real human beings with 'immortal' souls and an eternal destiny—will never get beyond this first stage of human existence?"[28]

Modern science poses other abortion questions for the church. There is always the need for theology to keep abreast with the latest understandings of the biological processes. In a period of scientific explosion theology can hardly keep pace. One critical finding in modern biology is that conception, biologically speaking, is seen as a process beginning with the penetration of the outer layer of the egg by a sperm and concluding with the formation of the diploid set of chromosomes. This process takes at least a day, raising the question as to how one ought to understand the term "moment of conception" frequently used in church documents.[29] Some scientists go further, saying that biologically understood, conception occurs only after a lengthy process has been completed and is more closely identified with implantation than fertilization.[30] Despite such subtleties, official Catholic teaching maintains that abortion is wrong in any instance, including rape or as a direct way of saving the life of a pregnant woman. And this was the church hierarchy's thinking when it decided it had to confront the *Roe v. Wade* decision in 1973.

The Political Debate

The U.S. Supreme Court ruled in January 1973 that restrictive state abortion laws violated the Fourteenth Amendment to the U.S. Constitution. The judges declared that women have a constitutional right to abortion. The ruling, however, was not absolute. It left the decision to have a first-trimester abortion to the woman and her physician; it held that states could pass regulations to insure the health of the woman for second-trimester abortions; and they could prohibit third-trimester abortions. The only limitation on state authority in the third trimester was to assure access to abortions if needed to protect the life or health of the woman.

Until the ruling, political opposition to abortion by U.S. Catholics had been spotty and local. It had not been coordinated. The first attempt to counter the incipient legalization movement came in 1966 when Father (now Bishop) James McHugh of the Catholic Family Life Bureau started to monitor the various abortion laws across the nation. That year he invited local anti-abortion activists to a meeting to serve as advisers to a group he formed called the National Right to Life Committee (NRLC). These early efforts placed Catholics at the center of a movement, still in its infancy and largely aimed at maintaining the status quo. One of the activists' early attention-grabbing techniques was the displaying of vivid pictures of dismembered fetuses with unmistakably human features.[31] These early activists were self-financed and even complained that local clergy were slow to assist them. Their aim was to take on the abortion reformers whose stated limited purpose was to legalize abortion for "tragic" cases such as preserving maternal health or preventing pregnancies that stemmed from rape or incest. Abortion reformers argued that legalized abortion would merely end the need to find them in "back alleys."

By all accounts, when the *Roe* ruling came, it caught the U.S. bishops by surprise. The response was to mobilize anti-abortion activists at the national level and through local parish networks.[32] Cardinal John Krol, president of the National Conference of Catholic Bishops, and Cardinal Terence Cooke, chairman of the bishops' Committee on Pro-Life Affairs, accused the Supreme Court of opening the doors to the "greatest slaughter of innocent life in the history of mankind."[33]

At the time of *Roe,* contraception was the most prominent moral issue in the church, which was still in the throes of digesting *Humanae Vitae.* Abortion was a lesser concern, limited mostly to local activists. Even the Second Vatican Council, less than a decade earlier, had little sense that abortion would become the divisive issue it eventually became. The council was unequivocal in its condemnation of abortion, but gave it scant attention. Writing in the *Pastoral Constitution on the Church in the Modern World,* council bishops addressed abortion in only a few lines, condemning it with the following words: "Life must be protected with the utmost care from the moment of conception; abortion and infanticide are abominable crimes."[34] The word *abortion* is not even mentioned in the forty-five-page index of the American edition of the documents issued by the council.[35]

The U.S. bishops' political response, expressed in U.S. congressional testimony in 1974, was to support a human-life amendment to provide a basis "for the legal protection of the unborn child." In testimony that year and repeated in 1976, the bishops explained why they opposed legal abortion, tying it to a wider web of social and moral ills. They said preliminary statistics indicated legalized abortion had already increased the number of abortions and was producing new threats to women's lives. They said it was spawning an "abortion mentality," eroding human life in other spheres, most noticeably in the treatment of handicapped newborns. They said it was escalating the tendency to look to the quick and violent "solution" to social ills. "By isolating the pregnant woman in her 'right to privacy,' the court had done a disservice," the bishops testified, "both to her and to her child, cutting them off from the family and societal bonds which can support and encourage life-affirming attitudes."[36]

While they raised a number of social concerns, these were all tied together by a deeper concern, they said, one with a theological base. "All human life," the bishops stated, "from the moment of conception and through all subsequent stages, is sacred, because human life is created in the image and likeness of God."[37] The 1976 U.S. presidential election was the first to follow the *Roe v. Wade* ruling and the first in which the bishops' anti-abortion commitment became involved in national politics. The bishops found themselves attempting to conduct two political strategies. The first was to make abortion the church's most prominent political concern; the second was to place abortion within a broader pro-life context. The tensions involved in meeting these twin objectives were to last into the 1990s. "The Pastoral

Plan for Pro-Life Activities," released by the National Conference of Catholic Bishops in November 1975, encouraged the development of a tightly organized pro-life unit in each congressional district. The plan, in short, committed the bishops to raising the political profile of abortion during the 1976 election and to conducting a grassroots campaign to elect pro-life officials at every level of government.[38] At the same meeting in which the "Pastoral Plan" was adopted the bishops also released a series of policy statements covering a wide range of other political and social issues, each with a moral component. For these issues, nevertheless, there was no detailed blueprint for political action.

Some bishops, worried that the national conference leadership would look like a single-issue group, pressed for another document and came up with one called "Political Responsibility: Reflections on an Election Year." The document, endorsed by the U.S. bishops in May 1976, expressed their concerns "to call attention to the moral and religious dimensions of secular issues, to keep alive the values of the Gospel as a norm for social and political life, and to point out the demands of the Christian faith for a just transformation of society." The document specifically stated that the bishops "do not seek the formation of a religious voting bloc" and that they would not "instruct persons on how they should vote by endorsing candidates."

The "Pastoral Plan" and the "Political Responsibility" statement, taken together, presented the bishops with a political dilemma during the 1976 election campaign. Gerald Ford agreed with the bishops on abortion and little else, and Jimmy Carter agreed with them on a series of issues, but disagreed with them on abortion. As the campaign developed, it became clear the dilemma was not real.

For despite the 1976 "Political Responsibility" statement, the bishops' spokesmen made it clear that abortion was special.[39] The archbishop of Cincinnati and the president of the National Conference of Catholic Bishops, Joseph Bernardin, explained it this way:

> *Human life is threatened in many ways in our society. Abortion, however, is a direct assault on the lives of those who are least able to defend themselves. If the church seems particularly concerned about abortion at the moment, it is for this reason: if we become insensitive to the violation of the basic human rights to life, our sensitivity to the entire spectrum of human rights will ultimately be eroded.*[40]

That year Bernardin declared the Democratic Party's pro-choice abortion platform "irresponsible,"and as for the Republican Party's platform, the bishops expressed "support [for] the efforts of those who seek enactment of a constitutional amendment to restore protection of the right to life for unborn children." After a meeting with Carter and the U.S. bishops' Executive Committee, Bernardin expressed "disappointment" in the candidate's position on abortion. After meeting with Ford, the first issue Bernardin mentioned was abortion and said, "we are encouraged that the President agrees on the need for a constitutional amendment." Later Bernardin insisted the bishops were not backing a candidate; nevertheless, there was little doubt left in the minds of Catholics following the bishops' actions how they were thinking. In effect, the "Pastoral Plan" had negated the "Political Responsibility" statement, and the bishops fell into a pattern, which continued on into the 1990s, of leaving the appearance—despite disagreeing with presidential hopefuls on a host of other social issues—that they supported the anti-abortion candidate.

Carter won, and the bishops ended up feeling burned. As a result of their 1976 involvement they purposefully maintained a low profile during the 1980 presidential election campaign.[41] For example, when the two political parties released platforms that basically reiterated the various positions they had taken in 1976 the bishops did not react as they had four years earlier. There were no declarations of outrage at the Democrats or support for the Republicans. During the campaign the bishops decided not to draw public attention to their policy differences with presidential hopeful Ronald Reagan, who presented himself as the national spokesman for religious values. In 1983 the bishops released their pastoral letter, *The Challenge of Peace: God's Promise and Our Response*, criticizing U.S. nuclear deterrence, though not condemning it, and Bernardin publicly laid out a new consistent approach to human-life issues. The "peace pastoral," as it was often referred to, offered a conditional approval of the American nuclear arsenal and called for a bilateral halt in the development and deployment of new nuclear weapons. In the 1984 election, the bishops still found themselves agreeing with Reagan on abortion, but the peace pastoral was a direct challenge to his approach to U.S. military postures.

In the 1984 presidential campaign long-building divisions within the U.S. episcopal ranks became public, and it was the abortion issue that finally caused the split to occur. Fresh off the peace pastoral, having acted as committee chair for the drawing up of the pastoral, and apparently having learned a political lesson in 1976, Bernardin (in 1982 archbishop of Chicago and in 1983 a cardinal), began to push a "seamless garment," or consistent ethic of life theme. His first major address was to a gathering at Fordham University in December 1983 where he called upon Catholics to work on behalf of all the human-life issues. Meanwhile, Boston Archbishop (later Cardinal) Bernard Law, speaking in September 1984 for himself and the New England bishops, explicitly cited abortion as the most important issue of the campaign. Said Law: "While nuclear holocaust is a future possibility the holocaust of abortion is a present reality. . . . We believe that the enormity of the evil makes abortion the critical issue of the moment."[42] Archbishop (later Cardinal) John O'Connor of New York told an interviewer that "if the unborn in a mother's womb is unsafe it becomes ludicrous for the bishops to address the threat of nuclear war or the great problems of the homeless or the suffering of the aged."[43] The bishops' leadership was clearly talking at cross-purposes. Law and O'Connor were attempting to counteract Cardinal Bernardin's consistent ethic by drawing public attention back to the bishops' opposition to legal abortion. The "seamless garment" cause was taken up by a group of twenty-three bishops who belonged to Pax Christi USA, a Catholic peace organization. These bishops declared that "one cannot examine abortion as though that were the only moral issue facing our people." They called upon Catholics to examine the "entire spectrum of life issues." The two positions were the same as those articulated in 1976 in the "Pastoral Plan for Pro-Life Activities" and the "Political Responsibility" statement. Nevertheless, the arguments were not carried out on equal grounds because while episcopal supporters of the consistent ethic discussed issues and a moral vision, those taking the abortion-centered course focused on elections, candidates, and votes.[44] Additionally, the vocal opposition to pro-choice candidates, especially Catholic candidates, by Law and O'Connor and a handful of other bishops drew much media coverage. It led Mary McGrory of the *Washington Post* to write in September 1984 that "the hierarchy of the church is acting like an arm of the Reagan reelection committee."[45] Try as they might, issue as they repeatedly would statements calling for Catholics to examine political candidates after looking at all the political issues, the U.S. bishops from 1976 onward left the appearance that abortion was their primary concern—and that Catholic voters should act accordingly.

From early on, after deciding to step into the political area to fight abortion, the bishops faced the argument that they were imposing Catholic teaching upon a secular nation. Citing polls that found Catholic attitudes and practices regarding abortion virtually indistinguishable from those of non-Catholics, critics said the church was attempting to coerce behavior by legal means, having failed to do so by the cogency of their moral reasoning. They said this was the same mistake—the abuse of power—the Vatican made in *Humanae Vitae*.[46]

From the moment they began their political involvement in their anti-abortion campaign in 1974, the U.S. bishops insisted they were not trying to impose Catholic teaching. Rather they were speaking out on behalf of human rights—a concern of all Americans. Said the bishops:

> *We wish to make it clear we are not seeking to impose the Catholic moral teaching regarding abortion on the country. In our tradition moral teaching bases its claim on faith in a transcendent*

> *God and the pursuit of virtue and moral perfection. In fact, moral teaching may frequently call for more than civil law can dictate, but a just civil law cannot be opposed to moral teaching based on God's law. We do not ask the law to take up our responsibility of teaching morality, i.e. that abortion is morally wrong. However, we do ask the government and the law to be faithful to its own principle—that the right to life is an inalienable right given to everyone by the Creator. . . .*
>
> *We appear here today in fulfillment of our considered responsibility to speak in behalf of human rights. The right to life—which finds resonance in the moral and legal tradition—is a principle we share with the society and the one that impels us to take an active role in the democratic process directed toward its clear and unequivocal articulation.*[47]

The Catholic hierarchy's entrance into the young anti-abortion movement proved both an added strength and a liability. On the one hand, the church's unambiguous condemnation of all abortions provided a principled point of view, a rallying cry; on the other hand, the very absoluteness of that position discomforted many non-Catholics (and some Catholics) who shared a moral antipathy to abortion, but not necessarily in all cases.[48] Official Catholic teaching helped fire up the movement but allowed organizations limited flexibility, adding to internal tensions and later to splits within the movement. Further, the contraception issue provided more problems for some. The National Right to Life Committee, created by Catholic efforts, took no position on contraception. Some anti-abortionists, however, complained that this hurt their lobbying efforts. Unable to speak about viable contraceptive alternatives to abortion, legislators were less receptive to their pleas, they pointed out.[49]

The anti-abortion movement's political strategies were threefold throughout much of the 1970s and 1980s:

- Lobbying Congress and state legislatures in favor of an anti-abortion constitutional amendment
- Lobbying Congress and state legislatures for the elimination of any public funding of abortion services or abortion counseling
- Supporting presidential candidates who opposed abortion and who promised to appoint U.S. Supreme Court justices likely to overturn *Roe* or weaken it[50]

While the movement was largely, though not exclusively, Catholic in its earliest stages, by the mid-1970s, other religions and religious activists were getting involved, including the more theologically conservative Protestant denominations, such as the Missouri-Synod Lutherans and the Southern Baptist Convention. At the same time, the first evangelical Christian right-to-life organization, the Christian Action Council, was founded by a coalition of evangelical Christian leaders and became active. The fundamentalists gave the movement new energy. Increasingly it found itself gaining a receptive ear among members of the Republican Party, eventually helping to elect Ronald Reagan as president of the United States.

Internal movement politics, though buoyed by Reagan's 1980 election, continued to be complicated by moral and strategic disputes. Since the NRLC and the U.S. bishops supported measures such as the defeated Hatch Amendment (1983), which did not itself ban abortion but permitted states to vote on restrictions, they were at times accused by hardliners of betraying the movement. Some anti-abortion organizations refused any legislative compromise that did not abide by the principle that all abortion is murder.

There were other divisions among Catholics as they found themselves attempting to deal with the divisive abortion question. In October 1984, for example, the Washington-based, Catholic pro-choice organization, Catholics for a Free Choice, provided support for a full-page *New York Times* advertisement, "Catholic Statement on Pluralism and Abortion," which claimed that more than one abortion view existed within the church. Frances Kissling, president of the organization, argues that women must abe allowed to make their own ways through "the morass of conflicting opinions about sexuality, human life, personhood" to decide the abortion question. Among the *Times* ad signers were ninety-seven clergy and religious, mostly nuns, who came under attack from the Vatican for having attached their names to the ad. Two of the women, Barbara Ferraro and Patricia Hussey, sisters of Notre Dame de Namur, were eventually singled out. Their order's leadership met with the Vatican pronuncio in 1986, and following that meeting Ferraro and Hussey said they found it had been a patronizing attempt to treat them as "little girls." In July 1988, the two women resigned from the order and returned to work among the poor in Charleston, West Virginia.

The abortion issue continued to be especially difficult for some Catholic women. Tensions between them and the hierarchy gained greater prominence when Archbishop O'Connor said he expected all Catholic politicians to do all they could to restrict access to abortion. In 1984, shortly after he was installed as archbishop of New York, he publicly criticized then vice-presidential candidate Geraldine Ferraro, a Catholic, for what he called her misstatement of

Catholic teaching on abortion. The fact that she was the first woman vice-presidential candidate of a major political party in U.S. history further complicated the dynamics. Some said they saw in O'Connor's attack an antifeminist bias. They asked why he had not attacked pro-choice Catholic male politicians.

Ferraro had signed a letter from the Washington-based Catholic pro-choice organization, Catholics for a Free Choice, inviting members of Congress to a briefing on the problems associated with abortion for Catholic politicians. O'Connor strenuously objected to a section in the letter that asserted the "Catholic position on abortion is not monolithic and there can be a range of personal and political responses to it."[51]

Ferraro, under attack from O'Connor, said she had taken the term *monolithic* to refer to the views of individual Catholics rather than to Catholic doctrine as such. "The teaching of the Catholic Church is monolithic on abortion," O'Connor countered in the highly publicized controversy, "and it is stated in a letter signed by Ferraro that it is not monolithic. Now that, to me, is a pretty basic disagreement." In response, Ferraro conceded that "the Catholic Church's position on abortion is monolithic. But," she added, "I do believe that there are a lot of Catholics who do not share the views of the Catholic Church."[52]

The dispute with O'Connor did little to help the Mondale-Ferraro candidacy in the 1984 election. In this case, O'Connor had challenged a Catholic political candidate who had allegedly misstated the church's *moral position* on abortion. Two years later, the cardinal's vicar general challenged Catholic politicians who disagreed with the church hierarchy's *political position* on abortion. Such politicians, announced Bishop Joseph O'Keefe, would no longer be welcome to speak at official Catholic events in the archdiocese. Immediately Catholics asked if the speaker ban was directed at non-Catholic dissenters as well as Catholics. Or were Catholics the only ones to be so banished? The archdiocese, under attack, found itself having to back off a bit by saying the decisions would have to be left up to the local pastors.

New York Governor Mario Cuomo was another Catholic politician to find himself embroiled in conflict with O'Connor. Cuomo in 1984 had become a leading spokesman for the national Democratic Party in support of a women's legal right to terminate her pregnancy. As governor of New York, he consistently supported public funding for abortions for poor women in his state. In doing so he asserted his right as a Catholic layman and public official to disagree with a particular legal and political application of his church's moral teaching on abortion. He repeatedly said that while he personally opposed abortion, as a public official he would uphold the law, the right of a woman to have an abortion.

Cuomo's altercation with O'Connor led the prelate to say he could not understand how "a Catholic in conscience could vote for an individual explicitly expressing himself or herself as favoring abortion."[53] Cuomo then accused O'Connor of meddling in secular politics and of failure to uphold the separation of church and state. For certain members of the Catholic hierarchy, including O'Connor, the abortion issue had became the decisive political issue, the one defining issue above and beyond all others—the Catholic litmus test. These prelates, among its most conservative forces, expressed concern for the full range of social issues with moral components, issues such as aid to the inner-city poor, arms proliferation, public housing, health care, capital punishment, and matters of war and peace. On each of these issues, the Democratic Party appeared more compatible during the 1980s and early 1990s with the expressed positions of the United States Catholic Conference, the U.S. bishops' administrative body. However, for practical purposes, this did not matter to many of the U.S. bishops, especially those most vocally opposed to abortion. For them, the abortion issue was paramount. They held that all other moral issues meant little if respect for the lives of the unborn was not first established in law. Therefore, their most visible allies were anti-abortion candidates, most frequently found in the Republican Party.

Catholic pro-choice politicians found themselves under greater scrutiny than non-Catholics who may also have been pro-choice. Pro-choice Democratic candidates at the local, state, and national levels all felt episcopal heat during this period. This was, in part, the result of the visibility of the staunchly anti-abortion prelates, Cardinals John O'Connor of New York and Bernard Law of Boston. Both argued that abortion was the most significant moral and political issue of the time. Both found themselves in conflict with Catholic pro-choice politicians, the most celebrated being New York Governor Cuomo, who explained his reasoning in a highly publicized speech at the University of Notre Dame on September 13, 1984.[54]

At the outset of his speech Cuomo said: "I believe I have a salvific mission as a Catholic." Then he continued as follows:

> *Does that mean I am in conscience required to do everything I can as governor to translate all my religious values into the laws*

and regulations of the state of New York or the United States or be branded a hypocrite if I don't? . . . Must I, having heard the pope renew the church's ban on birth control devices, veto the funding of contraceptive programs for non-Catholics or dissenting Catholics in my state?

Cuomo reminded listeners that the bishops had given up their efforts to change the law on the sale and use of contraceptives. He said he was not challenging the church's teaching on contraception or divorce, but just pointing out that the application of one's beliefs to political debate varies according to circumstances.

Cuomo went on to say that the Catholic public official "lives the political truth most Catholics throughout most of American history have accepted and insisted on: the truth that to assure our freedom we must allow others the same freedom even if occasionally it produces conduct by them we would hold to be sinful."

He said: "The bald truth is that abortion isn't a failure of government. No agency or department of government forces women to have abortions but abortion goes on. . . . The failure here is not Caesar's. This failure is our failure, the failure of the entire people of God."

Cuomo's supporters claimed he had eloquently explained the responsibilities of a Catholic holding public office; his critics dismissed his speech as self-deceptive and an act of obfuscation. They pointed out he claimed to accept the church's teaching on abortion but acted as if he did not—unlike the death penalty, which he opposed and acted against.

Several years later, Cuomo reiterated his views in a speech he gave in Tucson, Arizona, in September 1989. This moved Bishop Austin Vaughan, a prelate in the New York archdiocese, in January 1990 while serving a ten-day jail sentence for blocking an entry to an abortion clinic, to offer Cuomo a dire warning. Cuomo, the bishop said, was running a "serious risk of going to hell" for his support of abortion. By 1990 the political winds were shifting within the Republican Party in some parts of the nation, including New York, where it reaffirmed its "historic commitment to the right of privacy and reproductive rights." The Catholic hierarchy in New York was left out in the cold, facing a rather dismal prospect. Both the Democratic and Republican Parties supported the right to abortion. Within that context, O'Connor in June 1990 went the distance. He raised the specter of excommunicating pro-choice Catholic politicians.

As the 1980s concluded, the U.S. Supreme Court was once again considering the abortion issue. The makeup of the Court, more conservative as a result of Reagan appointees, took up a Missouri case involving a law that prevented the performance of abortions by public employees or in taxpayer-supported facilities. In the 1989 case of *Webster v. Reproductive Health Services*, the Court upheld the Missouri law, returning to the states limited authority to restrict abortions. *Webster* made little new law, but it seemed to demonstrate, for the first time, that five members of the Court disagreed with the *Roe v. Wade* trimester analysis and would apparently allow significantly greater state regulation of abortion than had been permitted under prior Court decisions. The Court also upheld provisions in the Missouri law that require a physician, in a case in which he or she believes a fetus to be twenty weeks or more old, to determine whether it is viable, before an abortion is permitted. The Missouri case moved the abortion battle out of the courts and back into state legislatures.

In 1990, the Court ruled to support another restriction, this time that states may require teenage girls to either notify both parents before obtaining an abortion or request a judicial hearing. Then a 1991 Bush administrative order barred federally funded clinics from mentioning abortion as an option. A number of state legislatures voted on bills that would outlaw abortion except in cases of rape, incest, or to save the mother's life, but most did not pass or were vetoed by governors. The climate was changing. The political struggle was intensifying. Pro-choice advocates were feeling the heat. There was worry that *Roe* could be overturned.

Then, in 1992, in another landmark ruling on a Pennsylvania case, the Supreme Court essentially upheld *Roe*, but permitted states to place further restrictions on abortions, including parental or spousal notification and a twenty-four-hour waiting period before the procedure. As the abortion battle moved into the state legislatures both sides kept their eyes on polls that repeatedly showed American voters supporting the basic right of women to have abortions, though they also favored certain restrictions. The U.S. bishops, seeing the court battle as having ended, at least for the time being, had to rethink their strategies. They decided it was necessary to influence public opinion.

With this in mind, the U.S. bishops' Secretariat for Pro-Life Activities took out a multimillion dollar contract with Hill and Knowlton, a New York-based public relations firm. The bishops signed the contract in 1990 as part of a $3 million pro-life public relations effort. The Knights of Columbus funded the project amid criticisms the bishops had forsaken traditional moral persuasion for slicker, manipulative measures. The campaign was not exclusively political but promoted services for pregnant women and focused on increasing public awareness about abortion. For example, one theme stressed that most abortions—92 percent—were being performed in "non-hardship" cases, those not involving rape, incest, or threats to a mother's life. Hill and Knowlton also prepared "talking points" on abortion, wrote sample articles to appear on newspaper opinion pages, analyzed the political situation involving abortion in the states, and produced various publications. It appeared that the public relations firm seemed to have convinced the bishops they had to be more conciliatory if they were to win over the vast numbers that found themselves between the very polarized anti-abortion and pro-choice camps.

Another effect of the return of the abortion battle to the state level was that many politicians reflected popular views. This solidified abortion rights and weakened anti-abortion support within the Republican Party. The U.S. bishops were making few new inroads. Yet another trend emerged in the 1990s. With tight budgets and funding cuts being called for, there was less enthusiasm to set aside money to care for the many infants being born to "crack" mothers. Gradually a split grew in the Republican Party between moral and fiscal conservatives. The GOP could no longer be counted to maintain anti-abortion platforms at the state or national level.[55]

With the Supreme Court having upheld legalized abortion in 1989 and again in 1992 and with both national political parties either solidly supportive of abortion rights or at least lukewarm to rescinding those rights, the U.S. bishops appear in the mid-1990s to have little to show for two decades of high-profile anti-abortion political activity. Their continued commitment to anti-abortion political activities, coupled with the Vatican's strong backing of such activities, assures the Catholic Church will remain active in attempting to rescind or restrict abortion laws. The U.S. bishops remain committed to staying the political course, but other Catholics continue to question the wisdom of this approach. At issue is how to combat abortion in the political arena without appearing morally inconsistent and without sacrificing other political causes of social and moral consequence.

The consistent ethic of life approach does not forsake the political arena, but it stresses consistency and moral persuasion. It sees education as key. In every presidential election cycle since 1976, the National Conference of Catholic Bishops has issued statements on "political responsibility" that have urged Catholics to become politically involved. In these statements the bishops spell out the moral dimensions of a host of political issues. Since the early 1980s these statements have explicitly upheld—despite the prominent voices of "single issue" bishops to the contrary—the consistent ethic of life approach to the issues. The 1992 U.S. bishops' statement reminded Catholics that episcopal political responsibility does not involve religious leaders telling people how to vote. The statement expressed concern for issues including euthanasia, substance abuse, abortion, arms control and disarmament, capital punishment, discrimination and racism, the economy, education, family life, food, agriculture, environment, health, housing, and human rights, immigration, mass media, and refugees.

The bishops said the following:

> *We urge citizens to avoid choosing candidates simply on the basis of narrow self-interest. We hope that voters will examine the*

> *positions of candidates on the full range of issues, as well as their personal integrity, philosophy and performance. . . .*
>
> *We are convinced that a consistent ethic of life should be the moral framework from which we address all issues in the political arena. In this consistent ethic, we address a spectrum of issues, seeking to protect human life and promote human dignity from the inception of life to its final moment.*[56]

The statement aside, with some vocal, prominent anti-abortion prelates leading the charge, it was difficult to refrain from the impression that the Catholic hierarchy during the 1992 presidential campaign preferred the lukewarm anti-abortion Republican, George Bush, to the staunchly pro-choice Democratic candidate, Bill Clinton. As Clinton had said: "Our vision should be of an America where abortion is safe and legal and rare." That was not what some bishops wanted to hear.

On the twentieth anniversary of the Supreme Court's *Roe v. Wade* decision, January 22, 1993, with a Democrat stepping into the White House, owing little if anything to the Catholic hierarchy, with anti-abortion protesters, including prominent U.S. archbishops gathered nearby, Clinton, at the outset of his presidency, took the following actions:

- Lifted the so-called gag rule on abortion counseling at federally funded clinics in the United States.
- Ended restrictions on U.S. aid to international family-planning programs in countries that provide abortion-related services. These restrictions had essentially eliminated the U.S. role in worldwide population-control efforts.
- Lifted a federal ban on medical research involving fetal tissue.

- Returned to overseas U.S. military hospitals the right to perform abortions that are paid for with private funds.
- Ordered a review of restrictions on the importation of RU-486, the French abortion pill.

If there was little sympathy shown over the years by the bishops for the Democrats and for this presidential candidate, Clinton's actions indicated the feeling was mutual. Moreover, U.S. Catholics' views on abortion continued to drift away from firm support of official church teaching. One Gallup survey found that in 1987, 45 percent of Catholics said the church's opposition to abortion had strengthened their faith; in 1993, only 37 percent gave that response. In 1987, 19 percent said it weakened their faith; in 1993, 22 percent gave that response. The trend was for the official abortion issue to become less of a positive influence and more of a negative influence. Church leaders and the laity were headed in different directions.[57]

Many Catholics feel that the need to find a new and more successful approach is necessary. These Catholics, U.S. bishops among their ranks, say the church has no alternative. The "consistent ethic of life" is not without its shortcomings, but it provides another way. It is likely it will continue to rally and divide U.S. Catholics, including the hierarchy. The consistent ethic holds that without regard to its achievements, real or potential, human life has intrinsic worth and moral claims on the community.[58] Catholic teaching, said Cardinal Bernardin, is based on two truths about the human person: Human life is both sacred and social. "Because we esteem human life as sacred," he explained, "we have a duty to protect and foster it at all stages of development from conception to natural death and in all circumstances.

Because we acknowledge that human life is also social, society must protect and foster it."[59]

Bernardin went on to say that because human life is sacred, "the taking of even one life is a momentous event." He acknowledged that traditional Catholic teaching has allowed the taking of human life in particular situations by way of exception—for example, in self-defense and capital punishment. "In recent decades, however," he continued, "the presumptions against taking human life have been strengthened and the exceptions made ever more restrictive." The principle factor responsible for the new context, he says, is modern technology. New technology challenges life along its entire spectrum, cutting across such issues as genetics, abortion, capital punishment, modern warfare, and the care of the terminally ill, he says, adding that while each requires its own moral analysis, "they are all linked."

Cardinal Bernardin continued by saying: "The theological assertion that the human person is made in the image and likeness of God, the philosophical affirmation of the dignity of the person, and the political principle that society and state exist to serve the person—all these themes stand behind the consistent ethic." In the 1980s and early 1990s Bernardin spelled out his "seamless garment" vision as it spawned scores of organizations and followers. He and others of like mind say they have no illusion that articulating a morality that makes sense to Catholics and non-Catholics alike will change the political climate at any time soon. They say they are educating for the long haul.

Bernardin, of course, has attracted critics along the way. Some have praised him for articulating a moral vision based on principle but have attacked him for what they see as its uneven application. The church, these critics point out, categorically condemns those who destroy innocent life in abortion, but it does not categorically condemn those who may have to destroy innocent life in warfare. The specific issue revolves around the church's moral view of the building, stockpiling, and potential use of nuclear weapons, which are, because of the sheer magnitude of their destructive force, nondiscriminant. In the case of abortion, the condemnation is clear. In the case of the possible use of nuclear weapons, the church is not absolute. The U.S. bishops' 1983 peace pastoral argued that the stockpiling of nuclear weapons is morally acceptable because they are an effective deterrent and could conceivably be used in warfare. To have condemned their use categorically the bishops would also have to have condemned their stockpiling and construction, and this would have placed them in direct conflict with U.S. national nuclear policy. It was a step the bishops chose not to take.

A deeper pattern of church moral reasoning is involved here, and it goes back well beyond the work on the peace pastoral, which has drawn considerable praise for its moral reasoning and general stance in opposition to modern warfare. The church has traditionally divided its moral reasoning into two spheres, the private and the public. It is the private sphere that has governed the many church declarations on sexual matters. It is in this sphere that the church has operated freely, claiming total ownership of the discussion. In this sphere the church works out of absolute moral principles meant to govern with absolute clarity. Any breech of these principles means committing a sinful act, almost always a gravely sinful act. Sexual sins are viewed as serious sins. Artificial contraception, for example, is seen as intrinsically evil. Likewise homosexual acts. Abortion is also seen as a grave evil.

In the public sphere, however, the church has had to share ownership with the Caesars of the world. In this sphere, moral matters are more complex. There are more shades of gray. Expert testimony is sought. Here there is a noticeable absence of absolutes. Even New Testament pacifism is missing, replaced with qualifications and principles to be met if a Christian is to engage in a "just" war. Here proportional good is measured against proportional evil. Circumstances are considered. Situations surveyed. Here consequences are important and need to be considered before judgments are rendered.

In the early 1980s, the U.S. bishops went through three years of interviews; gathered testimony from defense experts, scientists, and theologians; and wrote several drafts before issuing their peace pastoral. In the mid-1980s, they went through the same process before writing a pastoral letter on the U.S. economy. These documents are among the more recent in more than a hundred years of Catholic social teachings, impressive statements by the church hierarchy on just wages, labor organizing rights, international development, hunger, a just world order, and dozens of other social justice considerations. While these are founded on basic Christian principles, their reasoning moves them into carefully nuanced examinations of the time and circumstances before drawing conclusions. By contrast, sexual sins remain absolute in nature and without nuance and without regard to circumstances. Unlike the carefully reasoned social teachings, the sexual teachings come out of a theology of fixed and uncompromising law. There remains, then, at the end of the second millennium of Christianity a serious gulf between the methodology of social and sexual morality. Many Catholics see this as a serious inconsistency in church moral reasoning.

As painful as such criticisms may be, there has emerged in the past two decades a clear movement toward a consistent moral ethic on life issues in the U.S. hierarchy. Led by Cardinal Bernardin, the U.S. bishops have increasingly preached the outlines of such a "pro-life" or consistent ethic of life approach to teaching morality. This is relatively new work. Inconsistencies remain in practical applications. For example, the church permits no exceptions to abortion and euthanasia mandates, but condones killing in "just wars" and in some cases condones capital punishment. To those who complain the U.S. bishops have emphasized abortion over all other issues, Bernardin responds that a particular emphasis may depend on the specific needs of a given time. The pace of change in an institution as large and as old as the Catholic Church is slow. Old mind-sets are not likely to change quickly. Nevertheless, movement toward teaching a consistent ethic of life, grounded in the sacredness of all life, is slowly gaining ground.

V

❖ ❖ ❖

Homosexuality

Shock waves from an incident in New York City's Greenwich Village on June 17, 1969, rippled out and have managed to disturb the waters of the Catholic Church in the United States ever since. That night New York City Police raided the Stonewall Inn, a gathering place in Manhattan for gays and lesbians who for years had came to the bars on Christopher Street where they were easy targets for police harassment. The police were concerned with liquor code violations and same sex dancing which was illegal at the time. What started that evening as a routine raid ended up in a riot. Police entered Stonewall demanding identification. The pattern of entrapment and extortion was not new. Police threw out some clients and arrested others, including inn employees. On the street outside an angry group of ejected patrons was joined by other gays and lesbians. Within minutes the numbers were in the hundreds.

As a police van arrived to take away those singled out for charges, the crowd started throwing coins and street debris at the police. They uprooted parking meters, overturned trash cans, and threw rocks at the police officers who fell back into the inn where they barricaded themselves and waited for reinforcements.

During the next few nights, hundreds of gays and lesbians, hearing of the incident and fed up with harassment, began to confront the police on the streets of Greenwich Village demanding the shakedowns end. Victimized by police for years, they had had enough and were standing together to say: "No more!"

Stonewall ignited an already fledgling gay and lesbian movement that spread across the nation. Gays and lesbians began to reject the term *homosexual* and began to speak with a new, self-affirming and self-defining consciousness. The movement produced marches, protests, sit-ins, and in some cases, disruptive demonstrations. Thousands, then tens of thousands, even millions eventually publicly claimed their gay identity, breaking silence. It was a nationwide "coming out of the closet." The days of hiding, self-hatred, and shame were ending. Not that the transition was without enormous personal turmoil. In the 1970s a new awakening was occurring in the United States and there was no turning back. Publicly declared gays and lesbians were gaining places along side heterosexuals in U.S. society and abroad. Gay oppression had turned to gay pride.[1]

The shift was especially difficult for the Catholic Church, including the many thousands of U.S. Catholic gays and lesbians who found themselves in love-hate relationships with their church. The history of Catholicism is replete with stories of gay bashing: witch hunts, Inquisition trials, and even burnings of homosexuals who were viewed as moral outcasts and sinners. The church, as a molder of the wider Western culture and as a product of its time, was often unforgiving in it treatment of homosexuals. According to traditional teaching, homosexual acts are intrinsically evil. Deliberate homosexual acts, the church has taught, are mortal sins, meaning that those who commit them will be damned unless they confess and are forgiven by a priest. But while the church has contributed to self-hatred in gays and lesbians, it has also been their spiritual home. It is said: "Once a Catholic, always a Catholic," meaning that whether or not they choose to practice their faith, Catholics are the products of its sacramental traditions, rituals, and worldviews. Many gays and lesbians, loathing their church's homophobic role in history, still find themselves looking to it for spiritual guidance and meaning. Tens of thousands have simply disassociated themselves from the institution; tens of thousands of others have managed to accommodate themselves, finding room somewhere under its large cloak.

Perhaps the most significant recent attitudinal change toward gays and lesbians has followed the realization that homosexuality for the most part is not chosen. By the 1970s the behavioral sciences were largely in agreement that homosexuality is a sexual "orientation." This makes a critical difference in Catholic morality. The church has never taught that *being* gay is sinful. It teaches that sin must involve a personal choice and where choice is absent, there can be no sin. Whether the product of inborn characteristics or environment or both, many people believe it is no longer reasonable to see homosexuality, when considered an orientation, as a moral failing. While the numbers continue to be debated, it is generally believed that up to 10 percent of the population is predominantly or exclusively homosexually oriented. Some place the figure lower; some considerably higher. As church time goes, it is still relatively new to think of homosexuality in a neutral way. It was, after all, only in 1973 that the trustees of the American Psychiatric Association voted to remove it from its list of psychiatric illnesses.

Meanwhile, the Catholic hierarchy, as teacher in matters of faith and morals, could hardly ignore the implications involved in this new approach to homosexuality. After all, some have reasoned that if homosexuality were not a choice and if a sizable portion of the population is born with the orientation, then it must be part of God's mysterious plan of creation. But why? Moreover, the ethical questions are not easily resolved. By the same reasoning, if some people are born alcoholic, does that mean alcoholism is a part of God's creative design? With new scientific discoveries related to homosexuality surfacing, ethicists are being forced to ponder these matters anew. And what are the responsibilities to gays and lesbians as well as the larger human family? Examining these questions could not be done without eventually considering what this means with regard to the morality of homosexual acts, viewed by the church as gravely wrong.

The Vatican's first response came in 1975 in the *Declaration on Certain Questions Concerning Sexual Ethics*. In that statement, Rome distinguished between "transitory" and "permanent" homosexual inclination and implicitly distinguished between tendencies and acts. The former may not be morally wrong, but the latter most definitely and in all cases are. What this means, however, is that homosexuals, while inclined toward their own sex through no choice of their own, cannot ever act upon those inclinations. An entire group of people can never expect to experience physical intimacy. The church has always taught that celibacy is a "gift" given to a relative few. People "are called" to celibacy. Those who have been given the call have traditionally been encouraged to enter the clerical or religious life to serve as priests, brothers, or women religious.

The most recent explanation of Catholic teaching on homosexuality appears in the revised *Catechism of the Catholic Church*, published in English in 1994.[2] It includes the following:

> *The number of men and women who have deep-seated homosexual tendencies is not negligible. They do not choose their homosexual condition; for most of them it is a trial. They must be accepted with respect, compassion, and sensitivity. Every sign of unjust discrimination in their regard should be avoided. These persons are called to fulfill God's will in their lives and, if they are Christians, to unite to the sacrifice of the Lord's Cross the difficulties they may encounter from their condition.*
>
> *Homosexual persons are called to chastity. By the virtues of self-mastery that teach them inner freedom, at times by the support of disinterested friendship, by prayer and sacramental grace, they can and should gradually and resolutely approach Christian perfection.*

Many other Catholics have been forced to rethink their idea about homosexuality in the decades following the Stonewall incident. Well-publicized pockets of homophobia aside, many U.S. priests, women religious, and laity have taken initiatives aimed at assisting and welcoming gays and lesbians into parish life. Moral theologians, meanwhile, have reexamined church teachings, chipping away at old assumptions, integrating new ideas. They have looked at

Scripture and Catholic natural law formulations—the twin pillars of Catholic moral teachings.

Repeated prohibitions of homosexual acts are found in the Bible. Homosexuality is called "unnatural" and a "perversity" (Romans 1:26–27) and a sin that can exclude one from entry into the kingdom of God (1 Corinthians 6:10). More ominous is the punishment visited by God upon Sodom for the assumed sin that was named after that ill-fated city (Genesis 19:1-29). Some Catholic moral theologians have countered that the Bible needs to be understood in its cultural, historical, and religious context and must be looked at through the latest analytical techniques and that "simply citing verses from the Bible outside of their historical context and then blithely applying them to homosexuals today does grave injustice both to Scripture and to people who have already suffered a great deal from the travesty of biblical interpretation."[3] These theologians say that as often as it refers to the sinfulness of Sodom, the Old Testament never explicitly identifies Sodom with the practice of homosexuality.[4] Involved in the story of the male visitors to Sodom, they say, is the sexual violation of *rape*. The New Testament, meanwhile, presents Jesus as referring to the proverbial wickedness and punishment of Sodom, but with no indication of the specific nature of its sinfulness.

The Catholic Church's stand against homosexuality is also based on the belief that homosexual acts are unnatural. These are unnatural for the same reason artificial contraception is unnatural: the church teaches that genital sex acts must be open to the potential for procreation, that procreation is a fundamental, God-given purpose of sexual intercourse, and that any sexual genital expression that excludes the possibility of procreation is unnatural. Some moral theologians speak of this as being "act centered" morality. Theological revisionists prefer a "personalist" approach, one that views human nature and natural law from a wider perspective. Acts, they say, should never be seen apart from human relationships. They further argue that the behavioral sciences have revolutionized the way the modern world looks at nature and humanity and that twentieth-century insights must be integrated into Catholic moral teachings. Given the current starting point of natural law theology's view of sexuality—that sexual acts must be open to procreation—it is not lost on either the traditionalists or reformers that to change teachings on homosexual acts would not be without effect on church teachings regarding artificial contraception. By the same token, a change in church teaching on contraception could have an impact on its views on homosexuality.

The revisionists, meanwhile, are divided as well. Some say that homosexual acts must be judged with the same Christian criteria as heterosexual acts, confined to loving, faithful relationships. Others view homosexual acts as imperfect, but given that no one chooses a homosexual orientation, it is unrealistic and perhaps unjust to demand that the homosexual person live a celibate life. This position is sometimes referred to as a theology of compromise. Its argument: Mutual love in a stable and monogamous homosexual relationship is a lesser evil than a life without intimacy or a life of promiscuity.[5]

Internal Church Skirmishes

Catholics were confronting a number of moral issues in the early 1970s. In the wake of *Roe v. Wade* Catholic bishops were calling the laity to political battle; many were still reeling as a result of *Humanae Vitae*, the birth control encyclical.

Homosexuality was an issue to few Catholics. The big story at the time was word of the unprecedented numbers of priests and nuns resigning from their ministries, often to marry. Yet gay issues were making inroads. A struggle had started for the hearts and minds of U.S. Catholics. If their thinking on homosexuality was to change, it would require much education, and then even with education there were no assurances that their ideas or judgments would change. If attitudes toward African Americans and toward civil rights gains of the 1960s were any measure, results would be mixed. The lesson, it seemed, is that Americans can change, but legislation helps move them along. Gays and lesbians knew they would have to become active in local and national politics. This, too, would be difficult for the church, especially for those who had held onto older ways of thinking.

Perhaps expectedly the first internal church skirmishes surrounding homosexuality occurred on the political field. This story begins in 1971 with the hopeful experiences of a young Catholic nun, a School Sister of Notre Dame named Jeannine Gramick. That was the year she recalls meeting a young gay Catholic in Philadelphia named Dominic Bash who asked her, "What is the Catholic church doing for my gay brothers and sisters?"[6] The question challenged her to study the topic of homosexuality, eventually leading her to meetings with a group of Catholic and Anglican gay men. After a newspaper account of her associations with the men appeared in a Philadelphia newspaper, she received more than a dozen responses, one from Robert Nugent, a Philadelphia diocesan priest. He was in transition from parish work to an unofficial leave of absence. In his letter to Gramick, Nugent suggested he might help out. She responded, and the two began to meet with the gay men, counseling them and celebrating home liturgies. Soon the two began to write and lecture on issues of pastoral care for gays and lesbians, then to lobby for legislation to secure gay rights. When Gramick testified in support of a gay rights bill in Baltimore, Archbishop William Borders, who opposed it, registered a complaint with her religious superior. It was a minor skirmish; there would be larger ones to come.

While it was not planned, and it was hardly the first time, what was emerging was a conflict between two components of the Catholic faith: a gospel-based call to compassion and a call to uphold traditional church teachings. Some, of course, would say the two cannot be in conflict, that true compassion requires upholding all church teachings. But that is not the way many gay and lesbian Catholics saw it. To them old traditions and prejudices stood in the way of Jesus' teachings. This conflict was to characterize much of the tension and debate in the church on homosexuality for the next quarter century.

Nugent, meanwhile, found himself in a similar conflict with church authority. His testimony on behalf of a gay civil rights bill at a Philadelphia City Council hearing did not please Philadelphia Cardinal John Krol, who had sent a member of his staff to testify against the bill. After continued pressure from the Philadelphia archdiocese, Nugent left in 1975 to join a religious order, the Society of the Divine Savior, known for its sympathetic attitudes toward gay and lesbian concerns. The priest moved to Washington, D.C., where he continued his work with gays and lesbians. There he began to associate with a newly founded Catholic peace and justice center, the Quixote Center; in 1976, Gramick also joined the staff. In 1977, their joint work and organization was formalized under a new name: New Ways Ministry.

Part of the intention of the Second Vatican Council had been to open the church to renewal and to engage ordinary Catholics to come alive in their faith by living it out in the world. Basically, this meant living good lives by working for peace, justice, and mercy. It was in this light that Gramick and Nugent saw their work. They had been greatly influenced by the council and now were attempting to live it out. As new English-language liturgies were introduced and old Latin rituals were set aside, as altars were turned around so priests could face their parishioners, as nuns put away their old religious garments, as interfaith activities grew, the Catholic Church, it seemed, was setting out on a fresh course. Catholicism was less stodgy; the church, as the council bishops had wanted it, was entering the modern world. An institution that had for centuries placed its heaviest emphasis upon further defining and bolstering traditional doctrine after the Protestant Reformation was now putting on a pastoral face. Many U.S. Catholics felt good about their church. It had problems, but there was a sense that work was being done to face them. Instead of confronting a secular world, going to war with it, this post-conciliar church was embracing it in the hopes of transforming it. But that involved being transformed as well.

The Catholic Church in the 1970s and 1980s issued a number of statements on homosexuality and took many new initiatives. Some were intended to reaffirm traditional teaching, others to clarify, still others to cover new ground. Taken together, these reflected much of the anguish and hope found in the wider society.

Church Initiatives

In 1975, in the *Declaration on Certain Questions Concerning*

Sexual Ethics, the Vatican Congregation for the Doctrine of Faith offered the first official contemporary statement dealing with the pastoral and moral issues of homosexuality. For the first time a Catholic document granted the legitimacy of the distinction between a "transitory" homosexual orientation and a "definitive" homosexual orientation. Although it granted the validity of the distinction, it did not explore its implications for moral judgments.[7]

It did respond to arguments about allowing for expression of the orientation: "Some people conclude that their tendency is so natural that it justifies in their case homosexual relations within a sincere communion of life and love analogous to marriage insofar as such homosexuals feel incapable of enduring a solitary life." The document, however, is clear that there can be no justification for homosexual acts. "No pastoral method can be employed which would give moral justification to these acts on grounds that they would be consonant with the conditions of such people."

The declaration reasserted church teaching based on natural law theology. "According to the objective moral order," the document stated, "homosexual relations are acts which lack an essential and indispensable finality," meaning they cannot lead to having children. The church teaches that some natural law precepts are knowable and understandable to all—not just to Catholics. This is because it is based upon knowable, universal characteristics that guide all moral behavior. These are nature's norms; not the church's. The church merely helps interpret and proclaim these to the world. Among these norms is the belief that homosexual acts are unnatural and a sin against God's creative design of male-female complementarity.

Also in 1976, the U.S. bishops offered a balanced view of official church teachings in *To Live in Christ Jesus*, a letter on moral values. They spoke out against antihomosexual prejudices and once again distinguished between a homosexual orientation and homosexual acts:

> *Some persons find themselves, through no fault of their own, to have a homosexual orientation. Homosexuals, like everyone else, should not suffer from prejudice against their basic human rights. They have a right to respect, friendship and justice. They should have an active role in the Christian community. . . . Homosexual activity, however, as distinguished from homosexual orientation, is morally wrong. . . . [B]ecause heterosexuals can usually look forward to marriage, and homosexuals, while their orientation continues, might not, the Christian community should provide them [homosexuals] a special degree of pastoral understanding and care.*

Bishop Francis Mugavero in a 1976 pastoral letter on sexuality upheld the heterosexual norm while judging other orientations rather mildly, stating they represented "less adequately" the full spectrum of human relationships.[8]

The landmark book *The Church and the Homosexual*, by John J. McNeill, a Catholic priest and psychotherapist, was published in 1976. McNeill recounted the joy he felt when he was able to announce at a New York liturgy service for Catholic gays and lesbians that he had received an official *Imprimi Potest*, an approval from his superiors in the Jesuit order to publish the book on condition that he distinguish his views from official church teaching. The book had been four years in the making, including two years of intensive scrutiny by moral theologians in the United States and

Rome. He had reason to be elated. His was one of the first theological works in modern times calling for a complete revision of traditional church teaching on homosexuality. McNeill recalled that its publication buoyed his feelings that the spirit of the Second Vatican Council was still alive in the church.

The permission, he felt, upheld evidence coming from the fields of Scripture study, history, psychology, sociology, and moral theology—evidence he had gathered in his research—that offered a credible challenge to traditional church teachings about homosexuality. His book, he believed, would help usher in a much-needed public debate within the church, eventually leading to the church's revision of its understanding of homosexuality.

In his book, McNeill argued that the church inherited an erroneous interpretation of the story of Sodom and Gomorrah. The biblical account of the destruction of those cities has been linked with homosexual activities since earliest Christian times. But McNeill, with the backing of several biblical scholars, contended that the reason for God's vengeance against the two cities is never specified as homosexual.

He also contended that Christianity was unduly influenced by antisexual strains in Stoic philosophy and by a strong aversion toward Greek homosexuality by early Jewish Christians. He argued that homosexual behavior can be morally good and urged the church to review its blanket proscription. The church's view of homosexuality, he stated, has often been founded on attitudes that do not take into account modern behavioral science's concepts of human nature. Sexual relations can be morally justified if they are true expressions of human love, he concluded.

McNeill examined the two principal factors often proposed as supporting the traditional church teaching condemning homosexual acts—the procreative meaning of sexual intercourse and male-female complementarity. He asserted the nature of an authentic love relationship should no longer be viewed simply for its biological aspect. He also argued male-female relationships need not be the norm. A male or female is not just the product of biology, he argued, but is also a free human cultural creation. He pointed to the suffering involved in many relationships in which males have dominated females. He suggested, instead, that the critical theologian—and church—must try to liberate humanity from sexual stereotypes to fashion cultural identities making it possible for human beings to achieve the fullness of true personal relationships.

The joy of having received permission to publish his ideas, however, was short-lived. One year later, the Vatican Congregation for the Doctrine of Faith ordered the removal of the book's *Imprimi Potest*. Furthermore, Rome imposed a blanket silence on McNeill, forbidding him to discuss homosexuality in public. "Instead of allowing public debate on homosexuality, the church fell back on its 'creeping infallibility,'" he later wrote, "claiming that its teaching was based on 'divine revelation' and, therefore, was not open to change, regardless of any new evidence to support that change."[9] Rome maintained that McNeill had been giving a false impression that the church was changing its teachings about homosexuality, or was about to do so. This, it stated emphatically, was not the case.[10]

In 1977, *Human Sexuality: New Directions in American Catholic Thought*, an important work intended to break new ground in theological and pastoral approaches to homosexuality, was published. Appearing in book form, it was actually a report that had been commissioned by the Catholic Theological Society of America. The project ran several years and involved many Catholic theologians in the writing and review stages. The five theologian authors said they were presenting their work "in the spirit of the Second Vatican Council" to help "beleaguered pastors, priests, counselors and teachers." They intended it to stimulate further discussion. The report covered a wide range of sexual issues. The commission devoted several pages to homosexuality, affirming homosexual acts as moral within a restricted framework. The commission wrote the following:

> *Homosexuals have the same rights to love, intimacy, and relationships as heterosexuals. Like heterosexuals, they are also bound to strive for the same ideals in their relationships, for creativity and integration. The norms governing the morality of homosexual activity are those that govern all sexual activity, and the norms governing sexual activity are those that govern all human ethical activity.*
>
> *The question arises at this point: Are homosexuals, by reason of their condition, denied by God and nature the right enjoyed by heterosexuals to the intimate, sexual expression of love? . . . Is it to be presumed that homosexuals by virtue of their condition, have been guaranteed by God the "charism" of celibacy? (The data of the behavioral sciences seem to indicate the contrary.) . . . Heterosexuals are free to choose or not to choose a life of celibacy. Are homosexuals denied that free choice? . . . Heterosexuals may see continence as a call in life. Must homosexuals see continence as their destiny?*[11]

Although the work was criticized by church authorities, the

commission's conclusion was widely received and affirmed by the majority of mainline contemporary theologians.[12]

In 1980, Bishop (later Archibishop and Cardinal) Joseph Bernardin, speaking at the synod "On the Family" in Rome on behalf of the U.S. bishops, called for a more positive theology of human sexuality. He noted that in many parts of the world there was a significant gap between church teachings on sexual matters and the ideas of both the clergy and laity. He suggested this was undermining church authority. The church's moral teachings, he said, are seldom accepted solely on the argument of authority but had to be perceived as "reasonable, persuasive and related to the actual experience."[13]

During 1980, *Christianity, Social Tolerance, and Homosexuality*, by a young medieval historian at Yale University, Dr. John Boswell, was published. In his book, Boswell argued that church attitudes about homosexuality had not always been harsh, that the classical scriptural texts used for the traditional condemnation of homosexuality will not bear the weight put upon them, and that Catholic religious life has always provided a comfortable environment for homosexuals.[14]

In 1981, the Archdiocese of Baltimore established one of the first official diocesan ministries for lesbian and gay Catholics after issuing a theological rationale for the ministry. The statement said that the homosexual orientation is "in no way held to be a sinful condition" and that, like heterosexuality, it represents the starting point for one's response to Christ.[15]

New Ways Ministry, the national Catholic gay and lesbian ministry founded by Gramick and Nugent in 1977, sponsored its first national symposium on homosexuality and the Catholic Church in 1981. The papers from this event were later published in a book titled *Homosexuality and the Catholic Church.*

In 1983, the Archdiocese of San Francisco issued the first comprehensive pastoral plan for ministry with homosexual people. That same year, 1983, the Washington State Catholic Conference, consisting of the bishops of three dioceses of Washington State, published *Prejudice against Homosexuals and the Ministry of the Church* in which the bishops suggested that Catholic teaching on homosexuality needs "rethinking and development." They also urged the church to undertake "ongoing theological research and criticism, with regard to its own theological tradition on homosexuality, none of which is infallibly taught." Archbishop Raymond Hunthausen, one of the Washington bishops, also welcomed Dignity, an organization for Catholic gays and lesbians, founded in 1969 and with a membership of about five thousand, and about one hundred U.S. chapters, to celebrate its biannual convention Mass in Seattle's St. James Cathedral in 1983. Hunthausen then came under attack from the Vatican for allegedly failing to uphold Catholic orthodoxy. Rome stripped the popular archbishop of some of his episcopal authority while appointing an auxiliary bishop to oversee certain aspects of archdiocesan life, including its ministry to gays and lesbians.

An anthology of theological and pastoral articles on homosexuality by Robert Nugent entitled *A Challenge to Love: Gay and Lesbian Catholics in the Church* was published in 1983. It contained an introduction by Walter F. Sullivan, bishop of the Diocese of Richmond, Virginia. The Vatican tried unsuccessfully to prevent the work from being reprinted; it did succeed in forcing the bishop to have his name removed from the book's cover.

During this period, a number of Catholic gay and lesbian organizations formed. Some like Dignity and the Conference for Catholic Lesbians offered various forms of support to gay and lesbian Catholics. Some others including Communications Ministry, Inc., Christian Community Association, and Rest, Renewal and Re-Creation aided gay clergy and religious. Still others such as New Ways Ministry, SIGMA (Sisters in Gay Ministry Associated), and the Consultation on Homosexuality, Social Justice and Roman Catholic Theology promoted discussion and provided information and resources to both the homosexual and heterosexual communities.[16]

By the early 1980s, lesbian and gay Catholics had reason to believe they were making significant gains within the church—not evenly and not without some continued local harassment and setbacks. They had clearly gained the attention of many bishops and theologians who were, indeed, rethinking long-held views on homosexuality. This was taking place in the wake of the energy still generated by the Second Vatican Council and its commitment to renewal. Many Catholics believed the council had set into motion energies that would continue for decades, if not centuries. Like a ship at sea, an institution as large and as old as the Catholic Church changes direction slowly, almost imperceptibly.

Even as these new energies were moving the homosexuality discussion in new directions, other signals were also being sent out, these from Pope John Paul II, elected pope in 1978. His pontificate was gaining momentum and despite having taken the names of his reformist predecessors, he was of different mind.

This pope wanted the post-Vatican II "experimentations"

to end. He felt it was necessary to restore orthodoxy within the church. Furthermore, those pushing for change, it became clear, were suspect. Some, including Catholic theologians, were labeled dissenters. Some theologians were told they could no longer teach in Catholic settings. Within a few years of the opening of his pontificate an entirely new mood was settling in. Caution was the prudent path. Career-minded bishops spoke less of the fruits of the Second Vatican Council. Many began to worry publicly about church renewal having gone too far. Soon caution gave way to fear, and Catholics began to talk more privately. The term *chill factor* surfaced. It was being felt throughout the church. Don't take risks; try nothing new; assert traditional teachings. This is how one best protected one's place in the institution—or advanced within it. Curiously, Rome's new demands had little or nothing to do with basic theological doctrines, which were not being debated. There was no fight over the meaning, for example, of the Trinity, the Incarnation, or the Resurrection. The major issues were the church's moral teachings, and almost always those specific moral teachings having to do with sexuality or sexual ethics.

For many reform-minded Catholics, it was shocking to see the church returning to its old ways when teachings had come as dictates and had to be accepted without discussion—even by Catholic theologians. Hopes for more democratic initiatives within the church faded. Rome also investigated bishops. The disciplining of the warm and generous Raymond Hunthausen, archbishop of Seattle, upset not only the members of his archdiocese but Catholics across the nation. Bishops resented the action because it brought great strife to the U.S. church and broke the unstated and long-held rule that a local bishop is head of his local church, in communion with Rome, but not just a Roman delegate.

What this all meant to the study of homosexuality by moral theologians was not difficult to decipher. Any attempt to break new ground in this area would not be taken kindly by the Vatican. To the contrary, such scholarship would likely lead to trouble. For Catholic gays and lesbians, the pontificate of John Paul II would be especially difficult. They knew the signals coming out of Rome in the early 1980s did not auger well. The pope, for example, said there would be no more talk about women's ordination. Nor was the celibacy rule for priests to be discussed. Pope John Paul II repeatedly demanded that Catholics accept church teachings on contraception and abortion. It was not until 1986, in the eighth year of Pope John Paul's pontificate, that the Vatican issued its first major statement on homosexuality. On October 31, 1986, Cardinal Joseph Ratzinger, prefect of the Vatican's Congregation for the Doctrine of Faith, charged by the pope with upholding doctrinal orthodoxy, released a document entitled *Letter to the Bishops of the Catholic Church on the Pastoral Care of Homosexual Persons.*

Most of the letter covered no new ground. It cited Scripture and church tradition to uphold the church's strict judgment against homosexual acts, which were viewed as gravely wrong in all circumstances. What was new was the language that followed and its characterization of the homosexual orientation:

> *Although the particular inclination of the homosexual person is not a sin, it is a more or less strong tendency ordered toward an intrinsic moral evil; and thus the inclination itself must be seen as*

an objective disorder. Therefore special concern and pastoral attention should be directed toward those who have this condition, lest they be led to believe that the living out of this orientation in homosexual activity is a morally acceptable option. It is not.[17]

Whatever else the Vatican had said, what was heard loudest were the words "objective disorder." Reactions to the letter among U.S. Catholics, including bishops, clergy, and laity, ranged from lukewarm to hostile. Among Catholic lesbians and gays there were anger, tears, and even laughter. Some gay and lesbian organizations could only ridicule what they saw as hopelessly misguided thinking on Rome's part. The U.S. Catholic hierarchy did not seem pleased either. Most bishops chose silence; few printed the full text in their diocesan newspapers, although printing the entire text is generally the practice with important statements. Many were reported to have been personally upset by the letter. That the letter was written in English, and not in Latin or Italian, simply confirmed to some that it had been aimed at the English-speaking countries, particularly the United States.

For Jesuit Father John McNeill the letter proved to be too much. For ten years he had observed the silence imposed upon him by Rome by not speaking publicly on the issue of homosexuality. He had agreed to the silence, he later explained, in the hope that the church would consider the evidence in his book and begin a process of reevaluation. McNeill said he recognized that the U.S. bishops were making positive moves. They had made pastoral initiatives and had called for legislation to protect the civil rights of gays and lesbians, he recalled. "But every time any move was made toward a better understanding and spiritual care of gay people, the Vatican intervened demanding that the Catholic Church in the United States maintain a homophobic stance on all gay issues."[18] The "Ratzinger letter," as it came to be called, finally moved him to break the silence. "Since most gay people experience their homosexual orientation as part of creation, if they accept this Church teaching, they must see God as sadistically creating them with an intrinsic orientation to evil," Father McNeill commented.[19] As a homosexual and a psychotherapist, he explained that he understood the devastating pain involved in the church's attitude toward gays and lesbians. "In my more than twenty years' experience of pastoral care with thousands of gay Catholics and other Christians, the gay men most likely to act out their sexual needs in an unsafe, compulsive way and, therefore, to expose themselves to the HIV virus, are precisely those persons who have internalized the self-hatred that their religions impose on them."[20] One week after Ratzinger released his letter, McNeill issued a statement to *The New York Times* and the *National Catholic Reporter* condemning the Vatican document. His statement resulted in his dismissal from the Jesuit order.

The Ratzinger document was widely seen as an effort to halt church initiatives viewed by Rome as weakening traditional teachings. The Vatican was trying to turn back the tide on what it saw as creeping secularism inside the church. Shortly after the publication of the 1986 letter, polls conducted by *Time* magazine and the *Los Angeles Times* indicated that 68 and 67 percent of Catholics, respectively, agreed with the teaching that homogenital acts are morally wrong. Two years later, however, after much public discussion generated by the letter, Catholic support of church teaching banning all homosexual behavior had dropped to

58 percent, according to the *San Francisco Examiner*. For Catholics under the age of forty this figure was even lower. The letter was apparently not succeeding as Vatican officials hoped it would.

As far as Rome was concerned, a basic tenet of Catholic teaching was at stake, one that had been held in place for centuries—the condemnation of all homogenital acts. The Ratzinger letter spoke about the need to clear up "confusion" on homosexuality or any approach "that somehow tacitly approves of it." The Vatican wanted to make it clear that any theological arguments leading to or supporting homosexual acts were unacceptable.

The Ratzinger letter also took another step in Rome's counteroffensive, demanding that all Catholic gays and lesbians who did not adhere to official church teachings on homosexuality be denied the use of church property. The tension between the Vatican and Catholic lesbians and gays reached a new high. More than any other Catholic gay and lesbian organization this directive appeared aimed at Dignity, which for years had taken the position that gays and lesbians are called to affirm their sexual orientations and to express it in a manner consonant with Christ's teaching of love. The organization had become a challenge to official church teachings. It would not deny gays and lesbians their proclaimed right to sexual activity. The Dignity organization was appalled by the Ratzinger statement. In a meeting in Bal Harbour, Florida, the next year, it responded to Ratzinger's decree by boldly affirming that they could express their sexuality physically in a manner that is "loving, life-giving and life-affirming." Dignity–New York City staged what they called the "cathedral project" to protest their expulsion from a Jesuit-run church. Gay Catholics attended masses at St.

Patrick's Cathedral and stood throughout New York Cardinal John O'Connor's homily until they were stopped by a court order. In the months that followed, all but a handful of U.S. dioceses and archdioceses expelled Dignity from church buildings. Within five years, the organization's membership dropped from about five thousand to under three thousand. Remaining chapters continued to meet off church property. In the early 1990s, Dignity opted to downplay differences with church authority in order to find ways to exist in local dioceses as opportunities occurred. Some archdioceses, Chicago and Seattle, for example, began to sponsor weekly masses for Catholic gays and lesbians. Many gay and lesbian Catholics felt alienated from the church, maintaining their Catholic identities in small groups but keeping their distance from the institution. Many others simply left the church altogether.

Five years later, as the nation geared up for the November 1992 elections, gay rights legislation was set to appear on a number of state ballots. Family values were a major national election theme with gay rights becoming a target of the Right. In June 1992, the Vatican issued another directive to American bishops entitled *Some Considerations Concerning the Catholic Response to Legislative Proposals on the Non-Discrimination of Homosexual Persons*. The document claimed that discrimination against homosexuals is not unjust and is even desirable in areas such as employment of teachers or athletic coaches, housing, adoption, foster care of children, and service in the military. It stated that support for gay rights represents an attack on "family values" and could be seen as supporting a "homosexual lifestyle." Immediately, the directive came under attack by progressives, who said the Vatican was meddling in U.S. politics.

Conservatives, meanwhile, praised the move, calling it a needed initiative to help clear up the moral climate. The June 1992 document, from the Congregation for the Doctrine of the Faith, included the following:

> *Recently, legislation has been proposed in some American states which would make discrimination on the basis of sexual orientation illegal . . . Such initiatives, even where they seem more directed toward support of basic civil right than condonement of homosexual activity or a homosexual life-style, may in fact have a negative impact on the family and society. . . .*
>
> *The intrinsic dignity of each person must always be respected in word, in action and in law. But the proper reaction to crimes committed against homosexual persons should not be to claim that the homosexual condition is not disordered. When such a claim is made and when homosexual activity is consequently condoned, or when civil legislation is introduced to protect behavior to which no one has any conceivable right, neither the church nor society at large should be surprised when other distorted notions and practices gain ground, and irrational and violent reactions increase. . . .*
>
> *Even when the practice of homosexuality may seriously threaten the lives and well-being of a large number of people, its advocates remained undeterred and refused to consider the magnitude of the risks involved.*[21]

Many gays and lesbians took the words as not only justifying violence against them but fomenting more to come. Further, it appeared that the document suggested that it is gay activists and the professionals who try to help gays achieve self-acceptance who are responsible for the AIDS epidemic. The reaction from within the Catholic gay and lesbian communities was predictably negative.

Dignity/USA Vice President Marianne Duddy, for example, said it was "incomprehensible" that the institutional church could presume to issue such a statement. The organization issued a statement that in part read: "The Vatican position is an affront to the conscience and sensibilities of all persons, homosexual, heterosexual, Christian and non-Christian. It has no place in a society that seeks justice." [22] New Ways Ministry called the Vatican statement "unfortunate" and said it represented "an attempt to impose a unified ideology that appears out of touch at least with contemporary and firsthand awareness of these issues in our society."[23]

More telling was the reaction of one of the most prominent church groups in the United States, the Conference of Major Superiors of Men, which represents the heads of U.S. male religious orders. The organization issued a statement that revealed the depth of the breach between the Vatican and U.S. Catholic priests on the homosexuality issue:

> *. . . this statement clouds the institutional Church's stated views on justice and human rights. We view this statement as a hindrance to the church leaders of the United States in this most difficult and sensitive area of human living. . . . We are shocked that the statement calls for discrimination against gay men and lesbian women. We find the reasoning for supporting such discrimination to be strained, unconvincing and counterproductive to our statements and actions to support the pastoral needs and personal dignity of such persons. . . . Moreover, we find the argument used to justify discrimination based on stereotypes and falsehoods that are out of touch with modern psychological and sociological understandings of human sexuality.*[24]

Warned Mary Hunt, coordinator of Maryland-based

Women's Alliance for Theology, Ethics and Ritual (WATER): The cost to the Catholic episcopacy of the Vatican document supporting discrimination against homosexuals in certain circumstances could be very high indeed: public revelation of the names of gay Catholic bishops. "I think there are gay men who will begin to 'out' [reveal] people's names; [bishops] living duplicitously will find themselves 'outed,' and I predict in very high places."[25]

A handful of U.S. bishops risked Vatican displeasure by continuing to speak publicly in support of gay and lesbian rights. For them it was not just a "rights" issue, but a gospel demand, they said. One, Detroit Auxiliary Thomas Gumbleton, reacted by saying:

> *This statement is clearly based on an ignorance of the nature of homosexuality. It is also totally in conflict with Gospel values that condemn discrimination and insist that we recognize the dignity inherent in all persons. . . . I cannot in good conscience accept the statement as consistent with the Gospel nor can I justify implementing it.*[26]

Speaking at a Chicago symposium sponsored by New Ways Ministry March 28, 1992, Gumbleton said, "The church should affirm and bless the gay community for teaching what it means to love."[27] Gumbleton, one of three U.S. bishops who appeared on the panel, said he did not endorse homosexual activity. Rather, he was there to praise "the beautiful expressions of love and care within the gay and lesbian community toward those afflicted with AIDS. Nowhere do we find the resurrection more meaningful than in the community affected by AIDS," Gumbleton said, and nowhere else is "the grace of God as powerfully active." He and his episcopal colleagues, William Hughes of Covington, Kentucky, and Kenneth Untener of Saginaw, Michigan, received a standing ovation after their presentations to about five hundred Catholics involved in gay ministry.

Gumbleton spoke of his own agony on learning that his younger brother was gay. For a few months, he said, he refused to write or visit his brother. But his attitude changed, he said, after he met a seventy-year-old widow whose son had died of AIDS. She told Gumbleton she held her son in an embrace that "lasted as long as he lived," and she intended to work for the dignity of gay people for the rest of her days. Noting that a considerable "rigidity" remains in Catholic homosexual ministry, Gumbleton said some church authorities "are not happy that we [bishops] are here; so I have to be careful what I say." He urged the assembly to "wait with the church until more and more bishops, priests and pastoral ministers come to a better point of compassion, understanding, love, and care."

In 1994, Father Robert Nugent and Sister Jeannine Gramick, whose often troubled but thriving ministry to gays repeatedly placed them at the center of controversy in the church, were back in the spotlight again, the subjects of a revived Vatican investigation. Ten years earlier the Vatican had ordered them to end their association with New Ways Ministry, the group they cofounded in 1977. The order came at the urging of Washington Cardinal James A. Hickey, who disapproved of their presence within the archdiocese, where the group is headquartered. His efforts culminated in their resignation from New Ways. The priest and nun did not, however, cease their ministry to homosexuals. In 1994 they were called to defend their ministry and writings for the fourth time before a Vatican-appointed three-member commission charged with determining if they were in step with official church teaching on homosexuality. The Vatican Congregation for Institutes of Consecrated Life and Societies of Apostolic Life appointed the commission to determine "the present faithfulness" of the pair's work. The commission's chair was Detroit Archbishop Adam J. Maida, elevated to cardinal by Pope John Paul II in November 1994. The Vatican investigation of Gramick and Nugent's work actually began in 1988, then lay dormant until 1994. Since the late 1970s, both Nugent and Gramick have been able to claim the support of their respective religious communities. At the request of the former Congregation for Religious and Secular Institutes in the late 1970s and early and mid-1980s, their communities three times evaluated Nugent and Gramick's ministry. Both orders judged their work and teachings to be orthodox.

AIDS

In early February 1989, the Centers for Disease Control in Atlanta reported 48,582 Americans had died from AIDS-related causes. The number had exceeded the number of Americans who died in combat during the Vietnam War, officially set at 47,328. (There were 10,799 non-combatant American deaths in Vietnam.) No longer could there be any doubt that AIDS in the United States had become a disease of epidemic proportions. The church like other American institutions was slow to comprehend this or the challenge it presented.

It has been correctly pointed out that AIDS is a disease that plagues the entire human family, but in the United States it initially entered the Catholic discussion within the context of concerns especially related to the gay communities. In the early 1980s, the disease was still in its infancy and largely confined to the gay communities of San Francisco and New York as well as a few other pockets. Few in the church were examining it seriously. It had, however, come to the attention of a few journalists, one being Bill Kenkelen, the San Francisco-based reporter for the *National Catholic Reporter*. A gay Catholic, Kenkelen was aware of how the human immunodeficiency virus (HIV) was causing havoc in the lives of San Francisco gays. He began to write about AIDS patients, recording their voices and pleas. His first major article appeared in *NCR* in July 1984 under the banner: "AIDS: Its Victims Are This Century's Lepers."[28]

The piece quoted a Long Island, New York, chaplain, Holy Cross Father Norbert Sinski, then counseling AIDS patients. "They really are lepers," he said. "People look at them and say, 'It's your own damn fault.' They see it as evidence of a punishing God." That attitude was still common in the nation. AIDS, after all, was still primarily a "homosexual disease" despite evidence it was spreading among heterosexuals and drug users, by blood transfusion, and by infants' contact with infected mothers during the process of birth. Education came slowly. Even in May 1986, elderly Philadelphia Cardinal John Krol told a reporter the spread of AIDS was "an act of vengeance" against the sin of homosexuality.[29] Kenkelen died from AIDS-related causes on October 14, 1991.

The AIDS issue, meanwhile, was working its way into the church in other ways. At first isolated, then more frequent published reports surfaced of Catholic priests and brothers who were dying from the disease.[30] This information was not something church authorities were eager to see publicized. Nor could they completely cover it up. Many priests were known locally and shared with friends and communities the nature of their illness, often in the hopes of helping lift the stigma attached to AIDS. One of the most notable cases involved Father Michael Peterson, a forty-four-year-old Washington, D.C., archdiocesan priest, physician, and psychiatrist. In a public letter he wrote shortly before his death he said: "I hope that in my own struggle with this disease, in finally acknowledging that I have this lethal syndrome, there might be some measure of compassion, understanding and healing for me and for others with it—especially those who face this disease alone and in fear." Peterson was buried after a mass on April 13, 1987, in St. Matthew's Cathedral officiated by Washington Archbishop James A. Hickey. Some 180 priests attended the packed service. From that day on, it seemed, AIDS ministries within the Catholic Church went public. What had been isolated and optional was seemingly a requirement of proper pastoral care.

AIDS posed other problems for the church. Some U.S. religious orders, fearing both the potential of a tarnished image and the cost of paying for long-term AIDS care, began to test applicants for evidence of the virus. Other orders flatly opposed such actions.[31] A divisive and telling internal church conflict broke out in December 1987. That month, in a rare public episcopal fight, conservative bishops took on the Administrative Board of the United States Catholic Conference, a group of about forty bishops, after it issued an AIDS statement, "The Many Faces of AIDS," that cautiously condoned the use of condoms to prevent the spread of HIV. Cardinal John O'Connor called it a "grave mistake." The board's statement read: "Abstinence outside of marriage and fidelity within marriage as well as the avoidance of intravenous drug abuse are the only morally correct and medically sure ways to prevent the spread of AIDS." However, recognizing the pluralistic nature of U.S. society, "the church could tolerate the inclusion of information about prophylactics in public education programs." In March 1988, the Vatican sided with those bishops who wanted no mention of condoms.[32] That sealed the fate of the administrative board's AIDS statement. Explained Archbishop (later Cardinal) Roger Mahony of Los Angeles: "Not only is the use of prophylactics. . . technically unreliable; promoting this approach means, in effect, promoting behavior which is morally unacceptable." The final draft was criticized by public health officials who saw it running counter to efforts trying to increase condom awareness as a means of fighting the virus.

More, however, was a stake than this AIDS statement. For the Vatican to concede that in some circumstances, however rare, the use of condoms constitutes a lesser evil is, in effect, to set aside centuries of traditional deductive theology, an approach that moves from principle to reality. Reform-minded moral theologians have been arguing for an inductive approach, starting with situation and moving to teaching. The Vatican absolutist approach has brought forth the act-centered theology long associated with Catholic teachings. It leads to the teaching that artificial contraception, all abortion, and all homogenital acts are gravely immoral. No exceptions. To say that, however deplorable, some circumstances justify the use of condoms—even if the intention has nothing to do with preventing births—opens the door to other conditioned applications. This could, in turn, unravel traditional Catholic sexual moral theology.

In the debate over condoms, theology was not mentioned—at least not publicly—among the bishops. But it was tied into the issue. As a result of holding to principle without exceptions, teachings are precise, but to many Catholics unreasonable. While many applauded the bishops for holding out against the use of condoms, many others were dispirited by the whole affair. As it stands, even Catholics within marriage are forbidden the use of condoms, even if a spouse carries the HIV and its use is to prevent the spread of the disease. If condoms were allowed to fight AIDS, then why not to plan families? And if condoms were allowed to plan families, then has not the church been wrong all along on contraception? This was the question Pope Paul VI fretted with in 1968 before reaffirming church teaching banning artificial contraceptives. Twenty years later, the sexual issue remained very much an authority issue, and many would say that issue could not be understood apart from the composition of the church's all-male, celibate, clergy caste.

VI

❖ ❖ ❖

Celibacy

When Tristar Pictures released *Basic Instincts* in 1992, filmmakers sent out word that Sharon Stone, acting in a sexually evocative police interrogation scene, wore no underpants. It was not long before audiences were flocking to the movie. When the film later came out in video, reports surfaced that many copies were being damaged by renters who had repeatedly halted tapes at the point of the allegedly revealing scene. Stone had become a new sex symbol, and Hollywood had a $350 million blockbuster.

In the United States, sex is practically a way of life. It is everywhere around us. It speaks to us and moves us. It drives motion pictures, cable television, magazines, fashions, cosmetics. Advertising uses sex to sell everything, from tobacco to automobiles, jeans to beer, mouthwash to refrigerators. It shapes our consciousness and unconsciousness. Madison Avenue knows this and invests tens of billions each year to elicit sexual responses. Sex is used—and abused—in other ways, too. The Federal Bureau of Investigation reports that pornography—not "soft" skin flicks shown in hotel chains, but the crude variety that features violence to women and exploits young children—is an $8 billion to $10 billion U.S. industry.

Step back for a moment and consider the vowed celibate. Imagine what it is like to live by the vow of celibacy in such an environment. The Catholic Church teaches that celibacy, the abstinence from all sexual contact, comes as a gift of God and is given to relatively few. Since the twelfth century, the vow of celibacy has been required of Catholic priests of the Latin rite, those who live in the West. Catholic priests, both diocesan clergy who work in parishes and members of religious orders, vow celibacy to help them devote their lives to the service of God. In so doing, the church teaches, they better position themselves to dedicate their lives to the service of others. Women religious, or nuns, as they are frequently called, vow celibacy for the same reasons. As a result, untold thousands of Christians have lived by the sacred vows of celibacy throughout the ages—monks in monasteries, nuns in convents, parish priests and bishops. Untold thousands more have taken the vow, but have failed to live up to it. In this, they are perhaps not unlike married persons who fail to live by their pledge of fidelity. Since early church history celibacy has been held in special esteem, viewed as a higher state of life. Most Catholic saints have been celibate men or virgin women. Recent scholarship holds that celibacy was originally an initiative of women that was condemned by the church "fathers." Then, when they realized it couldn't be stopped, they "coopted" it so as to better control the practice.[1]

Today, mandatory celibacy is increasingly coming under attack. It is being challenged from within the church by those who see it as outdated and dysfunctional, and it is being assaulted by a culture that relishes sex. Church leaders say that celibacy makes a strong countercultural statement to the world in a time such as this. Undoubtedly this is the case when the vow is kept, but indications are that large segments of the clergy do not maintain the vow. The arguments for and against celibacy are at times mundane, at times heady. They way one looks at celibacy today can be influenced by the way one views the church. Traditional Catholic theology taught a model of church that placed it against the prevailing culture, saw it as embodying all that is good while living in an evil world. The Second Vatican Council emphasized a model of church that placed it *within* the culture but not *of* it. This notion of the church sees it as living simultaneously in two worlds while teaching that the union of the two can only occur beyond history, with the final coming of the reign of God. Given this model of church, the role of the Catholic Church in transforming the world is more subtle. Within such a theology, mandatory celibacy, as an intentionally countercultural statement, makes less sense. Within this model of church, what is required of the Catholic Church involves assessment and listening to the "signs of the times." As conservative theology has reasserted itself in the church during the pontificate of Pope John Paul II, however, it has supported church adherence to mandatory celibacy.

Is celibacy today a reasonable vow? Is it reasonable to expect one to maintain the vow, given the nature of Western culture? These questions have not been lost on the tens of thousands of Catholics who have vowed themselves to celibacy. They have not been lost on millions more who ask if mandatory celibacy is functional or even healthy. After pondering these questions and watching priests struggle, and sometimes fail, many Catholics are asking for an end to mandatory celibacy. They are not against celibacy, but they want it to be optional. If it was optional, they say, the church would see a dramatic increase in priestly vocations, and married priests would instill a healthier and more balanced theology of sexuality in the church. Of course, many others disagree with these arguments, not least of all, the hierarchy, or at least the most important member of the hierarchy, the West's last absolute monarch, Pope John Paul II. His adamant support of celibacy has made it a somewhat muted issue in the church. The Vatican does not want the subject discussed and sees optional-celibacy advocates as nothing less than "dissidents." Few priests and bishops talk about it publicly. Many clergy, especially prelates from non-Western cultures without histories of celibacy, continue to push for more discussion. Those efforts, however, have gone almost nowhere in recent years.

Try as the Vatican may, the issue of optional priestly celibacy does not disappear. Underneath the surface of church operations, it appears to be gaining momentum, not as a result of any victory in a battle of clashing theologies, but under the weight of enormous problems facing the Catholic priesthood. There is a "something's got to give" mentality in the church. The priesthood, as it exists in the West, as it has existed for many centuries of Catholic history, is struggling. It is gravely ill and breaking down. Some say it is in a nosedive, a state of collapse. Some argue it has already died and what the church is experiencing today is a painfully drawn-out funeral vigil. And if that is true, what comes next? A married priesthood, even women's ordination, these Catholics say. They are convinced it is only a matter of time. Without such changes, they argue, the church will never break out of its old, outdated, irrelevant, and incredible sexual teachings. And only with such changes, do they see much hope for the Catholic Church in the twenty-first century.

Married priests? Women's ordination? Changes in centuries' old sexual teachings to be relevant to the world today? Conservatives see such talk not as solutions to church ills, but as symptoms of creeping secularism within the church. Optional celibacy is anathema inside the Vatican. Of all the sex-related issues that face the church today none appears to touch deeper nerves at the highest level of the church than those that directly involve the makeup and function of the clerical ranks. The bottom-line question has been, Who are to be the priests of the church? The Vatican's firm response, with as few exceptions as possible, has been, celibate men, only celibate men.

No doubt, celibacy is a healthy way of life for many priests. Just as certainly, it is not for many others. Some psychiatrists and psychologists who have studied celibacy and counsel priests say it is neither wise nor reasonable to commit oneself to lifelong sexual abstinence. Richard A. Gardner, professor of psychiatry at the Columbia University College of Physicians and Surgeons, says celibacy is a nearly impossible requirement today:

> *Perhaps such [sexual] inhibitions could be accomplished in years in remote villages in Ireland, Poland, and Italy where past exposure to sexual stimuli was limited. Today that is far less likely. From their earliest years, children are bombarded with sexual stim-*

> *uli. Younger and middle-aged priests were raised in this world, and even older ones have been belatedly brought into it. The church is misguided in believing it can take a young person who was brought up in this world, put him in a seminary and fashion an asexual being.*[2]

This is the kind of talk that riles many church celibates, especially those who believe modern social science cannot get a fix on the life of the spirit. Spirituality is not something that is precisely measured, dissected, or understood by academics, they say. Father Raymond J. Gunzel is such a critic. He is a U.S. priest who counsels other priests and has written extensively about celibacy and the lives of priests who live by the vow. According to Gunzel, celibacy is possible—but only through regular contemplative prayer. "The gift of celibacy," he says, "can be called forth as a living and creative presence . . . only through the re-establishment of contemplative prayer as the primary and foundational value in all Christian vocations."[3] He is hardly alone in his assessment, but priests like Gunzel appear to be a diminishing breed.

Priest Shortage

That the Catholic Church in the United States faces a growing priest shortage is an undisputed reality, especially for those millions who find themselves unable to count on having a priest in their local parish. There are simply not enough to go around. The result is that thousands of churches, especially those in rural and in inner-city areas, have closed. Many more are threatened. Meanwhile, U.S. Catholic ranks, now at 60 million, swell. The number of ordained priests, however, has been falling steadily for twenty-five years. With older priests retiring and dying and fewer younger men ready to take their places, the prognosis is that the situation is going from bad to worse. In the process, a number of studies have pointed to celibacy as a major cause of the shortage. A 1990 U.S. study, for example, found celibacy to be the most significant roadblock to the priestly life by young Catholic men.[4]

The origins of the current shortage date back to shortly after the Second Vatican Council and the late 1960s when, almost overnight it seemed, thousands of priests, asking to leave their ministries, began to petition Rome for dispensations from their vows. Most who left—some say nine out of ten—eventually married. In the United States alone, an estimated twenty thousand priests have departed the priesthood in the past twenty-five years. The phenomenon has not been limited to this nation. Rather, it has been a worldwide movement. An estimated hundred thousand priests have left worldwide, according to reports by organizations of resigned priests. The Vatican downplays such figures, placing the number at around sixty thousand. It appears that it cites official requests for dispensation; however, many priests leave without every asking for permission. The Catholic hierarchy has a tendency to underreport departures, especially when the priests in question leave without going through the formal process.

Catholics have a difficult time explaining why the bottom fell out of the priesthood after the Second Vatican Council. Some point to church disillusionment after Pope Paul VI's 1968 birth control encyclical, others to a feeling of letdown after the excitement of the years of the council (1962–65); still others to wider opportunities for service in secular society. In nearly all cases, there appears to have been some inner need to share their lives with others, most often with women in marriage.

These dropout figures do not tell the entire story, even the most critical one. The more potentially threatening trends for the Catholic priesthood in the West come out of Catholic seminaries, which today hold only a fraction of the number of candidates compared with a generation ago. In 1965, some nine thousand seminarians were studying theology in U.S. seminaries, the last step before ordination; thirty years later, the figure had fallen to under three thousand. As a result many seminaries have closed; others have consolidated. In the early 1960s, rectors could turn down candidates, taking only the best applicants. In the 1990s, rectors welcome most comers. The church has made efforts to maintain standards, but there is an almost universal recognition among those connected with seminaries that standards have fallen significantly. So the worry of having fewer priests is compounded by that of having priests of only modest talents.

All of this has caused the Catholic clergy to undergo consolidation, i.e., managing a number of parishes as a nonresident pastor, as lay Catholics assume more church roles. Many have viewed this as a healthy trend, and some see it as part of a transition to a more lay-controlled and lay-led church of the future, even as prelates cling to old ways. In other words, practice may be getting ahead of theory. Some theologians say this has always been the way the church has evolved. But as lay ministers enter into new roles within the church, they continue to find that all final authority rests in the hands of the clergy. According to church law, the bishops are responsible for the administration of the church, and, of course, only celibate men can be bishops. So there is change without change, and this conflict is adding to tensions within the church. It has been the priests, more often, who have been caught in the middle. Many already face the nearly impossible task of carrying the major administrative duties of a parish (or two) while conducting the full scope of sacramental rites, including baptisms, weddings, funerals, and daily masses. And at day's end, most are expected to return to the loneliness of a no-longer-bustling and socially supportive parish rectory.

Social scientists first began to study the priest shortage in the 1970s. Alarmed by reports of priest resignations, they gathered available data. Later, as still more priests left, these scholars intensified their efforts, studying trends while trying to develop models and projections. Their work, however, was often hampered by incomplete data. By the mid-1980s, even more alarmed and now encouraged by worried bishops, they again intensified their efforts. By then the Catholic Church was already feeling the pinch of the priest shortage. With the assistance of a $400,000 grant from the Lilly Endowment Foundation, the U.S. bishops contracted with sociologists Richard A. Schoenherr of the University of Wisconsin and Lawrence A. Young of Brigham Young University to conduct detailed research. It was to be the most comprehensive study yet. It was to take years of research but establish beyond doubt where the church would be hit hardest by the shortage and how the crisis would work itself out. As the project's findings were gradually released through private interim reports to the hierarchy, a number of bishops became upset over the gloomy projections. Several reportedly sought to squelch the entire study, exhibiting a kind of "slay the messenger of bad news" mentality. By 1990, after the third private interim report was presented, the bishops decided to cease sponsorship of the research altogether. Schoenherr remarked that the unexpected cutoff left him and his fellow researchers "high and dry."[5] For their part, the bishops said they were withdrawing support because of delays in data processing and the necessity of rewriting and reediting portions of the material. They were, they said, simply fed up.[6]

Undeterred, the sociologists acquired the means to continue their research independent of ecclesial support. In 1993 they published their final findings in a book entitled *Full Pews and Empty Altars: Demographics of the Priest Shortage in United States Catholic Dioceses*. Almost immediately, episcopal efforts began to discredit and downplay the research. In an article published in a Catholic weekly and widely reprinted in local Catholic newspapers, Los Angeles Cardinal Roger Mahony declared, "I reject that pessimistic assessment and feel that the Catholic church in our country has been done a great disservice by the Schoenherr report." The cardinal claimed that Schoenherr, a resigned priest, had been using the study to push his "personal agenda": optional celibacy for priests. The study, Mahony said, "presumes that the only factors at work are sociology and statistical research. That is nonsense. We are disciples of Jesus Christ. We live by God's grace, and our future is shaped by God's design for his church—not by sociologists."[7] Schoenherr responded that sociology does not claim to provide the whole truth or give the final answers, only to state something that is true and worth consideration. The episode revealed the deep suspicion that characterizes many bishops' views of social science when it is applied to the church. The two worlds simply don't mix, some say. It also further reveals what many Catholics see as a major—some say insurmountable—church problem: institutional denial, an unwillingness by the hierarchy to accept and face bad news.

What does the Schoenherr and Young study report? It offers evidence of a 40 percent reduction in the number of diocesan, or parish, priests (as opposed to members of religious communities) from 35,000 in 1966 to 21,000 in the year 2005. It also projects the U.S. Catholic population expanding from 45 million to 74 million during that forty-year period. The study was thorough. It involved the creation of a registry of every diocesan priest in 86 of the then 180 U.S. dioceses between 1966 and 1985—including age, year of ordination, and information on deaths, retirements, resignations, and moves outside the home diocese. In all, some 36,000 priest histories were compiled. The following were among the findings:

- The decrease in priestly ordinations is the most significant factor in the overall clergy decline, far more significant than resignations, retirements, or other factors.
- Ordination rates continue to fall, with 47 percent fewer men ordained during 1980–84 than during 1966–70. By the mid-1990s, the decline for the period could plunge to 69 percent, averaging a 32 percent drop per decade.
- Nationally, resignations from active priestly ministry peaked in the early 1970s, when 4.6 percent of the active clergy ages twenty-nine to thirty-four were resigning annually. Resignation rates then dropped notably: resignations were cut in half during in the late 1970s and 1980s. However, resignations have continued at moderately high rates. In the 1990s, between 35 and 40 percent of each year's newly ordained priests are needed to fill

vacancies created by continuing resignations.

- By the year 2000, one of every three priests in some dioceses will be retired.
- Because of steady growth in church membership, the layperson-to-priest ratio will double from 1,100 Catholics per active priest in 1975 to 2,200 per active priest in the year 2005.

The Schoenherr and Young study scrupulously stuck to the data but added personal conclusions in the last three pages of the book. There researchers declared the following:

> *We believe the church is being confronted with a choice between its sacramental tradition and its commitment to an exclusively male celibate priesthood. One of the most critical aspects of this confrontation is that most church leaders have failed to accept responsibility for the choice. Instead they focus on stopgap solutions to the ever-worsening priest shortage while hoping for a dramatic increase in vocations. . . . We speculate further that, to preserve the more essential elements of Roman Catholicism, the nonessentials—first compulsory celibacy and later male exclusivity—will need to be eliminated as defining characteristics of priesthood."*[8]

One of the distinguishing characteristics of Catholicism is its sacramental tradition. The church has placed heavy emphasis on the Eucharistic liturgy as the central worshiping experience for Catholics. The Eucharistic liturgy is the reenactment of the Last Supper at which Jesus broke bread, offered wine, and shared it with his disciples. This celebration has continued throughout church history, and the church has taught that only ordained Catholic priests can celebrate the Eucharist. In so doing, Catholics believe it becomes the living presence of Christ. This church doctrine is called transubstantiation. Without an ordained priest, this central celebration cannot occur, the church holds, although, with the growing priest shortage and with the perception among some Catholics that this involves an injustice, liturgies involving the sharing of bread and wine occur without ordained priests. The church hierarchy frowns on these activities and says they are illicit and do damage to church unity.

It is easy to see that the growing priest shortage within the church involves essential teachings of faith and practice. It is for this reason that many Catholics argue that maintaining the celibate clerical state, in spite of a priest shortage that is leading to less frequent Eucharist celebrations, involves grave injustices to the faithful. These Catholics say the hierarchy is more concerned with maintaining an arbitrary discipline to hold together an authority structure than it is with making the Eucharist available to the faithful.

With a keen sense of the pressures building in the church, Milwaukee Archbishop Rembert Weakland became the first U.S. Catholic archbishop in recent memory to publicly propose the possibility of a married priesthood. In a pastoral letter in January 1993, he said that under certain circumstances, he would be willing to ask the pope to ordain a married priest. Weakland also indicated that he would not defy the pope on the celibacy matter.[9]

The United States is by no means the first nation to feel the priest shortage. It has long been the way of life in large parts of Asia, Africa, and Latin America where it has existed for decades, if not centuries. The bishops of Indonesia have repeatedly requested that the Vatican allow them to ordain married men as priests so the church's sacramental work can grow on the outer islands. In many parts of Latin America, Catholics see a priest only once a year, if that often. In Africa, unlike the West, where there is little or no celibacy tradition, the idea of unmarried priests makes little sense, and missionaries report it impedes the growth of the church. In those parts of Africa where Catholicism has spread in this century, reports flourish of priests and even bishops who commonly live with women. Few of the faithful appear to object.

HOMOSEXUALITY

With the increasing openness of homosexuality in society, the question of homosexuality in clerical ranks was bound to come up. AIDS was also helping pry it open. There are no reliable statistics on this subject. While it has been a concern for some time to many U.S. Catholics, the U.S. bishops have adamantly refused to gather information on the sexual inclinations of its priests. In one of the few studies based on hard data—1,500 interviews between 1960 and 1985—Richard Sipe, a Maryland psychotherapist and author of the 1990 book *A Secret World: Sexuality and the Search for Celibacy* (Brunner/Mazel, Publishers), concluded that about 20 percent of fifty-seven thousand U.S. clergy and religious priests were homosexual and that half of these were sexually active. Since 1978 the number of gay priests has been rising significantly, Sipe maintained.

Father Andrew Greeley, a church sociologist, estimated that a quarter of the priests under thirty-five are gay, and half of them may be sexually active.[10] The conclusions of other church observers vary widely. Some put the percentage at up to 50 percent, especially among younger priests.

Others place them closer to Sipe's figures. About a quarter of the gay priests that Sipe studied countered loneliness with long-term liaisons. Other gay priests justified their sexual activities by defining the vow they took as calling them to stay "celibate" but not necessarily "chaste," meaning no marriage but occasional male liaisons.[11] Most U.S. Catholic seminaries accept gay candidates, but they cannot be ordained unless they agree to be celibate. The screening system is not infallible, however; nor are policies consistent. Some seminaries reject all gay candidates; others limit the number they will accept. On the other hand, in some cases there have been reports of predominantly gay seminaries and homosexual climates within them that became so pronounced that heterosexual seminarians felt uneasy and ultimately left.

A number of reasons are offered for the phenomenon of an increasingly gay priesthood. As thousands of priests left to marry, the proportion of gays in the priesthood generally increased. Others add that gays have long been attracted to the priesthood, the only difference now being they are more public about their sexual preference. Is a heavily gay priesthood a problem? Those who say it is argue that large numbers of gay priests make the priestly vocation less attractive to heterosexual candidates. Others suggest that gay priests—given that priests commonly live in some form of male community—are more likely to be tempted to act out their sexual inclinations. Meanwhile, many Catholic gays and lesbians say they get annoyed when people speak of the "gay clergy problem." They view it as one more form of gay bashing, or homophobia. Nevertheless, what appears to be the growing "gayness" of the U.S. Catholic clergy remains a serious concern for many in the church. However, the church is not yet concerned enough to support a survey to give statistical form to the phenomenon. Again, some Catholics see this as part of a larger problem of denial among the hierarchy.

The History of Celibacy in the Church

Celibacy is a church discipline; not a theological requirement. Pope John XXIII reportedly once said he could end it with a stroke of the pen. When Catholic bishops speak of celibacy, they often tie it to two New Testament verses. In Matthew 19:12, Jesus says ". . .some, because they have made themselves eunuchs [have renounced marriage] for the sake of the kingdom of heaven. Whoever can accept this ought to accept this." This same idea is echoed by Paul in his First Letter to the Corinthians (7:7) in which he says, "I wish everyone to be as I am, but each has a particular gift from God, one of one kind and one of another." Neither quotation, however, is a demand for celibacy. All of Jesus' apostles, including Peter, the first pope, were married. The earliest Christians largely operated in familial settings. Their communities had both married and unmarried ministers. Within centuries, the numbers of unmarried ministers increased, but many priests continued to marry. After the early Christian martyrdom period, monks began to show their commitment to their faith by living as celibates in monasteries. For many priests, however, celibacy continued as an option.

Beginning in the fourth century, laws of sexual abstinence emerged and were connected with liturgical services. It was widely believed sex was a cause of impurity and through sex women contaminated men. As a result, the church held that if a married priest had sexual intercourse, he needed to wait a full day before he was again "clean" enough to celebrate the Eucharist. The fear that women would "contaminate" the high priests had earlier been found in ancient Judaism as well as Greek and Roman cultures. Christians appeared to have inherited these fears. The Catholic Church's celibacy requirement, which grew out of abstinence laws, can be traced back to ancient convictions connected with ritual purity, the most important being that sexual intercourse (even in the confines of marriage) was unclean and unhealthy. The abstinence laws did not become a functional problem until the fourth century when Eucharistic liturgies became more common, even a daily occurrence. This required priests to abstain from sex on a more or less a permanent basis. Many resisted.[12] From the fourth through the tenth century, pressures for celibacy grew. Priests were prohibited from having sex in marriage; women continued to be seen as contaminants and barriers to priestly sanctity.[13] But the church was failing to convince priests to abstain from sex.

Not until the year 1139, at the Second Lateran Council, was the law of mandatory celibacy finally and officially imposed. The council asserted it did not regard any marriage entered into by a priest as valid. Those priests and nuns already married were told to separate from their spouses.[14] The move was vigorously resisted in various parts of Europe. In the centuries that followed, many priests, even bishops, continued to disregard church law and marry.

The introduction of church celibacy cannot be divorced from the history of the church in the tenth century, a particularly corrupt century for the papacy. At that time popes aligned themselves with the ruling aristocracy and were commonly married, and their wives birthed future popes. Pope Sergius III (papacy 904–11) was no clerical role model.

He had the close support of a man named Theophylactus, a wealthy nobleman, and Theophylactus' teenage daughter, Marozia, by whom Sergius had an illegitimate son—the future Pope John XI. Marozia was eventually responsible for the election of three popes including her son.[15] Pope Sergius was only one of a number of popes of his ilk during that period. Efforts were made in the following two centuries to clean up the papacy. Pope Gregory VII (papacy 1073–85) was noted for his reform efforts, among them pushing celibacy upon a reluctant clergy. To Gregory, priestly marriage was concubinage. Gregory called upon people to boycott married priests.[16] Meanwhile, the roles the wives of married priests played, especially in passing on property to their heirs, was of no little concern to church leaders. Property inheritance became a vexing church problem. Imposing mandatory celibacy was viewed as one way of assuring that the church would be able to keep property while limiting the influence of women. Gregory spoke of "sundering the commerce between the clergy and women through eternal anathema."[17]

Several centuries later, with corruption again rampant in the church, Martin Luther protested clergy abuses, including those he saw resulting from mandatory celibacy. Luther, a monk, married a former nun in 1525. Later in 1537, he wrote of the church's effort to enforce celibacy:

> *They were completely unjustified in forbidding marriage and in burdening the divine state of the priesthood with the demand of continual celibacy. In doing so, they have acted like anti-Christian, tyrannical, unholy, scoundrels, occasioning all sorts of terrible, ghastly, countless sins against chastity, in which they are caught to this day.*[18]

The Council of Trent (1545–63) again reinforced celibacy. It did this by requiring that Christian marriages be witnessed by a priest. Effectively, this made it impossible for priests who were continuing to marry clandestinely to do so with the church's blessings. It was one more strike against the married priesthood.[19] There was little question after Trent about the importance of celibacy to the church. The council officially elevated the celibate state above that of married men and women, declaring, "If anyone says that it is not better and more godly to live in virginity or in the unmarried state than to marry, let him be anathema," that is, cut off from the church.[20]

In more recent times, when the church was again in a reformist mood, during the Second Vatican Council, many bishops wanted mandatory celibacy to be on the council agenda. It was not to be. Pope Paul VI, in a letter delivered to the bishops on October 11, 1965, forbade the council to discuss the subject. He had made a similar move once before when he had outlawed discussion of artificial contraception. Concerning celibacy, Paul wrote the following to the council members: "It is not opportune to debate publicly this topic which requires the greatest prudence, and is so important. Our intention is not only to preserve this ancient law as far as possible, but to strengthen its observance."[21] Bishops had written the pope beseeching him to let them discuss celibacy, but his secretary of state, Archbishop Paul Poupard, replied that Pope Paul feared a debate would "have serious consequences for priests, who were not all that solid."[22]

The upshot was that Paul VI developed an encyclical on celibacy instead. *Sacerdotalis Caelibatus,* meaning "On the Sacredness of Celibacy," was published two years later,

June 24, 1967, and it reiterated the church's celibacy requirement. In the encyclical Paul VI spoke of celibacy as a "dazzling jewel." Critics, however, have contended the encyclical contains an internal contradiction or at least internal tension.[23] It states that celibacy "is not, of course, required by the nature of the priesthood itself. This is clear from the practice of the early church itself and the traditions of the Eastern churches." But if celibacy is not *essential* to the priesthood, then efforts expended to prove it is "particularly suited" to the priestly ministry will never amount to the *necessary* link between priesthood and celibacy the encyclical wishes to assert. If the link were really necessary, it would admit no exceptions. And, of course, there are exceptions.

In reality, about 20 percent of Catholic priests are married with the pope's blessing. These, however, are priests of the Eastern Catholic Churches in such countries as Hungary, the Czech Republic, Slovakia, Ukraine, and Lebanon. They fall under the jurisdiction of the Vatican just as much as do the priests of the Western Church.[24] Historically, these churches successfully held out against the Vatican efforts to impose celibacy upon them. Further, scores of married Catholic priests currently work in the United States with Rome's blessing. These priests are Roman Catholic priests who during the past two decades have entered the church and who were formerly Episcopalian and Lutheran priests who were already married. Having converted to Catholicism, they have been allowed to stay married and became ordained Catholic priests. At least eighty such priests work with the blessing of the U.S. hierarchy. This has caused hard feelings among many Catholic priests who have resigned and left their ministries to marry and have been refused church permission to continue their work as priests.

Resigned, former, married, inactive, whatever one calls them, the priests who left have played important if unofficial roles in the church in recent years. The official church's initial reaction to their departures was to deny their existence, to put them out of mind. They were considered "fallen aways" and unhealthy models for those priests still in the ranks. In more recent years, partly out of need for assistance and partly out of recognition of long-shared values, the U.S. hierarchy has somewhat warmed up to these priests—although not enough to let them do priestly sacramental work. Nevertheless, many do it on their own in defiance of church law.

In many parts of the world these priests have drawn together and have organized. At first, they lobbied to be reinstated in the church as active priests. Failing to convince Rome, most eventually went their ways into other vocations. Their organizations, however, continue to flourish, even as their focuses have broadened to include wider church reform issues, including peace and justice matters and a vision of church including both women and married priests. Some of these inactive priests have become especially articulate critics of mandatory celibacy. In the United States, the organization, called CORPUS draws together resigned priests and spearheads church-reform issues. The organization involves many who have left their ministries, yet in some sense have stayed within the church, refusing to give up hope for eventual change in church law. Some even retain their Roman collars and prefer to be called "reverend." Formed in 1974, CORPUS was arguing, by the late 1980s, that church failure to allow an inclusive priesthood was crippling its teachings. Justice must be modeled before it can be taught, says CORPUS, which has survived and grown by gathering together those who refuse to give up hope for married and gender-equal church leadership.

Clergy Sex Abuse

Arlington Heights is a Chicago suburb and an unlikely setting for a revolt against the church, but that is precisely what happened in October 1992. What made the revolt even more implausible was that it involved otherwise moderate Catholics, mostly middle-aged and middle-class, part of the mainstream. They said they were fed up with what they described as their church's unresponsive, even arrogant ways. They portrayed Catholic bishops as closed and part of an old-boy network. These were by no means radicals who came for this three-day conference. No sign carriers. Not the types normally working the streets for political causes. They were straight out of the local parish or congregation. Or once had been. Bitter, confused, drained, but unquestionably determined, they came to Arlingtion Heights to find strength in each other and on a mission to change policy and structure in the Catholic Church.

It was a gathering of victims of sex abuse by members of the clergy. They preferred to call themselves "survivors." The gathering also included the victims' supporters. This was the first-ever national meeting of its kind. And while the conference was not limited to Catholics, most participants, it turned out, had ties to the Catholic Church. For three days they talked with and listened to each other. They heard experts speak on aspects of personal experience so painful, so numbing, so disturbing, that many could only sit in silence, staring into empty space. Often there were simply hugs and no exchanges of words. Those who made up the group understood each other in fundamental ways that required nothing more than to look into each others eyes. Each, it seemed, had two experiences in common. The first was the experience of being sexually abused at a young age by a member of the clergy. The second was the experience of making it public, of trying to bring it to the attention of a church official, often a bishop, only to be greeted by denial and cover-up. The process commonly led to further victimization, this time of a psychological order, entrance into a weird world where the perpetrator is portrayed as the victim and the victim as the perpetrator.

The conference, in the words of organizer Jeanne Miller, was three days of "breaking the cycle of silence."[25] Miller had been the primary organizer of a loose network of survivors of sex abuse by members of the clergy originally called VOCAL for Victims of Clergy Abuse Linkup, but which now simply goes by the name LINKUP. It claims to be a national response to an assault on innocence and faith. Referring to the pattern of abuse and cover-up, Miller told the gathering, "When someone talks to me about child molestation, I get the feeling they are telling me my story."[26]

Here are some of the stories recalled by those attending the gathering:[27]

- A middle-aged woman said she never knew she had been abused by a priest until one day when she was having her first body massage. Suddenly, as the masseuse touched her thigh the memories erupted within her. "It wasn't just like seeing him [the priest] do it to me," she said. "It was that I became that little girl again, screaming: 'Don't do it! Don't do it!' "

- Another woman said that she, too, had no memory of abuse until she read a story about clerical sex abuse in a newspaper. She stopped and broke into uncontrollable tears, she said, as vivid memories began to pour into her mind. Trauma, it appears, gets buried in the psyche only to resurface decades after the fact.
- A man in his late twenties, sexually abused by a priest for years while he was a young teen, said he suffers from psychological distress but cannot bring himself to enter counseling. The thought of it, he said, terrifies him. "How can you get therapy if the therapist is going to abuse you?" he asked, He no longer trusts anyone in counseling, he said.
- A man in his twenties recalls having gone to a priest counselor years ago for help after being sexually abused, only to be sexually abused for the second time.
- Two male survivors in their thirties recounted stories of abuse as altar boys. Both said they went along with it for years. Both said they felt singled out. It was "the special feeling of being treated like an adult, of being chosen," one said, explaining years later to himself why he went along with it.
- A man in his fifties spoke of the way his abusive experience as a youngster lowered his self-esteem throughout his adult life. He talked of the way it caused him to feel anger and how he, in turn, had often directed that anger at his own children. Abuse, it appears, ripples outward.

Back in 1985 the first indications of what eventually became a national church scandal appeared. Jason Berry, a freelance journalist, started by writing about a priest named Father Gilbert Gauthe, who was from Lafayette, Louisiana,

Berry's home diocese. Gauthe had been charged with abusing young boys over a period of years. Similar cases, meanwhile, were appearing in other states, but getting virtually no press coverage. Berry hooked up with the *National Catholic Reporter,* and soon the paper reported what initially turned out to be more than a dozen cases in other parts of the country, most involving multiple victims.

The most stunning thing to emerge, however, was the almost invariable pattern of church response: first a denial by the local bishop, then the reshuffling of the accused priest to another assignment and the discrediting of the accuser by church officials, and finally, the lawsuit. While probing the story, Berry heard other rumors about other priest offenders and pressed ahead with his investigation. He found priests with sordid pasts and young people in varying states of emotional, mental, and physical disarray. In his travels to dioceses across the nation, Berry also found parents embittered and frustrated by church leaders' apparent indifference to their complaints; law-enforcement officials hesitant to move against the church; top officials of the chancery withdrawing behind a curtain of testiness and secrecy.

As the record eventually showed, Gauthe's bishop, Gerard Frey, responded to the allegations against Gauthe by reassigning him. Gauthe's conviction led to a sentence of imprisonment for twenty years. As it turned out, the tragic saga of the Lafayette diocese, where another bishop was eventually sent to monitor Frey, provided Berry with an excellent case study of how abuse was also being handled elsewhere. At first few other publications picked up the growing priest pedophilia story. *NCR,* meanwhile, came under attack for allegedly defaming the church. However, within a few years the story of widespread sex abuse throughout the country had spread throughout the press and was on the covers of *Time* and *Newsweek* magazines, as well as the subject of television news specials.

The numbers of reported cases slowly mounted—200, 300, 400. Estimates by attorneys who specialize in cases involving abuse by clergy and estimates by journalists who follow such cases say that by the mid-1990s some 600 priests had been involved and the church in the United States had paid out more than $500 million in lawyer and settlement fees. One diocese, Santa Fe, New Mexico, threatened bankruptcy in 1994 because of abuse-case settlements. Church officials say the numbers are considerably lower but at the same time refuse to disclose any dollar amounts. The sex-abuse issue, at least one poll has shown, has discredited the church in the eyes of the laity more than any other development in recent years.

Although the Arlington Heights conference was not exclusively Catholic, most there expressed some past or current ties with the Catholic Church. Laced through participants' conversations were demands for a radical restructuring of authority and the institution of the Catholic clergy. Mandatory celibacy and an all-male priesthood were portrayed as major factors contributing to sexual abuse by members of the clergy. Richard Sipe spoke at the conference; he has probably studied the phenomenon of sexual abuse by clergy longer than any other Catholic professional:

> *The historical significance of this meeting, which transcends all of us individually and even the immediate subject matter, cannot escape any of us here. This meeting is the first of its kind ever to be held within Catholic Christendom. This is the first time a group of Catholic Christians has gathered to evaluate publicly the*

celibate/sexual functioning of its clergy. We stand on the brink of the most profound reformation of the Catholic clergy and its celibate/sexual system since the time when Martin Luther challenged clerical integrity, on October 31, 1517.

Child sex abuse, or *pedophilia* as it is technically termed, involves adult sexual molestation of a prepubescent child. To be attracted to children is considered a psychological disorder, and it affects a small proportion of the populace. Most pedophilia involves an adult male and a female child. Most abuse by clergy in other religious denominations involves such relationships, experts attest. In the Catholic Church, however, the pattern has almost always involved an adult male and a male child. Easy access to young boys has been offered as one reason for this phenomenon.

Sipe outlined four types of clergy abusers: those predisposed by a genetic lock, those predetermined by a psychodynamic lock, those conditioned by a social/situational lock, and those rooted in a moral lock.[28] The term *lock*, he said, means "that, given ordinary circumstances and nonintervention," those so disposed will inevitably become sexual abusers. According to Sipe, those in genetic lock never attain "normal" adult sexual patterns and, should they become sexually active, "will inevitably gravitate to minors." Psychodynamic lock is traced, he said, to factors within early relationships, often coupled with early sexual overstimulation and experiences, which conspire to lock the person at an early level of psychosexual development, making him "extremely vulnerable to regression and to sexual attraction to minors." Social/situational lock is specifically clerical. It is, he said, a state in which "conformity to set answers rather than free inquiry" is rewarded. Sipe said that, theologically, the celibate male priesthood is a man's world where God is Father, Son, and masculine Spirit. The ideal and only women venerated are mothers or virgins (forbidden objects of sexual fantasy). Emotionally, it is a world in which men are revered and powerful (pope, bishops, rectors) and boys are treasured as the future of the church. Sipe added the following:

> *It is clear that the institutional church is in a preadolescent state of psychosexual development. This is a period, typically prior to eleven years of age in which boys prefer association with their own sex; girls are avoided and held in disdain, often as a guise for fear of women as well as of their own as yet unsolidified sexuality. Sex generally is rigidly denied externally while secretly explored. The rigidity extends to strict rules of inclusion and exclusion. Control and avoidance are of primary concern.*

Priests in moral lock by design, he said, involve themselves sexually with minors because they want to.

Some put the figure of pedophiles in the Catholic priesthood at 4 percent. Sipe claimed that about 6 percent of the Catholic clergy (2 percent of priests are psychiatrically defined pedophiles, he claimed) have had sexual contact with minors. He said sex abuse by priests is caused in part by the church's demand for mandatory celibacy, a link denied by Catholic bishops. To these denials Sipe has responded that the hierarchy's unwillingness to see, or at least consider, the connection, speaks to the heart of the problem. "Denial," in this instance, has been described as the unwillingness of Catholic bishops to either acknowledge or handle the sex-abuse problem in a pastoral way. Sipe claimed, "The church knows and has known for a long time a great deal about the sexual activity of its priests. It has looked the other way, tolerated, covered up and simply lied about the broad spectrum of sexual activity of its priests, bound by the law but not the reality of celibacy."

Sipe, one of the church's most vocal critics of mandatory celibacy, listed fourteen points he feels the church needs to recognize before serious reform takes place:[29]

- Sexual abuse of minors by Roman Catholic clergy is a long-standing problem.
- The phenomenon of the sexual abuse of minors is a worldwide problem among Roman Catholic clergy.
- When the whole story of sexual abuse by presumed celibate clergy is told, it will lead to the highest corridors of Vatican City.
- Sexual abuse of children is part of a larger pattern of sexual involvement by priests with others—adult women and men.
- Seminary training does not prepare clergy for celibate/sexual reality. Seminary training produces many psychosexually impaired and retarded priests whose level of adjustment is adolescent at best.
- The celibate/sexual system that surrounds clerical culture fosters and often rewards psychosexual immaturity.
- The homosocial system of the hierarchy that excludes women categorically from decision making and power at the same time that it glorifies exclusively the roles of virgin and mother creates a psychological structure that reinforces male psychosexual immaturity and malformation.
- A significantly larger proportion of the clergy than the general population has a homosexual orientation.
- By refusing to deal honestly with the reality of homosexuality and the clerical state, Catholic teaching fosters

self-alienation of its clergy and encourages and enables identity confusion, sexual acting out and moral duplicity.
- The Catholic moral teaching on sexuality is based on a patently false anthropology that renders magisterial pronouncement noncredible.
- Clergy deprived of a moral doctrine in which they can believe are also deprived of moral guidance and leadership in their own lives and behavior.
- The hierarchy cannot claim ignorance of the sexual practices of their own—themselves and their fellow priests—and at the same time assert that they are credible and authoritative sources of leadership in sexual morality for the laity.
- The hierarchy cannot use the psychiatric system to deal with the problems of sexual abuse—whether with children, with adult women, or with adult males—and sidestep their personal and corporate roles as enablers.
- Child abuse by clergy, the tip of the iceberg, does not stand on its own. Difficult as it is to accept, the hierarchical and power structures beneath the surface are part of a secret world that supports abuse. These hidden forces are far more dangerous to the sexual health and welfare of the church than those that can already be seen.

Sipe's sweeping charges, while warmly received at the conference, are generally viewed by the Catholic clergy as unfair and overstated. They point, however, to the growing rift the abuse issue has caused within the church.

One of the questions that came up at the Arlington conference and continues to be asked within the church is whether sex abuse by priests is related to homosexuality in the priesthood. Pedophilia, the phenomenon of abuse of prepubescent children, appears not to be. However, ephebephilia, the phenomenon of abuse of postpubescent minors, seems to have links. While the former is a sexual disorder, the later involves an acting out of homosexual inclinations by gay Catholic clergy. Many cases that get reported as child sex abuse involve post-pubescent minors, those generally in the thirteen- to seventeen-year-old age group. So what may often get passed off as pedophilia, strictly speaking, involves homosexual activity by Catholic priests.

These relatively recent insights have fueled requests in some church circles for more thorough studies of the sexual orientation and activities (or inactivities) of the nation's Catholic priests. Meanwhile, no conclusive data say homosexual priests are more likely to break their vows than are heterosexual priests. Celibacy is clearly a struggle for both. According to St. Paul, Minnesota, attorney Jeffrey Anderson, who specializes in cases of sex abuse by priests, there are cases now in every one of the nation's 188 Catholic dioceses. One telling point Anderson has made is that he has never worked with a survivor on a lawsuit who had not first tried to settle accounts within the pastoral context of the church, that is, by seeking removal and treatment for a priest and compensation for therapy, but not necessarily by seeking damages in court. Survivors go to the courts, it appears, not as a first resort, but as a last resort.[30]

Complicating the church's sex-abuse problem is the fact that many who have accused priests have done so years after the fact. This is because of what psychologists call the phenomenon of delayed-memory syndrome. An ugly memory apparently can stay hidden for years until some experience triggers it and the person remembers. This is what a young man, Steven Cook, maintained in a

November 1993 lawsuit in which he accused Chicago Cardinal Joseph Bernardin of sexual abuse years earlier while Cook was a seminarian. Bernardin denied the allegations and was eventually vindicated in February 1994, when Cook recanted the charges, saying his memory was not reliable and that he could no longer "in good conscience" pursue the charges. But the damage had been done; Bernardin had been portrayed in parts of the media as a sex abuser. The cardinal said the experience was the most difficult of his life. In December 1994, Bernardin met with Cook, who apologized, and the two reconciled with each other. Wrote Bernardin of the meeting: "I told him that in every family there are times when there is hurt, anger, alienation. But we cannot run away from our family. We have only one family so we must make every effort to be reconciled."[31]

In June 1993, Pope John Paul II spoke out publicly for the first time on the crisis of sex abuse by U.S. clergy, saying to the U.S. bishops: "I fully share your sorrow and your concern, especially your concern for the victims so seriously hurt by these misdeeds."[32] The pontiff said he had become aware in conversations with visiting bishops of how much, "together with all the faithful, [they] are suffering because of certain cases of scandal given by members of the clergy." Pope John Paul's statement spoke of the special gravity of sin that gives scandal to children. Said the pope: "The gospel word woe has a special meaning" when applied to sins with children. He quoted Jesus' words in Matthew's gospel: "For him who gives scandal [to children] it would be better to have a great millstone hung around his neck and to be drowned in the depths of the sea." The pope's statement also attacked the media for sensationalizing clerical misdeeds and called for prayer as a path of reconciliation. His words were met with relief in some circles, skepticism in others. The papal statement was released less than a week after it was distributed in closed-door sessions to the U.S. bishops who were meeting in June 1993 in New Orleans. During that meeting, the bishops also dealt with the sex-abuse issue for the first time in a public session; they had discussed it at four earlier national gatherings in executive session. At the outset of the New Orleans gathering, Archbishop (later Cardinal) William H. Keeler of Baltimore, president of the National Conference of Catholic Bishops, announced the formation of a special committee of U.S. bishops to study the issue of sex abuse by members of the clergy. The committee, he said, was to make recommendations to the bishops about how better to respond to the problem. Special panels have been set up in nearly every U.S. diocese, often with lay members, to handle sex-abuse complaints. The U.S. bishops have resisted establishing national guidelines, saying these are local matters to be handled by the local bishop. The national committee has released no figures on the numbers of priests involved nor the amount of money paid in settlements, and it says it has not gathered the information.

When a priest is found to be an abuser, commonly he goes into treatment for periods of six months to a year or more. Some are then assigned ministries in which they will have no contact with minors. Others are simply removed from the priesthood. There is treatment, but apparently no cure for pedophilia. Doctors use a drug called Depo-Provera that quells the urge but does not eliminate it. Treatment centers using therapy report some success. But the danger of recidivism and the risks it poses normally rule out any placement in a parish situation.

Chicago psychologist Eugene Kennedy has for years

worked with the U.S. bishops in matters of clergy sexual misconduct. He has been among those calling for a thorough study of the current state of the Catholic priesthood, which he sees as in a state of collapse. He says he is disappointed that the bishops have failed to respond to the crisis and have avoided studying it. Without information, there can be no analysis, no diagnosis and no treatment, no path to restored church health. According to Kennedy:

> *What is at stake here is nothing less than the sacramental life of the church. . . . This is a problem not of the priesthood itself but of the clerical culture in which it is set. Nobody questions the centrality of the sacramental priesthood in Catholic life. Many believers soon will, however, unless the blight that seems to grow out of, and at the same time devour, clerical culture is honestly identified and dealt with in a serious manner.*[33]

The mounting problems within the Catholic priesthood the church faces have not moved Pope John Paul II to reconsider mandatory celibacy. To the contrary, the pope has continued to defend mandatory celibacy. He has done so repeatedly during his tenure as pope. He does not associate alleged illness in the priesthood with celibacy, but rather sees celibacy as the answer to church ills. The church, the pope has said, cannot adjust its rules to match the "different set of values" in today's society. He has insisted that celibacy signifies the "unconditional acceptance" of priestly ministry and is a gift to the whole church. "The fact that a society is no longer marked by Christian values" has brought confusion to marriage and priestly celibacy, but this, he has concluded, "should in no way discourage us from fulfilling our task."[34]

But it has discouraged Catholics, nevertheless. Priests are hurting, but no group of Catholics is more discouraged, more disaffected, than Catholic women.

VII

❖ ❖ ❖

Women and the Church

Sister Theresa Kane arrived at the National Shrine of the Immaculate Conception on October 7, 1979, in Washington, D.C., ready to face the new pope and a national television audience. As administrator general of the Sisters of Mercy of the Union in the United States and president of the Leadership Conference of Women Religious (LCWR), the umbrella organization for women leaders of religious orders, she was the logical person to address Pope John Paul II. An estimated five thousand nuns had packed the shrine dedicated to the Mother of God. Kane's remarks were to be brief. Pope John Paul II, on his first trip to the United States as pope, had a full day of appointments. She would have his attention for only a few minutes, and it would be a unique opportunity to speak her mind. In her wildest dreams, she thought she might even engage the pope in a conversation. Days before she had consulted with several other LCWR leaders. They offered support, but she knew she alone would be responsible for what she said that day. The acoustics were poor. The stand in the sanctuary had been placed so that she would face outward. This meant the pope would be to her side and slightly behind her as she spoke and she would be unable to see his eyes as she read her remarks. But that was of lesser consequence, for the time had come to express not only her thoughts but the aspirations of untold numbers of other Catholic women. In a clear booming voice she told the pope he needed to be mindful of "the intense suffering and pain that is part of the life of many women in these United States." Going on, she said,

> *As women we have heard the powerful message of our church addressing the dignity and reverence for all persons. As women we have pondered these words. Our contemplation leads us to state that the church in its struggle to be faithful to its call for reverence and dignity for all persons must respond by providing the possibility of women as persons being included in all ministries of the church.*[1]

Politely but unhesitatingly, Kane said what she thought needed to be said: Christian dignity demands that women be allowed to be ordained priests. The pope never responded.

That day Theresa Kane became a Catholic celebrity, admired for her boldness by many Catholics, admonished for her lack of respect by many others. Growing internal divisions within the Catholic Church on sexual matters took a public turn that day. One year later in Philadelphia at the conclusion of her term as LCWR president, she expanded on her Washington remarks:

The church preaches a message of "dignity, reverence and equality of all persons" to people and governments of the world, but it has yet to recognize the injustices it imposes on women. Until the institutional Catholic Church undertakes a serious, critical examination of its modes of acting toward women, it cannot, it will not, give witness to justice in the world. The challenge for women in the '80s is to confront and eradicate the systemic evils of sexism, clericalism, and paternalism.[2]

In just one generation the ordination issue, symbol of church injustice to large numbers of Catholic women, has generated widespread discontentment and alienation. Not that most women in local parishes are ready to actively protest, but they are less enthusiastic about raising their children in the faith. Approaching the outer edge of the beginning of the twenty-first century, an exclusively male Catholic priesthood is the most painful, most intractable, most divisive, and potentially most damaging issue facing the church. For millions of Western Catholic women no other issue is more dispiriting than their denial of the sacrament of ordination. Not only does it effectively keep them from all authority positions in the church, they say, but it is especially demeaning that men officially define women's roles, based on their sexual nature alone. For educated women such a situation, they say, is simply no longer acceptable, especially not in a church carrying out the mission of Jesus Christ.

An exclusively male priesthood, however, is and has for centuries been, the official teaching of the Catholic Church. The official church catechism states that only a baptized man can validly receive the sacrament of ordination because "the Lord Jesus chose men (*viri*) to form the college of the twelve apostles, and the apostles did the same when they chose collaborators to succeed them in their ministry."[3] Nevertheless, many Catholic scholars dispute this simplistic succession theory, pointing out that the sacrament of ordination did not develop until centuries after the life and death of Jesus and that both men and women hosted and prepared Eucharistic gatherings in the private homes of early Christians. Clearly, however, stripped of questions of justice, dignity, and authority, the issue of ordination centers on Catholic theology. However much Jesus esteemed women, the Catholic hierarchy maintains today, that Jesus distinguished between men and women—and the church must do likewise.

Women's advocates counter that Jesus' supposed choice of male apostles was the result of the cultural values of that time, including the values of the men who recorded the events and those who eventually chose what would come to be Sacred Scripture. In recent times, the ordination issue has been divided into two camps: the official church, which speaks of the "complementarity" of women, a kind of "two nature" theology of human sexuality. The church teaches that women are equal to men but by nature are different. The Creator intended that they "complement" men. Thus, their nature is different from men—and only men can "image" Jesus and officiate in the celebration of the Eucharist following Jesus' command: "Do this in memory of me."

Women's ordination advocates argue a "one nature" theology, saying that all are equal in the eyes of God. The ordination issue has forced theologians to ask if Jesus' gender is essential or accidental to the divine Redemption plan. Or to put it another way, was Jesus first and foremost a man or first and foremost a person who happened to be a man?

By extension, the same questions are asked of those he chose to be his apostles. Did their "maleness" somehow more precisely pattern Jesus? Rosemary Radford Ruether, professor of theology at Garrett-Evangelical Theological Seminary in Evanston, Illinois, and Catholic feminist theologian, put it this way in an open letter she wrote to the U.S. Catholic bishops:

> *You claim to affirm the equality of women with men in the image of God, yet you deny to women equality in Christ, who is, for Christians, the veritable image of God. Your contention that women do not image Christ, by their very nature as women and thus cannot represent Christ in the ordained ministry, is built on all the sexist presuppositions that you claim to oppose: that women are essentially inferior, lacking in the fullness of human nature, mentally, morally and physically; a defect in generation, as Aristotle and Thomas Aquinas, the fonts of your patriarchal anthropology, did not hesitate to assert.*[4]

Feminist theologians say that to argue that Jesus' sexuality is more important than his humanity is to fall into an unacceptable dualism that—despite protests to the contrary by the official church—perpetuates a male-centered and male-controlled church structure. To adhere to this traditional theology, they say, is to forever relegate women to lesser roles and assure continued oppression. For a religion whose doorway to the fullness of church authority and all final decision making is the sacrament of ordination, the outcome of this theological debate is of major consequence. It will shape Catholicism in the century ahead.

Yet ordination remains an ambiguous symbol for many feminist women today. On the one hand, it is a central and profound focus for the lack of equality in the church. On the other, many see today's clerical priesthood, with its distinctions between clergy and laity, as precisely the wider problem in the church. Many feminists argue that gaining the entrance of women into the present clerical structure will not solve but will exacerbate church contradictions. In other words, women priests alone, they say, will not solve the ills of the church. Only more thorough institutional reforms will attend to those needs.[5]

Nevertheless, for a generation now the ordination question has remained active, despite continued efforts by the Vatican to squelch discussion of the topic. An organized women's ordination drive began in the United States in 1974 when Mary B. Lynch asked people on her extensive Christmas-card list if it was time to ask the ordination question. Thirty-four people who said yes met in Chicago and planned a national conference. The first Women's Ordination Conference (WOC) occurred over a Thanksgiving weekend in Detroit in 1975 attended by some 1,200 women and men. Another 500 had to be turned away. Near the end of that gathering, women were asked to stand if they felt called to ordination: 280 stood up.[6] WOC was not expected to be a continuing program at the time. Twenty-two core commissions were organized at Detroit, however, and in 1976 the national organization became a reality. The following year, WOC member Ruth Fitzpatrick became its first full-time employee and began operating on a modest budget.

With the concurrence of Pope Paul VI, the Vatican Congregation for the Doctrine of Faith on October 15, 1976, approved a statement titled *Inter Insignores*, the "Declaration on the Question of the Admission of Women to the Ministerial Priesthood." Its primary argument for excluding women from priestly ordination was the allegedly unbroken tradition of restricting priesthood to men. The declaration's theoretical argument supporting the restriction was its contention that women are unable to fully represent Christ, that "women are incapable of acting *in persona Christi* in the consecration of the Eucharist."[7] *Inter Insignores*, conceding that "we are dealing with a debate which classical theology scarcely touched upon," nevertheless stated that "the Church, in fidelity to the example of the Lord, does not consider herself authorized to admit women to priestly ordination." The Vatican had spoken, but it was not the last word.

In June 1978, the Catholic Theological Society of America at its annual meeting received a report calling for the ordination of women and refuting arguments used in *Inter Insignores* that women are by nature unfit for the priesthood. The report held that "women's ordination is a question never before addressed to the church in a comparable set of circumstances. It demands a new effort at self-understanding and an openness to new practice under the guidance of the creative Spirit."[8] The Catholic Biblical Association of the United States added its voice to the critique of *Inter Insignores* in the issue of the *Catholic Biblical Quarterly* of November 21, 1979. An association task force held that "there is a serious logical difficulty about the historical argument that Jesus intended to exclude women from the priesthood." It held that the New Testament does not show that a theological decision was made to exclude women from the priestly ministry. Indeed, the report concluded that New Testament evidence "while not decisive by itself, points toward the admission of women to priestly ministry" since it refers to women as founding churches, acting as leaders, functioning in public worship, teaching converts and prophesying.[9]

Pope John Paul II was pontiff for less than a year and still a relatively unknown prelate when he visited the United States in 1979 where he reaffirmed Pope Paul VI's ordination views while speaking to a group of seminarians. A few years later, in 1983, he delivered the same message to a group of U.S. bishops in Rome. Nevertheless, some in their ranks, a minority, continued to offer support to the women's ordination idea.

In 1988, in a lecture Auxiliary Bishop Francis P. Murphy of Baltimore called for "an international commission to investigate the issue of women's priestly ordination." Murphy said he was "convinced that the commission would find compelling reasons for opening up the priesthood to women." He said that a "fundamental weakness" of the status quo position of the church is trying "to fit the experience of women into the traditional, male-dominated categories of church teaching, language and practice."[10]

Bishop Kenneth Untener of Saginaw, Michigan, speaking at the University of Notre Dame in 1989, admitted: "I feel sad that we seem reluctant to look at these issues from every side in a healthy conversation." He then raised questions about the Vatican's contention that the priest acts *in persona Christi* ("in the person of Christ") and therefore must be a male. Three years later, Untener reiterated his plea for a critical examination of the priestly ordination of women, "a task we must face with honesty and courage."[11]

In 1990, Bishop Matthew Clark of Rochester, New York, and chairman of the American bishops' committee on women, urged the church to explore "fully and courageously the issue of the ordination of women along with other issues of sexual morality. That same year the Assembly of Quebec Bishops suggested that it may be time to consider allowing women to be ordained as priests.

In 1992, Bishop John Cummins of Oakland, California, told his fellow bishops that the ordination of women had aroused "more dissatisfaction at home" than it did among the bishops. He cited "a universal change of consciousness—among this generation," indeed so much so that "the people who disagree on this [the exclusion of women from the priesthood] are among our very best people."[12]

Bishop William A. Hughes of Covington, Kentucky, said in a public talk in 1993 that both the ordination of women and a married priesthood should be considered as possible solutions to the church's "steadily worsening" priest shortage. "We need an open and sincere dialogue," he said.[13]

Meanwhile, Catholics in the pews were becoming more accustomed to the idea. A 1992 Gallup poll reported that "two-thirds of American Catholics favor opening the priesthood to women, an increase of 20 percentage points over just seven years ago."[14]

During his pontificate, Pope John Paul II continued to reiterate Pope Paul VI's position on the ordination issue. However, in a 1,146-word statement issued on May 30, 1993, John Paul went considerably further. In a document titled *Ordinatio Sacerdotalis* ("On Priestly Ordination"), he not only reiterated that the church does not have the authority to ordain women, but he went on to say that he was speaking "definitively" and that Catholics must stop discussing the issue. The papal statement declared that church teaching on ordination is "certainly true" and "requires the full and unconditional assent of the faithful." No pope had said that before.[15]

U.S. bishops, some begrudgingly, reaffirmed the papal declaration even as they admitted it would cause considerable pain for many. Restricting priestly ordination to men in the Catholic Church "does not limit the potential of women in the church," insisted Baltimore Archbishop (later Cardinal) William H. Keeler, president of the U.S. bishops' conference. "The church is completely committed to the equality of all persons in dignity and nobility." He urged "all those who may find this further affirmation of the church's authentic teaching difficult to accept to receive it lovingly, pray for understanding and to see in it a call for them to live out fully their fundamental Christian vocation according to the gifts that they have been given."[16] Chicago Cardinal Joseph Bernardin said he recognized that the letter "will be a disappointment to some" but emphasized that "it is our task as a community of faith to do all we can to enable all members—both women and men—to use their gifts to the best advantage."[17] New York Cardinal John O'Connor said, "I would say that anyone awaiting a change in the future is going to wait well beyond an infinity of lifetimes."[18]

Milwaukee Archbishop Rembert Weakland, long the most sympathetic of the U.S. archbishops to the women's cause, had urged that the church not close the door to women's ordination. In response to the pope's letter he admitted that he was among those who would have trouble with it. "I certainly will be obedient to this command," he said. "Yet, in a spirit of filial loyalty, I must also express my own inner turmoil at this decision. I know that in the long run my obedience will result in a deepening of my faith, but I state sincerely that it will not be done without much sacrifice and inner searching." Weakland then went on to ask a number of questions that he said needed to be answered in the wake of the papal pronouncement:[19]

- What effect will this declaration have on so many women and men, especially younger women and vowed religious, who still see this question as one of justice and equality, all protestations to the contrary not withstanding? How, as a bishop, am I to deal with the anger and disillusionment that will inevitably result? What can I do to instill hope in so many women living on the margins of the church?
- What effects will this declaration have on theologians still concerned about the theological underpinnings of the pope's teaching? Will they be able to express honestly their concerns? Will adherence to this judgment of the pope be a requisite for teaching as a Catholic theologian?
- What effects will this declaration have on men and women for whom the issue of the way in which the church exercises its authority is already a problem? For those still struggling with church teachings on birth control, will they have difficulty accepting that a single person alone can decide what they must in faith accept? Are they now to be put against the wall, as it were, over this issue?
- Finally, what effects will this declaration have on ecumenical dialogue? Because full communion among the churches ultimately must include the mutual recognition of ministries, will this declaration mean that full communion is ruled out with all except the Orthodox churches?

Weakland concluded: "The Holy Father has certainly thought of these consequences. Since this document is more dogmatic in tone, his pastoral concern may not be immediately obvious. We must trust that the Holy Father is sensitive to the reactions this declaration will cause."

The papal statement was not declared "infallible," but it was said to be "definitive" and this sent Catholic theologians scurrying to make sense of this never previously proclaimed category of church authority. As far as U.S. Catholic theologians were concerned, this represented a new level of church teaching, one that did not quite have the binding force of an infallible statement, but one that Catholics were to see as having the full weight of the office of pope behind it. Father Ladislas Orsy, a Jesuit church lawyer, said the statement was "less than an infallible definition." "Definitive," he said, was a "somewhat new" concept. "We don't have a long-standing tradition to understand it." he said.[20]

It says something about the church in the United States that after the pope demanded that discussion of women's ordination cease, it seemed to pick up momentum, at least outside episcopal ranks. It also got Catholics talking more about the proper use and abuse of papal authority. "This is the ultimate power play of a desperate monarchy that sees its time has gone," said Fitzpatrick, national WOC coordinator.

The old Vatican proverb, *Roma locuta, causa finita*, ("Rome has spoken; the case is closed") no longer seems to carry much weight in some Catholic circles. The papal pronouncement was variously described by women as arrogant, condescending, and patronizing. Within seventy-two hours of the statement's release, Ruth Fitzpatrick had appeared on several television shows, participated in numerous radio call-in programs, and done "more than 50" telephone interviews with journalists, from the BBC in

London to Anna Quinlan of *The New York Times.*[21] At the time of the statement's release, Fitzpatrick said she was planning the 1995 "20th anniversary gathering" of the first Women's Ordination Conference. Theologian Rosemary Radford Ruether, following the statement, wrote that "rather than convincing the 'faithful' that the ordination of women is not open to debate, the pope may be suggesting to Catholics that the infallible teaching authority of the pope is open to question." She went on to say that "the inability of the Catholic hierarchy to admit error of interpretation has become an increasingly burdensome barrier, not just to intellectual freedom in the church, but to faithfulness to the gospel, which demands at times repentance in order to be open to the grace of renewal of life." She called upon Catholic theologians to begin to face the "inappropriateness" of this barrier directly:

> *We need to examine what kind of assumptions about God and papal power lie behind a practice of refusal to allow discussion of ideas that have lost their credibility on the grounds that the church could not have erred. No new development on a number of the most critical issues facing Catholics will be possible unless the issue of inappropriate claims to infallibility is faced. The unintended benefit of this recent papal letter may be that this most-avoided topic has now become unavoidable.*[22]

Feminist Theology

Throughout church history and until only quite recently to be a Catholic theologian was to be a man. Almost always it meant being a priest. It meant being cut off from women, their experiences, their thoughts, their feelings, their voices. It meant being part of a special and esteemed group within the church, the clergy. It meant being entrusted not only with writing theology, but proclaiming it, preserving it, and enforcing it. It meant having the the power to define sin, judge it, and forgive it. It meant standing at the crossroads of eternity and helping to play traffic cop, helping to decide who goes to heaven and who goes to hell. The awesome power of the priesthood has been unparalleled by any secular creation. Only in the past generation, however, have large numbers of women come to say that a priesthood that is all male has worked against them. In the face of this exclusion and claiming to be outsiders in a male-defined, male-controlled, male-centered church, women have begun to talk, to share stories, to record their experiences and to analyze it all. This has come to be called "feminist theology."

While many Catholic feminists write theology, there is no "Catholic feminist theology" as such. Since some women in almost all organized religions say they share a sense of exclusion and oppression, the subject has crossed denomination lines and has exploded, finding energy in literature well beyond traditional classic theology. Feminist theology and spirituality have instinctively looked for bonds with other oppressed peoples, be they victims of sexism, classism, or racism. In the United States, feminist theologians have crossed traditional racial barriers, sometimes linking Hispanic, black, and white feminist concerns. Feminist theology differs in a number of ways from classical Catholic theology. While traditional sexual morality has often taught absolutes (such as, never birth control, never homosexual acts), feminist theology has emphasized context and circumstance. For example, What are the mitigating factors? Is the act the lesser of two evils? Is it a nurturing relationship? While traditional theology has started with abstract thought and uses deductive reasoning, feminist theology more often starts with experience and reasons inductively. While traditional theology makes claims to knowing divine Revelation, feminist theology says that what passes for "divine" Revelation is only a *male perception* of divine truths. The feminists make the point that traditional theology is incomplete because it has ignored centuries of women's experiences. Catholic feminists see church teachings on sexual matters as intended to keep them in their places and far from church authority. Catholic sexual teachings, as feminists see it, more often than not helps to perpetuate patriarchal structures by preserving male authority over women's sexuality. Feminists bitterly reject this approach, adding that credible sexual ethics can never emerge from an all-male clergy.

Many consider feminist theology a branch of "liberation theology," although it has its own separate origins. Liberation theology also grows out of the experiences of oppression and is based on the insight that the God of Israel and the God of Jesus Christ sides with the poor and stands in solidarity with the marginalized and outcasts of history. Though liberation theology is most often associated with Latin America from which it came in the late 1960s, starting with Gustavo Gutierrez's groundbreaking *A Theology of Liberation*, liberation theology is more broadly conceived to include all theology being done by any marginalized people or group.

Feminist theology sees women as a marginalized group. As a path to their own liberation, feminist theologians critique the church, rejecting all notions of male dominance, including male God imagery; androcentric, or male-centered, thought; and all patriarchal structures. Many men have joined with women in making such critiques, further strengthening the movement. With feminist ideas growing among many educated and articulate Christian women, and with these ideas already taking hold among Third World women, feminist theology represents an enormous challenge to the Catholic Church, some say the greatest challenge since Martin Luther nailed his ninety-five theses on the door of the castle church at Wittenberg on October 31, 1517. Others go on to say that if Catholicism cannot find a way to meet this challenge, it has only modest hopes for survival, at least in its current form. The problem for the hierarchy is that educated women—including mothers, who are the traditional faith teachers—are quickly coming to accept the feminist critique. They may not leave the church as a result, but they do not support the old institution with traditional intensity. They find their own ways. Meanwhile, what the feminists say they offer the church is not simply a challenge; they see it as an opportunity to rediscover authentic Christianity and revitalize the faith. They see it as as an effort to separate religious incidentals from real Christianity. However one views it, feminist theology is, indeed, revolutionary. It is bringing to light Christian perspectives lacking for centuries, those of half the human race.

Tracing Origins

The seeds of contemporary Christian feminism were planted during the first women's movement, which began in the United States more than 150 years ago. Work for women's rights took hold in the 1840s and led to a historic meeting at Seneca Falls, New York, in 1848. That gathering took place in a Methodist church. While some of the nineteenth-century feminists eventually broke their ties with the

Christianity, others remained active in promoting the cause of women within churches, arguing for the admission of women to seminaries and to the ministry, as well as for voting rights.[23] The twentieth-century women's movement has similar connections within churches and has led to splits within churches. Christian feminists, advocating the ordination of women and expanded roles in ministry, seminary education, and decision making, are part of the wider women's liberation movement. It was only in the late 1950s and early 1960s that universities and seminaries began to open themselves to women studying religion and theology. It was at that period that Mary Daly became the first woman to go to Europe to earn a doctorate in sacred theology, the early standard degree for a seminary teacher. She is now on the faculty at Boston College. Catholic feminists look back to some of Daly's works as groundbreaking, citing in particular the 1969 publication of *The Church and the Second Sex* and the 1973 publication of *Beyond God the Father: Toward a Philosophy of Women's Liberation*. Daly's works put forth some of the original critiques of patriarchal structures and church use of androcentric language patterns as integral aspects of women's oppression. Also considered foundational were the writings of Rosemary Radford Ruether, including her 1974 publication *Religion and Sexism* and her 1975 publication *New Woman, New Earth*. Yet another pioneering effort was the 1979 publication *Kiss Sleeping Beauty Good-Bye* by Madonna Kolbenschlag, the first work to link the study of myth with a theological and psychological perspective on women. Elisabeth Schussler Fiorenza's 1983 work, *In Memory of Her: A Feminist Reconstruction of Christian Origins*, is yet another example of formative femininst theology. As for the goals of Christian feminism, Schussler

Fiorenza has written: "Only as we, women and men, are able to live in nonsexist Catholic communities, celebrate nonsexist Christian liturgies and call on God with many names and images will we be able to formulate a genuine Christian feminist spirituality."

By the mid-1970s, virtually every Christian college or university with a graduate school had begun to have master's degree programs in fields such as religious studies, religious education, pastoral studies, youth ministry, and theological specialties such as exegesis or biblical languages. These programs became populated with women who furthered the feminist discussion as they shared their stories. When academic institutions began to offer doctor's degrees in various sacred sciences, women entered those programs as well. When women graduates began to teach and reflect on the meaning of Christian faith from their perspectives, social sciences and religious studies began to cross-fertilize. All this was adding to the expanding feminist movement. By the mid-1980s, the validity of the feminist critique of patriarchy had become a given in most Catholic women's circles outside the ranks of the most traditional Catholics. Curiously a good number of Catholics continued to see feminism in a negative light, even as they supported feminist causes.

Meanwhile, Catholic women theologians were gaining wider acceptance in the traditionally male-dominated field of Catholic theology. In part this was the result of the influence of the wider women's movement. It also resulted from the recognition that much of the women's scholarship was both competent and imaginative. Many of the women who entered theology in the 1970s continued to publish in scholarly periodicals, to write books, and to work in seminaries, colleges, and universities, and in parishes and dioceses. Eventually they became active in the Catholic Theological Society of America (CTSA), the most noted American theologicial organization. By the early 1990s, almost a fifth of the CTSA's more than 1,400 members were women. Sister Agnes Cunningham of the Servants of the Holy Heart of Mary became the first woman CTSA president, elected to a 1977–78 term; Monika Hellwig became the second, 1986–87; Holy Name Sister Anne E. Patrick became the third president, 1989–90, and Lisa Sowle Cahill became the fourth, 1992–93.

Meanwhile, the ideas and critiques of feminist theologians were spreading well beyond academic circles into other church areas and were inspiring many women to enter church ministries, whether those ministries were open to them or not. By the 1990s women outnumbered men in many Protestant and interdenominational seminaries; they were studying beside men in some Catholic seminaries, even as the priesthood continued to be closed to them. An estimated 15 percent of Catholic seminary faculty nationwide is now made up of women. For these feminists the process has been painfully slow. Even in those Christian churches that now allow the ordination of women—the United Church of Christ, the American Baptist Convention, the Presbyterians, the Methodists, two of the Lutheran synods, and the Episcopalians—difficulties remain in accepting women in leadership positions in local congregations.[24]

Any effort to neatly categorize feminist theologians is bound to fall short. By the nature of their work, they cross traditional boundaries as they seek new ways to develop church. Some have placed them into two general camps: the reformist feminists, who remain Christian and seek to reclaim Christian symbols for feminism, staying committed to renewing the church, and the radical or, as some say, the post-Christian feminists, who view Christianity as inherently sexist and incapable of reform. But even such a general distinction draws criticisms from some feminists. Ruether is one who takes issue with those using the word *radical* as a measure of how distanced one gets from the official church. She argues that feminist theology is better served by linking the word *radical* to a fierce justice commitment and to authentic Christian teaching.

One of feminist theology's early tasks has been to critique the past, with a particular focus on those aspects of the Christian tradition that have denied the importance and validity of women.[25] Feminist theologians see this belittlement reflected in countless ways, beginning with Scripture. They start by citing Old Testament passages that associate women and evil, especially those that depict women as temptresses, as in the Adam and Eve story. Of course, the subjugation of women preceded Hebrew and Christian biblical writings, dating back to antiquity where it was common to view women as a source of disease and bad spirits, especially during menstruation when intercourse was often prohibited. Both pagans and Jews looked upon menstrual blood as infectious and poisonous.[26] For example, in the Old Testament book of Leviticus (15:19–24) God defines a menstruating woman as unclean for seven days, and anyone who touches her or anything she has touched or anything touched by someone she has touched, as unclean. Such attitudes were common at the time and were widely shared by the early Christians. The subjugation of women by men was reflected in New Testament injunctions as well. For example, Christian women were told to be silent in the Christian assemblies and were to subordinate themselves to male "headship." Early Christian writers, again reflecting broader cultural currents, had little understanding or sympathy for women's bodily functions, which they commonly feared. Around the year 200, the church father Clement of Alexandria (c. 150–211/15) warned men not to have intercourse with menstruating women, claiming that children conceived during menstruation would be born impaired. In the Judeo-Christian tradition, menstruation had the added disadvantage of being tied to sin, commonly seen as the the result of God's punishment after Eve tempted Adam to eat of the Tree of Knowledge. Clement was only one of a number of early church writers to express virtual contempt for women. He once observed that a woman should properly be shamed when she thinks "of what nature she is."[27]

In such writings are found examples of long-held male prejudices as well as the early beginnings of church structures built to help keep men pure and women at a distance. It was not long before these notions worked their way into church theology and traditions, becoming integral to Christian reflections, especially those dealing with sexual morality. Augustine, writing in the fourth century, for example, noted that "the good Christian likes what is human, loathes what is feminine." Eight centuries later, Thomas Aquinas wrote that "woman is defective and misbegotten" and that "it is not possible in the female sex that any eminence of degree can be signified."[28]

Today's feminist theologians, equipped with new tools for studying Scripture, have worked to separate cultural prejudice from essential Christian teachings. They have called for new scriptural interpretations and the reading of

Scripture and church documents with a highly critical eye, one that takes into consideration the cultural prejudices of the times in which they were written. Shussler Fiorenza advises women to read the Bible "against the grain," looking behind the words to discover how and why authors constructed their stories as they did. Most feminists scholars agree that scholarship will never reach a culture-free understanding of core Christian beliefs. Nevertheless, they say the effort to separate authentic teachings from dominating cultural forces must continue.

Schussler Fiorenza described the scholarship as follows:

> *All interpretations of texts depend upon the presuppositions, intellectual concepts, politics, and prejudices of the interpreter and historian. Feminist scholars, therefore, rightly point out that for all too long the Christian tradition was recorded and studied by theologians who consciously or unconsciously understood them from a patriarchal perspective of male dominance. Since this androcentric cultural perspective has determined all writing of theology and of history, their endeavor is correctly his-story. If women, therefore, want to get in touch with their own roots and tradition, they have to rewrite the Christian tradition and theology in such a way that it becomes not only his-story but her-story as well, recorded and analyzed from a feminist point of view.*[29]

According to Schussler Fiorenza, the purpose of feminist theology is not just to understand the Christian tradition and texts within their historical settings, it "is to liberate Christian theologies, symbols, and institutions" from what has "stimulated and perpetuated violence, alienation, and oppression." The task, then, is never-ending; it is seen as a call to constant church renewal. She says that feminists view

Christian faith and life as caught in the middle of history and in need of constant "prophetic criticism."

Many Christian feminists see their work as the product of personal experience and scholarship, moving freely from one world to the other, using both as sources of reflection. Storytelling, or the sharing of experiences in the face of patriarchal structures, has been essential to these women and has helped fuel their spirits and scholarship. The starting point for many has been the common experiences of discrimination and oppression, things they share with other societal victims. Schussler Fiorenza, recalling her early struggles to make her way in a largely male church, writes of her early years at the University of Notre Dame where, in 1973, she was called to deliver a speech following the *Roe v. Wade* Supreme Court decision. Her recollection helps in an understanding of the way women face challenges in traditionally male-run church institutions and points to how a Catholic feminist's thinking differs at times from that of Catholic men.

With the university organizing lectures to denounce the abortion decision, she remembers being called upon by friends and students to speak her mind. Somewhat reluctantly she agreed to speak, beginning by paraphrasing Matthew 23, a Scripture passage in which Jesus spoke to the crowds and to his disciples warning them of the hypocracy of the high priests. She said that since "the scribes and Pharisees have taken their seat on the chair of Moses. Therefore, do and observe all things whatsoever they tell you, but do not follow their example. For they preach but they do not practice."

She then went on to say that she did not want to discuss the "difficult question" of when human life begins in the womb, but to consider the issue with the Matthew Scripture passage in mind. "At the end, the reading asserts that the central matters of this teaching are 'justice, mercy and faith.' Any moral teaching on abortion must be shaped by the concern for 'justice, mercy, and faith,'" she said, going on to say that "since Notre Dame subscribes to the teaching that abortion is morally wrong, it must at the same time seek to safeguard the 'weightier matters of the law'—justice, mercy, and faith." That, she said, would entail changes in policy in at least four areas of university life. She listed them:

> First, the university must make information about and access to birth control readily available. Campus ministry should advocate—rather than oppose—the dissemination of birth-control information and counseling through student medical services on campus. We must realize that many of our students are sexually active instead of closing our eyes to it. Availability of birth control does not foster premarital sex. Its absence increases the number of Notre Dame and St. Mary's students who end up in downtown abortion clinics.
>
> Second, we must reconsider our policy that expels pregnant unmarried women students but not their male partners from campus housing. Instead, we should provide nursery and day care facilities that would allow student mothers to finish their studies while their babies are cared for on campus. . . .
>
> Third, we must stop advocating adoption as the moral solution to the problem of abortion. The adoption business of bartering "white babies" is morally more offensive than the termination of pregnancy in the first weeks after conception. In many cases, the trauma of adoption is as great as, if not greater than, that of early abortion. . . .

> Finally, since Notre Dame has been traditionally a male, clerical institution, the administration and academic leadership of the university needs to communicate to women students and faculty that their intellectual gifts are treasured and their university contributions are respected. . . . A moral antiabortion stance requires that the university adopt for staff and faculty a paid-pregnancy and family-leave policy, establish a child care center on campus, develop an affirmative action program, institutionalize a job-share policy, and make possible tenurable part-time positions with all fringe benefits.
>
> As long as we do not practice what we preach, the woes and indictments that Jesus pronounced against the leaders of his own time are addressed also to us at Notre Dame. . . .[30]

Some years later, Schussler Fiorenza left Notre Dame, citing fears that "an intellectually responsible Catholic theology would not be possible in Roman Catholic institutions, but only in theological environments that guaranteed freedom of speech and research."[31] Other Catholic women with interests in religious studies or theology likewise gravitated to nondenominational settings.

The Christian feminists see critique as only part of their work. While "deconstruction," is required, they view themselves as involved in "reconstruction" efforts, giving women new self-understanding, energy, and life. In one example, Anne E. Carr, professor of theology at the Divinity School of the University of Chicago, puts it this way:

> *Christian writers have been inclined to speak of sin as pride, self-assertion and rebellion against God and of grace as the gift of self-sacrificial love. But in fact such categories relate more to the*

> *experience of men, in cultures that encourage them toward roles of domination and power. Women's temptation or sin, conversely, relates to lack of self-assertion in relation to cultural and familial expectations, failure to assure responsibility and make choices for themselves, failure to discover their own personhood and uniqueness rather than finding their whole meaning in the too-easy sacrifice of self for others. Reinterpreted by feminist theologians, grace takes on a wholly different character as the gift of claiming responsibility for one's life, as love for self as well as love of others, as the assumption of healthy power over one's life and circumstances.*[32]

The point the feminists make along the way is that women can bring new insights to theology and help the church, both women and men, form deeper understandings into long-held sacred truths. They do this by bringing themselves and experiences to the work of the church.

WOMEN-CHURCH

While feminist writers see much in historical Christianity that is deeply patriarchal and alienating, many do not extend this judgment to its founder, Jesus. Nor are they waiting for the official church to change before they take steps to change it. One of the clearest indicators of this impatience can be seen in a movement called Women-Church. Formed in the 1980s and generated by but not limited to Catholic women, Women-Church has sought separate space for women to worship together and discuss common concerns. It sees early Christianity as in line with a feminist transformation and calls on churches to reform themselves to be faithful to Jesus, who, they say, stood for justice and treated women justly.

The Women-Church movement and a 1985 book by the

same name written by Rosemary Radford Ruether (*Women-Church: Theology and Practice of Feminist Liturgical Communities*) claim that women, especially Catholic women, suffer from "linguistic deprivation and a eucharistic famine," and must work at being church. Women-Church says that women must neither entirely leave nor entirely stay within churches that do not meet their needs.

Some 1,200 women attended the first Women-Church gathering held in Chicago in 1983, entitled "From Generation to Generation: Women-Church Speaks." More than 3,200 attended the second national gathering held in Cincinnati in 1987, entitled, "Women-Church : Claiming Our Power." And more than 2,400 women attended the third gathering in Albuquerque in 1993, entitled "Women-Church: Weavers of Change." Women who have met in the name of Women-Church find support in each other, saying they seek out strictly feminist communities to worship as women in spiritually nurturing ways. They say they seek the creation of temporary separate bases from which both to critique the patriarchy and block its power. The Women-Church Convergence is a network of Women-Church organizations and groups rooted in the Catholic tradition but claiming to encompass a spirituality that goes beyond it. Women-Church claims it does not seek to establish alternative structures, saying that institutions will provide resources for their transformation but not for their competition.[33] Diann L. Neu and Mary E. Hunt are cofounders and codirectors of the Silver Spring, Maryland-based organization called WATER, the Women's Alliance of Theology, Ethics and Ritual, a feminist nonprofit educational center that began in 1983 as a response to emerging feminist needs. WATER sponsors a monthly Women-Church group and sees itself as supportive of the wider Women-Church movement. Neu maintains that Women-Church is growing and making a big difference in the way many women come to be church. Women-Church, she writes, "proclaims through sacrament and solidarity, story and song that women are church. This is different from merely belonging to a church or even leaving a church, since it signals that women are essentially what patriarchy has denied, namely, religious protagonists able to shape and create the reality called church."[34] Women-Church, while initially a U.S. phenomenon, has spread overseas and now claims an international following. "Liturgy and community, social justice and solidarity are what most women want when they become part of a Women-Church community or a women's spiritual support group," Neu explains. "Women come to these groups because we are starved for a language that sustains us spiritually, for a symbol system we can call our own. We yearn for rituals that speak to our concerns, needs, desires, dreams, and practices."

When feminist Christians gather in ritual or to share ideas, language usage is an essential concern. Because they view biblical texts as written by men in a patriarchal culture, they are particularly concerned that these texts be translated and interpreted, whenever possible, in ways that are not offensive to them. With this in mind, they ask the broader church first that the patriarchal character of the texts be acknowledged, then that efforts be made to distance contemporary culture from those cultures that produced the texts, and finally that nonsexist and inclusive language be used in translations and liturgies.

Sister Elizabeth A. Johnson, author of *She Who Is: The Mystery of God in Feminist Theological Discourse*, is an associate professor of theology at Fordham University, New York. After more than a decade of teaching at Catholic University of America, Washington. D.C., the Sister of St. Joseph left CUA, saying she needed greater academic freedom. In her 1993 book, she argues that it is vital to bring the feminine to the historically male-imaged God. All speech about God, she says, has a profound effect on listeners, adding that the historical model of the theistic God as monarch, with constant use of male imagery, has resulted in a mind-set that has permeated Christianity and most religions with patriarchy. Neither she nor most other feminist theologians propose switching the patriarchical for a matriarchical language. Rather, she says, the goal of feminist theology is "not to make women equal partners in an oppressive system," but rather to bring about justice and transform the system. Emphasizing that women have been marginalized throughout history, she says that if men feel threatened by inclusive language they are only beginning to imagine what it must have been like for women throughout the centuries. Johnson poses the following question: "If it is not meant that God is male when masculine imagery is used, why the objection when female images are introduced?" Answering her own question, she says that "an intrinsic, literal connection between God and maleness is usually intended, however implicitly."

Sallie McFague, professor of theology and former dean at Vanderbilt University Divinity School, is considered one of the more innovative feminist theologians in her exploration of new images of God.[35] She makes the point that all talk about God is metaphorical, not descriptive. Royal imagery, talk of "king" and "kingdom," which is hierarchical, she says, is not inclusive and is no longer appropriate God talk.

In a time when kings were part of people's daily experience, she says, one might make a case for such a model, but today, king imagery is anachronistic and oppressive as well. She prefers God language such as "the spirit that is the breath, the life of the universe, a universe that comes from God and could be seen as the body of God." This model, she contends, is today more appropriate than the model of God as "an other-worldly king whose human subjects, living as 'resident aliens' on earth, work toward a coveted afterlife with God in some other place." To consider the universe as God's body, McFague says, "is neither idolatry nor pantheism: The world, creation, is not identified or confused with God. Yet it is the place where God is present to us." She calls this understanding "panentheist," God being in all finite creatures, and they in God. "Yet God is not identical with the universe, for the universe is dependent on God in a way that God is not dependent on the universe." She says that in panentheism "God is embodied but not necessarily or totally." McFague has grabbed the attention of many Christian woman who see in her writings both a restoration of the religious mystery and language that is inclusive and does not alienate feminist sensitivities.[36]

Inclusive Language

By contrast, the Catholic hierarchy has found it virtually impossible to come up with language that is acceptable to Catholic feminists. Some examples from recent church experience help illustrate the problem. In the mid-1980s, the world's bishops decided it was time to pull together in one book the church's teachings as an aid to catechists, those who teach the faith. The project was to take years to complete with the official text being written in French.

Translations were to be based on that text. Heading the effort in the United States was Father Douglas Clark of Richmond Hill, Georgia. His job with a team of other linguistic experts was to translate the French text into readable and acceptable English. He eventually set out to write his translation using modestly inclusive language. In doing so, he did not follow some personal whim or feminist agenda. Rather he followed, apart from common sense, a National Conference of Catholic Bishops' statement of November 1990 entitled "Criteria for the Evaluation of Inclusive Translations of Scriptural Texts Proposed for Liturgical Use." It made the points that some "segments of American culture have become increasingly sensitive to 'exclusive language,' i.e., language that seems to exclude the equality and dignity of each person regardless of race, gender, creed or age" and that "English vocabulary itself has changed so that words that once referred to all human beings are increasingly taken as gender-specific and, consequently, exclusive." The bishops' 1990 statement concluded: "The Word of God proclaimed to all nations is by nature inclusive, that is, addressed to all peoples, men and women. Consequently, every effort should be made to render the language of biblical translation as inclusive as a faithful translation of the texts permits."[37] Clark labored for months, and his translation gained the support of some of the nation's most conservative bishops, including Cardinal Bernard Law of Boston, an early catechism project backer. However, before its release, the Vatican became concerned that Clark's text did not adequately depict Catholic doctrine—and the inclusive language was the principle reason for the problem.

Meanwhile, French, Italian, and Spanish versions of the catechism had already been published. Months passed, then a year, and finally after two more years of work, the Vatican, having taken back the writing project, finished its task of converting the entire catechism into exclusive language. It was a frustrating moment for U.S. Catholics. The final work read like something written in the 1940s. Thus, for example, the catechism, officially published in 1994, begins with these exclusive words:

> *God, infinitely perfect and blessed in himself, in a plan of sheer goodness freely created man to make him share in his own blessed life. For this reason, at every time and in every place, God draws close to man. He calls man to seek him, to know him, to love him with all his strength. He calls together all men, scattered and divided by sin, into the unity of his family, the Church. To accomplish this, when the fullness of time had come, God sent his Son as Redeemer and Savior. In his son and through him, he invited men to become, in the Holy Spirit, his adopted children and thus heirs to his blessed life.*[38]

It was precisely the kind of language many Catholic women cite when they say the church is not sensitive to their needs and, intentionally or not, excludes and demeans them. The text—intended to teach the faith—ended up only further alienating many Catholics, women and men, who have grown accustomed to reading and hearing inclusive language in their daily lives and even in many of their local parishes. Many U.S. Catholics interpreted the Vatican translation, whether true or not, to be a power play, as if to say Rome runs the church and that's the way it is meant to be. Many Catholics were angered by the action, not least among them feminists who were fed up with exclusively male gender imagery.

The Vatican, however, was not yet finished. Later in the year, in October 1994, reports surfaced that several months earlier the Vatican Congregation for the Doctrine of Faith, which oversees doctrine and is headed by Cardinal Joseph Ratzinger, rejected for liturgical and catechetical use a Bible translation, the New Revised Standard Version (NRSV), written in inclusive language and already officially approved by the U.S. bishops and Vatican liturgists three years earlier. This time the Vatican doctrine watchdogs, apparently under pressure from conservative Catholics in the United States, overruled the U.S. bishops without offering a public explanation. Again, the Vatican said inclusive language had failed to stay faithful to scriptural truths. This action was viewed as another power play and a further centralization of church decision making, perhaps unprecedented in Catholic history. Each time the Vatican moved against what it viewed as unfaithful language, it was acting against what is called "horizontally" inclusive imagery, that is, language that deals with human imagery and not divine imagery, such as *humanity*, not *mankind* and *brothers and sisters*, not *brethren*. By feminist standards the "inclusive language" overruled by Rome was modest indeed, making no effort, for example, to portray God also as Mother.

The NRSV Bible had been produced by an ecumenical team of scholars under sponsorship of the National Council of Churches. The Catholic edition had been reviewed and approved by Catholic scholars who were shocked and dismayed by the ruling. Following the news of the action, the executive board of the Catholic Biblical Association responded with an urgent appeal to the U.S. bishops to stand firmly against what it termed the "demeaning" Vatican action. "The church's credibility is involved," the ten-member board said in a letter they sent to the president of the U.S. bishops' conference, Archbishop William Keeler of Baltimore. "We are deeply concerned about the implications of this [Vatican] approach to something that impinges so directly on the pastoral efforts made by the American hierarchy," the Catholic Biblical Association wrote.[39]

While inclusive language was the immediate issue, the broader issue for Catholic feminists was the place of women in the church. The Vatican actions added to a sense of alienation many Catholic women already felt. While estrangement is not unique to Catholic women, it appears in greater numbers in the Catholic Church than in other denominations, according to some surveys. Four out of five Catholic women who participated in one study said they often felt alienated from the institutional church because of gender-exclusive language and emphasis on the strong male imagery of God.[40]

Letter on Women

For at least a generation, beginning with *Humanae Vitae*, the encyclical that reaffirmed the church's opposition to artificial birth control, and *Roe v. Wade*, the Supreme Court decision legalizing abortion, the gap between Catholic women and the church hierarchy appeared to grow by the year. Even women opposed to the legalization of abortion expressed indignation when they saw male prelates monopolizing the abortion debate. The feeling was widespread among women, regardless of outlook, that the formation of an abortion morality without women's input simply could no longer do. As tensions around a host of issues dealing with women's issues grew the bishops found themselves under substantial pressure to provide relief. Word continued to be sent to Rome that U.S. Catholics were becoming increasingly disaffected with the church. Dating back to the early 1980s, for example, the bishops sent word to Rome that the exclusion of girls as altar servers was causing morale problems in the parishes. Rome said it would take the matter under advisement, doing nothing to forward the discussion. The result was that in parishes throughout the country, priests simply went ahead and allowed the practice. Most bishops were forced to look the other way. Some, under pressure from conservatives who reported infractions to Rome, spoke out against altar girls, knowing full well that parishes would continue to disregard their words. It ended up being a kind of game—but at the cost of the continued erosion of church authority. It wasn't until 1994 that Rome finally sent word that girls could serve at the altar, at the discretion of the local bishop. All but two bishops gave their blessings to the practice. The two who did not, Bishops Fabian W. Bruskewitz of Lincoln, Nebraska, and Bishop John R. Keating of Arlington, Virginia, notoriously conservative prelates, argued that allowing girls to serve at the altar would discourage young boys from becoming priests.

Through the 1980s, the altar-girl issue was just one more visible sign, along with exclusive language and the male domination of the abortion discussion, of Rome's recalcitrance and its seeming unwillingness to understand U.S. culture. It was one more issue women could point to, along with the usual list of gender-related topics, that, they said, forced them into a distinct "second class" citizenship within the church. In an ironic twist, the growing priest shortage was at the same time forcing the church increasingly to rely on women to help keep the church operating, especially in rural areas. In a number of cases, bishops were forced to choose between closing a parish or placing a woman in charge as a parish administrator. In theory, a priest would remain the official pastor, perhaps occasionally visiting the church, but in reality it was a woman's operation. By the early 1990s, there are some 240 "priestless" parishes in the United States. Three-quarters of them were "pastored" by women. Some of the women in those leadership positions were among the most talented in the church, having been scrutinized carefully before being allowed to take on a parish. Reports showed that the early reluctance of some parishes to give up their priest quickly turned around as parishioners, guided by the woman administrator, found that their parish continued to function smoothly. In some cases, the loss of a priest forced the laity to take greater responsibility for the parish operation, and this had the unexpected result of raising parish involvement and morale. Nevertheless, whoever is running the parish, church law demands that the final responsibility rests with an ordained priest. Further, as the trend of women administrators spread, Rome sent word to the U.S. hierarchy to cut back on the practice. Some women found that their contracts were not being renewed. Faced with a woman heading a parish, some dioceses appeared to opt for closing the church.[41]

Under pressure to somehow improve the status of women in the church, the U.S. bishops in 1983 set out to write a pastoral letter dealing with women's concerns. Many Catholic women were suspicious of the idea from the start. Some believed that a group of men could never pull it off and wanted to watch at a distance. Others hoped the process might sensitize the prelates to women's growing disenchantment. Finally, there were those who were outspoken in their opposition to the idea. Women aren't the problem, they argued: Patriarchy is the problem; sexism is the problem; male chauvinism is the problem; a skewed, distorted, and enslaved theology of God is the problem. Write papers about those issues, but don't write one about women.[42] The Vatican, meanwhile, harbored its own doubts. Some in Rome thought it would not be wise to write a pastoral on the subject. It would be better, they said, if the U.S. bishops wrote a study guide or a discussion packet or a diocesan information program, but not an official, open, teachable pastoral letter on women.

The idea was first put forth by Bishop Michael McAuliffe of Jefferson City, Missouri, in 1982. It was not until two years later, one year after the bishops officially approved the idea, that they announced the formation of a six-bishop drafting committee headed by Joliet, Illinois, Bishop Joseph Imesch, who was to work with the help of seven women consultants. Through 1985 and 1986, an estimated seventy-five thousand women participated in consultations sponsored by the U.S. bishops in dioceses, on college campuses, and on military bases across the nation. The bishops listened to a cross section of Catholic women, including mothers, professionals, housewives, theologians, leaders of Catholic women's organizations, and members of religious orders. In April 1988 after long deliberations and writing, the committee issued its first draft. It was punctuated throughout with the diverse and sometimes critical voices of women heard in the consultations. With the draft in hand, the bishops began stage two of the process, more nationwide consultations with women gathering still more reactions for yet another stab at the letter. Meanwhile, in June 1988 the U.S. bishops at a gathering in Collegeville, Minnesota, met to discuss the first draft. Their reactions, too, were varied and recorded to be incorporated into the second draft. The following September, Pope John Paul II met with a group of U.S. bishops at the Vatican and spoke to them about the first fruits of their efforts:

> *In dealing with the specific rights of women as women, it is necessary to return again and again to the immutable basis of Christian anthropology as it is foreshadowed in the scriptural account of the creation of man—as male and female—in the image and likeness of God. Both man and woman are created in the image of the personhood of God, with inalienable personal dignity and in complementarity—one with the other. Whatever violates the complementarity of women and men, whatever impedes the true communion of persons according to the complementarity of the sexes offends the dignity of both women and men.*
>
> *Through the first draft of your proposed document on the concerns of women for the church and society, I know that you are making real efforts to respond with sensitivity to these greatly varying concerns, by presenting women as partners in the mystery of the redemption as this mystery is lived out in our day. You are rightly striving to help eliminate discrimination based on sex. You are also rightly presenting Mary, the mother of God, as a model of discipleship and a sign of hope to all, and at the same time as a special symbol and model for women in their partnership with God in the ministry of the church.*
>
> *Throughout the whole church a great prayerful reflection still remains to be made on the teaching of the church about women and about their dignity and vocation. I have already announced my own intention to publish a document on this subject, and this document will come out shortly. The church is determined to place her full teaching, with all the power with which divine truth is invested, at the service of the cause of women in the modern*

> *world—to help clarify their correlative rights and duties, while defending their feminine dignity and vocation. The importance of true Christian feminism is so great that every effort must be made to present the principles on which this cause is based, and according to which it can be effectively defended and promoted for the good of all humanity. The seriousness of this commitment requires the collaboration not only of the entire college of bishops but also of the whole church.*[43]

Weeks later Pope John Paul II issued his own letter on women, titled *Mulieris Dignitatem* ("On the Dignity of Women"). The letter stressed "complementarity" as the anthropological and theological foundations for assessing the dignity of each sex. It spoke out against the discrimination toward women who, the pope said, "ought to be recognized as cooperators in the mission of the church in the family, professional life and the civil community." It went on to stress the church's high esteem "for virginity and reverence for motherhood" calling Mary the "exemplar of life for all Christians, but especially for women."[44]

While supportive of women's roles in the world, the statement's theology was traditional and ended up serving as a theological guide for the U.S. bishops' second draft, released in March 1990, and all subsequent drafts. Partnership was to be replaced by complementarity as the official norm in male-female relationships within the church. That one letter by a pontiff can have this effect speaks to the power of the office of the papacy in the modern age. Yet ideas rarely die. Sometimes they go underground or simply await to be expressed on another day—as even the pope would learn.

That second draft took a conservative turn; some of the

women's voices that had appeared in the first draft were dropped along the way. Whereas the first draft held open the possibility of discussing matters such as birth control and ordination of women to the priesthood, the second draft deleted controversial issues and affirmed the church ban on ordination of women. The second draft, meanwhile, had a stronger defense of church teaching on birth control and eliminated the following controversial passage: "Consulting with women on matters pertaining to birth control will contribute to church teaching on sexuality." The second draft contained no fewer than twenty references to the pope's letter that made a special point to emphasize the "complementarity" versus equality of women and men. The second draft contained a section about Christian feminism, distinguishing it from "radical feminism" and warning against goddess worship, changing sexual morals, and a pro-choice abortion stance. The second draft did endorse inclusive language at a human level (*humanity*, instead of *mankind*, for example), but cautioned against applying it to God-language, including references to God the Father.

The bishops had planned to debate and vote on the document at their annual Washington meeting in November 1991, but in September the Vatican stepped in, requesting that the discussion be postponed pending further consultations with Vatican officials and other leading bishops from around the world. For those U.S. bishops who wanted to get on with it and for women still hopeful that the pastoral might actually say something positive, the Vatican intervention amounted to obstructionism.

Conservatives, however, celebrated the move, recognizing that it could only mean the pastoral would take an even more conservative bent. In May 1991, the U.S. bishops' drafting committee spent two days at the Vatican in consultations and left openly discouraged. By then, the U.S. bishops had been involved in the process for nearly eight years, and they were weary, increasingly torn between the demands of Rome and the expectations of U.S. women. The Vatican told the visiting delegation it thought it best that the pastoral be downgraded to a simple statement, that there needed to be more in the document on the humility of Mary, and that the complementarity of women should be further emphasized. It was not what the bishops wanted to hear. Interviewed by telephone from Rome, a beleaguered Bishop Imesch said he was disappointed following the meeting. "I think we put in a significant amount of time; we had considerable consultation," he said. "I think what we have expressed are the concerns of American women. I don't think we can alter what their feelings are, what their impressions are, what their reality is. If that is not acceptable, then I don't know where we go from here."[45] Imesch said the Vatican consultants expressed the belief the U.S. pastoral drafters had not spoken "sufficiently as bishops" but simply repeated the concerns of women. Some consultants, he said, also criticized the drafting committee for consulting only "radical" feminists. "We clarified that the women we consulted would hardly be called radical feminists," Imesch countered—but to no avail. The Rome consultants also said that the pastoral should include a more in-depth treatment of "biblical anthropology" in light of the pope's letter on women. The U.S. delegation was further told that the pastoral needed to develop the "Marian dimension" of the church, Imesch said. That dimension, spelled out in the pope's letter, included "the aspect of servanthood, lowliness and humility, which is emphasized in the life of Mary," he said. Five Vatican officials and bishops from thirteen countries besides the United States had been involved in the meetings. Imesch said it was impossible to convey to them the thoughts and feelings of U.S. women that had come out of many years of consultations.

Commenting on the meeting, Monika Hellwig, Landegger Professor of Theology at Georgetown University in Washington, D.C., said it showed that the U.S. bishops were "caught in a trap." There was no way they could compromise between expectations of American women and those of the Holy See, she said. As for calls for more Mariology and anthropology, she said they masked a "hidden agenda" that included centralization of power at the higher levels of the institution. "I don't throw myself heavily into [advocating] women's ordination because it's useless to tackle that issue head-on while the hidden agenda is not confronted," said Hellwig, adding that "some of the greatest pressure" for women priests is coming from parts of Asia, South Africa, and Latin America because of priest shortages—belying claims made by conservatives that ordination is primarily a U.S. women's concern.[46]

Back from Rome, Imesch's committee returned to the drafting board. In March 1992, the bishops' administrative committee, consisting of several dozen bishops, approved sending a third draft to the bishops for discussion at a June meeting to be held at the University of Notre Dame. That draft, while accommodating Vatican concerns, condemned the "sin of sexism" while giving strong support to the church's "unbroken tradition" of calling only men to ordained priesthood. It was released for public consideration in April 1992. While retreating on theology, the bishops pledged to work toward improving wages for women and guaranteeing equal treatment for all persons under the law. With regard to their own house, they said the ability of deacons and priests to work cooperatively with women was considered so important that a seminarian's "incapacity to treat women as equals" ought to be considered a "negative indicator for fitness for ordination." The third draft, meanwhile, expanded on the second draft's description of Mary as a disciple, placing new emphasis on her role as "mother of the church" and a person who practiced "obedient faith." Gone from the document were the second draft's statements encouraging "participation by women in all liturgical ministries that do not require ordination"; discussion of Christian feminism; the rationale for not ordaining women to the priesthood; and quotations from Catholic women who commented on church teaching during a series of consultations.

At their June 1992 Notre Dame meeting, the bishops took a straw vote on the third draft and decided to move ahead toward a final vote the following November. But it was still unclear whether they would be able to agree by then on what to say or how to say it. The third draft received mixed reviews among the bishops. Of those who spoke up, the majority appeared to want it to take a more conservative tack. Archbishop William J. Levada of Portland, a strong conservative voice in the church, agreed to write the fourth draft. At Notre Dame, along with Auxiliary Bishop Alfred C. Hughes of Boston, Levada had issued a minority report to the third draft, objecting that it had not adequately upheld official church teaching on women. Meanwhile, a growing number of more progressive bishops were saying they simply wanted the pastoral letter shelved. They felt it had become too much of an embarrassment to the bishops' conference.

The following September, the administrative committee

released the fourth and what turned out to be the final draft of the pastoral, making no recommendation on how the full body of bishops should handle it. The fourth draft decried sexism but added other evils adversely affecting women. Among these other evils, it cited the sexual revolution, some forms of feminism, and social laws and policies that try to treat men and women alike. It called for advancing the rights and dignity of women in society and the role of women within the church—provided they did not go beyond the strict limits set by official church teaching.

When the vote finally came, two days into the bishops' November 1992 meeting, 137 bishops voted in favor and 110 voted against. According to conference rules, 190 votes, or two-thirds of the 285 eligible voting bishops, were needed for approval. Never before in the history of the bishops' quarter-century-old conference had a pastoral letter—the most authoritative conference teaching statement—been rejected. After nearly ten years, what turned out to be a fiasco was finally over. A number of factors led to the pastoral's defeat, including the fourth draft's sharp move to the Right and episcopal reaction to that shift. Early in the debate, Archbishop Weakland spoke against passage, warning it could create a reaction within the church as far-reaching as that caused by *Humanae Vitae*, the 1968 papal encyclical prohibiting artificial contraception. Passage, he said, "would lose another generation, especially another generation of very wonderful women." Known to be the most progressive U.S. archbishop, Weakland's views carried significant weight in the bishops' conference, although it, too, had shifted to the Right considerably during the pontificate of Pope John Paul II by his supervision of consistently conservative episcopal appointments. Another factor had been heavy lobbying by Catholic groups, especially women who told local bishops of their opposition. And finally there was a strong resentment among many U.S. bishops that Rome had inserted itself too forcefully into the deliberations.

Many Catholic women said they were pleased by the final vote. One was Loretto Sister Maureen Fiedler, a leader of an organization called Catholics Speak Out, which lobbied against the pastoral. She said that "massive grass-roots lobbying" led to the pastoral's defeat and that Vatican pressures further separated the bishops from Catholic women and, in the end, helped assure the pastoral's defeat. With each passing draft, the voices of Catholic women had faded, replaced by increasingly traditional church exhortations on women's roles within the church. As for many U.S. women, with some exceptions on the Far Right, the end came with both tears and laughter, the former because of the pain so many felt, the latter from watching the spectacle of men pronouncing on women's concerns as a means to placate their growing anger.

Near the end of the ten-year process, after the third draft had been released and before the fourth was written, Dominican Sister Maria Riley wrote an analysis of the situation from a Christian feminist perspective.[47] Referring to the third draft, she wrote the following:

> *While clearly condemning "sexism as a moral and social evil," the document has no analysis of patriarchy, the political, economic, social, cultural and ecclesial structure that sustains and legitimates the sin of sexism. Without such an analysis, the recommendations for eradicating the sin of sexism are limited to individualistic "conversion of heart" and changing sexist atti-*

> *tudes. Granted, such conversion is central to the Christian message. However, many people, women and men, have been through this conversion of heart over the past several decades, but the patriarchal structures remain securely in place, particularly in the church.*
>
> *In the process of developing the three drafts, the committee has obviously worked to articulate a theological anthropology that seeks to avoid the dualism obvious in many church documents when discussing women and their "proper roles," "according to their nature," implying that woman's nature is different from man's. However, the bishops are a bit disingenuous when they condemn "some theorists" who suggest a dual human nature without admitting that the church itself, through its traditional approaches to women, has, in fact, promoted this kind of dualism. The question of how to express both the radical equality and the sexual differences between women and men will continue to be a central debate in theology, social theory and social policy for some time to come. . . .*

There was a twist of irony to the conclusion of the story of the bishops' pastoral letter on women. Less than a week before the bishops gathered in Washington to vote to scrap the effort, the Anglican Church voted its approval of women's ordination. That vote assured that the issue of the ordination of Catholic women would not be divorced, in anyone's eyes, from the bishops' deliberations. Said the visibly disappointed Bishop Imesch when it was nearly all done: "A number of bishops are very uncomfortable with the prohibition on discussing the issue of women's ordination. They have difficulty with saying this is a nondiscussable issue." The debate on ordination of women in the Catholic Church, he said, "will proceed with or without us."

Imesch's assessment appeared correct. In the months that

followed, Catholic episcopal voices were no longer heard in the women's ordination discussion, which continued unabated. The Women's Ordination Conference went ahead with plans for its 1995 meeting. Out of deep conviction but also seemingly feeling the need to defend his position, Pope John Paul repeatedly defended his ban on the ordination of women as priests. He even suggested that attempts to reverse it were misguided efforts to attain power. In one instance, in a twenty-page apostolic letter to priests to mark 1995 Holy Thursday ceremonies, the pope, speaking on the importance of women in the lives of priests, reiterated his conviction that the priesthood, on biblical grounds, is the sole province of men because Jesus chose only men as his apostles. "By the will of Christ only men are admitted," he wrote.[48] In his letter, the pontiff challenged dissidents who have claimed the ban on women priests is discriminatory. "Today in some quarters the fact that women cannot be ordained priests is being interpreted as a form of discrimination," he wrote. "But is this really the case? Certainly, the question could be put in these terms if the hierarchical priesthood granted a social position of privilege characterized by the exercise of 'power.' But this is not the case: the ministerial priesthood, in Christ's plan, is an expression not of domination but of service!" Many Catholic women, of course, saw it differently. "Men fear the fact that women might treat them the way they treat women," Ruth Fitzpatrick, national coordinator of the Women's Ordination Conference responded.[49] "It is like the South during the civil rights era. Whites were afraid that blacks, if they got power, would lynch whites the way whites lynched blacks. We're not going to 'lynch' men. But I still don't understand why they are so terrified of opening the door to women."

In his letter, the pope repeated his complementarity theme, saying the importance of women is in their role as mothers and nurturers. He lauded the world's 950,000 Catholic nuns for their "guarantee of selflessness."[50]

Only weeks before, however, leaders of the Jesuit order, the Catholic Church's largest male religious order, after ten weeks of meeting in Rome for their 34th General Congregation, issued a statement on women in sharp contrast to those that had come out of the Vatican over the years. At the conclusion of their gathering, attended by more than 200 Jesuit leaders from around the world, the order issued a series of statements outlining the mission and goals of the coming years. Since the order normally meets for a general congregation once every dozen or so years, what the Jesuits had to say was viewed in the church as important themes, the outlines of a twenty-first-century Catholic vision of church. It was all the more important, then, that the Jesuits issued a uncompromisingly strong affirmation of the roles of women in church and society. The Jesuits even went beyond the theme of "partnership" into one of "solidarity." They came to the belief that they needed to issue a statement on women in their assessments concerning the pressing social justice needs of the modern world. The Jesuit statement began by acknowledging the traditional "dominance of men in their relationship with women."[51] It lamented this relationship and the way women continue to face discrimination and violence throughout the world. "The original plan of God was for a loving relationship of respect, mutuality and equality between men and women, and we are called to fulfill this plan," the letter stated. Then, speaking with considerable candor about the failings of their religious tradition, the letter asked Jesuits to undergo a conversion of heart:

. . . we Jesuits first ask God for the grace of conversion. We have been part of a civil and ecclesial tradition that has offended against women. And, like many men, we have a tendency to convince ourselves that there is no problem. However unwittingly, we have often been complicit in a form of clericalism which has reinforced male domination with an ostensibly divine sanction. By making this declaration we wish to react personally and collectively, and do what we can to change this regrettable situation. . . .

Many women have helped to reshape our theological tradition in a way that has liberated both men and women. We wish to express our appreciation for this profound contribution of women, and hope that this mutuality in ministry might continue and flourish. . . .

We invite all Jesuits to listen carefully and courageously to the experience of women. Many women feel that men simply do not listen to them. There is no substitute for such listening. More than anything else it will bring about change. Without listening, action in this area, no matter how well-intentioned, is likely to bypass the real concerns of women and to confirm male condescension and reinforce male dominance. Listening, in a spirit of partnership and equality, is the most practical response we can make, and is the foundation for our mutual partnership to reform unjust structures.

Second, we invite all Jesuits, as individuals and through their institutions, to align themselves in solidarity with women. The practical ways of doing this will vary from place to place and from culture to culture, but many examples come readily to mind:

- *Explicit teaching of the essential equality of women and men in Jesuit ministries, especially in schools and universities.*
- *Support for liberation movements for women which oppose their exploitation and encourage their entry into political and social life.*

- *Specific attention to the phenomenon of violence against women.*
- *Appropriate presence of women in Jesuit ministries and institutions, not excluding the ministry of formation.*
- *Genuine involvement of women in consultation and decision-making in our Jesuit ministries.*
- *Respectful collaboration with our female colleagues in shared projects.*
- *Use of appropriately inclusive language in speech and official documents.*
- *Promotion of the education of women and, in particular, the elimination of all forms of illegitimate discrimination between boys and girls in the educational process.*

The Jesuits are one of the most influential forces within the Catholic Church. That they saw the need to speak out on the women's issue as they did could not go unnoticed. It almost certainly added to the enormously explosive energies building within Catholicism surrounding questions of gender and sexuality as the Church approached another century and millennium. At a critical point in church history, the Vatican, it seemed, was controlling the immediate church agenda, but not the wider church dynamics. The outcome of the struggle to integrate women into the authority structures was far from completion. Women's voices were not going away, and large numbers of them have continued to demand radical reform. Catholic men, meanwhile, it seemed, were of divided mind on the issues, but growing numbers, reflecting women's views, could no longer separate these questions from the basic justice concerns of the church.

VIII

Carnal Love

The Franciscan priest Richard Rohr is a popular preacher and founder of the Center for Action and Contemplation in Albuquerque, New Mexico, where he offers retreats and teaches through storytelling. He tells the story of an experience he had in the Philippines and the insights it gave him about how different cultures view sexual acts differently.[1] Rohr spoke about masturbation, but told the story through the eyes of a young Filipino Franciscan.

"I sometimes wonder why I became a Franciscan," Rohr recalled the young man saying. "I hope this doesn't shock you, but when a young Filipino boy can first get the seed there's no shame associated with that. That first masturbation is a moment of glory and breakthrough. I know you won't understand this, but I came running into the schoolyard with the seed in my hand. All my classmates came crowding around me, and I exclaimed, 'I got the seed, I got the seed.' All the little guys were looking at it, and this meant that I was a man. Now why would that be bad or displeasing to God?"

The young Franciscan continued: "Then this old Franciscan walks up and says, 'What's that in your hand?' So I told him it's my first seed, and he said, 'Go wash your hand and don't come back.' And I could not understand. Why would that be displeasing? Why would the seed God put in our body be something I should be ashamed of?"

The church has long taught that masturbation is a serious sin. This negative view stems from centuries'-old Christian notions that see sex acts, unless intended for procreation, as sinful. This, in turn, can be traced to the Judeo-Christian Creation story: Adam and Eve, the Temptation, the Fall, concupiscence, and the banishment from Paradise. This leads to the Christian salvation story: the Incarnation, the life of Jesus, his death on the Cross and his Resurrection after three days. For ages this sacred story of good and evil has been set in the context of human sin and God's grace. The church, meanwhile, views itself as taking the place of Christ on earth to be God's visible sign of love, a source of grace, of sacraments while acting as an intermediary between sinful people and their divine Creator.

This story was also heavily shaped by idealist Greek philosophy, the teachings of Plato in particular. Many ancients viewed sex as the lowest part of human nature while seeing life as a conflict between the dark and light forces. Their dualistic thinking eventually permeated Christian thought: good and evil, grace and sin, soul and body. Above all, sex and by extension the temptresses, women, were viewed as threats to salvation. Christianity became so influenced by this thinking that sex within marriage was also suspect. Thomas Aquinas (1225–74) argued that the celibate life is to be preferred because it is "unseared by the heat of sexual desire."[2] Following Augustine's (354–430) theory on original sin, Thomas Aquinas also argued that Jesus had to be conceived virginally because sin is transmitted by the male seed.[3] Throughout virtually all of church history the only moral justification for sex in marriage was intercourse with the intention of procreation.

All this negativity, Rohr has written, is ironic for a religion that believes that God became flesh. "Of all the world religions," he wrote, "Christianity has the biggest bias against the body. This is a disastrous theology. If I were Satan, and if I wanted to destroy Christianity, I would work overtime to tempt Christians to hate the flesh. Because we are the only religion that ever believed that God became flesh."

Rohr continued: "The incarnation means that God moved from spirit to word to flesh. Jesus took on a body. He had genitals. He sweated. He defecated. It is an extraordinary leap to believe that God entered this world. And yet, as I have traveled the earth and seen different religions, I found we have the most negative attitude toward our body. Our bodies carry the most shame and guilt just for being a body. Maybe it's not so extraordinary. That's the way evil disguises itself. It turns the good around."[4]

Some of this Catholic negativity has begun erode, but only slowly and not without considerable resistance from powerful elements in the church hierarchy. The first historic breakthrough occurred in the mid-1960s at the gathering of bishops in Rome for the Second Vatican Council. For the first time, marital sex was dignified and conjugal pleasure was blessed and depicted as enhancing mutual respect and love, not merely contributing to the continuation of the human race. The breakthrough came with the promulgation of the council document, *The Church in the Modern World*. This is what it said about full sexual sharing:

> *Such love, merging the human with the divine, leads the spouses to a free and mutual gift of themselves, a gift proving itself by gentle affection and by deed. Such love pervades the whole of their lives. Indeed, by its generous activity it grows better and grows greater. . . .*
>
> *This love is uniquely expressed and perfected through the marital act. The actions within marriage by which the couple are united intimately and chastely are noble and worthy ones. Expressed in a manner which is truly human, these actions signify and promote that mutual self-giving by which spouses enrich each other with a joyful and a thankful will.*

This more supportive view of marital sexuality was part of a wider shift that occurred in the church during the council. The very language and image of God, of church, and even of sin changed dramatically at that time, setting the church on an entirely new course.

The traditional view of God as a God of judgment, deciding to send some to heaven and others to hell, was transformed into a God of compassion and love, a God who understands and forgives. Both the preconciliar and postconciliar notion of God, of course, show up throughout the Judeo-Christian story. One or another, however, has generally dominated the Catholic psyche.

The image of God was not the only important image to change at the council. The bishops who gathered in Rome rewrote the very definition of church. Traditionally viewed as an institution made up of a hierarchy of bishops, priests, and nuns with the laity at the bottom of the pyramid, the church was redefined by the council as the "People of God." The consequences of this change for most Catholics were enormous.

The concept of medieval monarchical hierarchy was replaced by one of bishops as pastors and shepherds. The notion of a church frozen in tradition and time was replaced by a sense of people on a journey in time. The notion of working for personal perfection to gain heavenly reward was replaced by the idea that the Christian task is to work as peacemakers and builders of justice to bring about the reign of God on earth. As the People of God make their way, they do not always have the answers. Traditional Catholic triumphalism was replaced by the need to "discern" the Spirit of God in the world and to be guided by the "signs of the times." Thus "truth" is no longer something merely proclaimed but is discerned through prayer and experience. The new Catholic vision is bold and empowering. This is the church not existing to fight the world but to be a leaven within it—to guide, mold, and shape the world as it learns from modern insights wherever they might be found.

Gone or diluted in this postconciliar notion of church was the idea that all authority trickled down from the pope and the bishops; truth was no longer an exclusively episcopal domain, even as the bishops remained the principle preservers and teachers of faith. The vision of church as the People of God allows for Catholic experience, as a teaching guide, to again emerge. Catholic tradition has long placed trust in the "sense of the faithful," that is, it has taken seriously those beliefs that emerge out of Catholic experience.

Without affirmation by the people, a church teaching becomes suspect. It follows that any overwhelming rejection of an official church teaching by the laity is reason to believe that teaching is in error. Many Catholics argue that this is precisely the case with regard to official church teaching on birth control, rejected by nine out of ten adult Catholics in the United States as well as by most priests and many bishops. Some would extend that argument to include other church teachings on sexual morality.

Finally, another major shift occurred at the Second Vatican Council, involving the language of sin. Traditionally, Catholics were taught that there are two kinds of sin: mortal and venial. If one dies in the state of mortal sin, that is, before confessing to a priest and receiving absolution, mortal sin means eternal damnation. To die in the state of venial sin means to be sent to purgatory, a kind of temporary hell where the soul remains until purged of all sin. After Vatican II, this traditional language was replaced with a new language that sees sin as human failings involving more immediate and worldly consequences, both personal and social in nature. Instead of threatening hell, Catholic religious education textbooks began to speak of the consequences of the misdirection of sex, including premarital sex. Such consequences include possible pregnancy, sexually transmitted diseases, and a diminished relationship. For example, explaining why the Catholic Church teaches that premarital sex is wrong, a popular high-school religious textbook states the following:

> *The church sees sexual relations as an expression of deep love between two people—love so profound that the two individuals pledge themselves to mutual, lifelong commitment in marriage.*

The sexual intimacy that expresses that love should be the full meeting and sharing of body, mind and heart; it is not to be taken lightly, as mere recreation for people who are not committed to each other.

We are sexual beings, blessed with sexuality so that we can bring about new life—children, love between a man and woman, and other relationships that flow from creating family. Sexuality, like all fragile gifts, must be handled with care. It requires stability based on the commitment that marriage promises.[5]

Decades, even centuries, from now church historians may look back at the Second Vatican Council's stress on God's love and mercy as its most lasting legacy. How the church looks at itself, its mission, its teachings, all are shaped by the way the church imagines God and teaches about God. Intended or not, the God of love has resulted in a lifting from the collective Catholic psyche of the fear of sin and hell. This does not mean Catholics have stopped believing in sin or hell, although some have. It means rather that they are less inclined to think that an all-merciful God could create anyone to be condemned to eternal damnation. And as the council challenged Catholics to take Scripture more seriously, to pattern their lives on the life of Jesus, to formulate conscience, to take responsibility for their actions, many began to question traditional church teachings, especially those dealing with sexuality. For many those teachings simply did not square with gospel values, at least they did not appear to emerge out of those values, and certainly they did not square with personal experience. Among those who found teaching in conflict with experience were married couples facing birth control, gay and lesbian persons facing church prohibitions of homosexual acts, and women being told they could not speak of God as mother or encourage daughters to be priests in the church.

Catholicism from the mid-1960s to the mid-1990s has been a somewhat schizophrenic religion torn between those who embraced Vatican II and wanted more and those who were troubled by its results and wanted less. The church of the past generation has been in conflict between those Catholics who saw in the council's actions the birth of more mature religious belief and those who saw in them the weakening of old practices and structures. Few Catholics who were adults at the time of the Second Vatican Council are indifferent to it. While verbally endorsing the reforms of the council, the pontificate of Pope John Paul II has worked to restore traditional teachings. In the forefront of this restoration effort has been the pope's emphasis on traditional Catholic morality, especially in regards to matters of sexuality.

While the Second Vatican Council remains the most formative Catholic event since the Protestant Reformation, more than a few of those theologians who most actively embraced its changes have in recent years been marginalized by the Vatican, some having been termed Catholic "dissenters." Nowhere has the conflict been more striking than in the field of moral theology, which is undergoing enormous change and, at the same time, enormous resistance to that change. The current state of Catholic moral theology has been described "as changing from a classicist worldview, composed of static essences, abstract and universal principles, deductive reasoning, preestablished norms, and authority to a post-Enlightenment worldview that is historical, dynamic in its understanding of reality, inductive in its method, and open to new data and experience in its formulations of moral truth."[6]

Considering for a moment the question of masturbation, the newer theology would hold it is not necessarily an "intrinsically evil" act and that circumstances would have to be weighed before forming a moral judgment. An inductive approach to considering masturbation might suggest that if it becomes habitual it might be a symptom of some other serious problem. The traditional moral theology, meanwhile, would view masturbation as a serious sin, an offense against the natural order as intended by God and taught by the church. This teaching dates back to Thomas Aquinas, who wrote the book on natural law theology and viewed the secretion of semen as in accord with nature only within marriage and during a sexual act intended for procreation.[7] Following this reasoning, the 1994 official *Catechism of the Catholic Church*, employing a traditional classicist approach, calls masturbation an "intrinsically and gravely disordered action."[8] The catechism, quoting from *Persona Humana*, a document published by the Congregation for the Doctrine of Faith, says the following:

> *By masturbation is to be understood the deliberate stimulation of the genital organs in order to derive sexual pleasure. "Both the Magisterium of the Church, in the course of a constant tradition, and the moral sense of the faithful have been in no doubt and have firmly maintained that masturbation is an intrinsically and gravely disordered action." "The deliberate use of the sexual faculty, for whatever reason, outside of marriage is essentially contrary to its purpose." For here sexual pleasure is sought outside of the "sexual relationship which is demanded by the moral order and in which the total meaning of mutual self-giving and human procreation in the context of true love is achieved."*

But even as this debate about moral theology continues and keeps young, bright Catholic theologians from entering the field of moral theology, a whole new field of theological and philosophical discussion has erupted in Catholicism in the past two decades fueled by the discoveries of modern science, by the growth in ecological awareness and sensitivities, and by a widespread hunger for meaning and contemporary spirituality. All this at first may seem removed from a discussion of sexuality. But it is not. Religions come to express and teach sexual values and ethics through religious stories, in the case of Christians, those contained in Scripture and passed down through church teachings. During the past twenty years, however, large numbers of Catholics are among those who have found new spiritual energy in another religious story, the creation-centered story, the story of the universe. While the traditional creation story begins with Adam and Eve, the new creation story beings with the big bang billions of years ago. This sacred story is not necessarily incompatible with the old sacred story, but it can lead to different insights and values, even different ways of ordering the moral issues of the day. This new sacred story has been gaining increasing attention among Christians, and since it is helping to shape the way many Christians look at themselves, creation, and relationships, this sacred story deserves further exploration.

Creation-Centered Spirituality

Catholicism expresses a belief in a Trinitarian God: Father, Son, and Holy Spirit. Or to use inclusive and nonsexist language: Creator, Redeemer, and Holy Spirit. At various times in church history one of the three images of God has stood out. In the West, the second person of the Trinity, the Christ figure, seems to have most shaped Catholic thought. In the East, the third person of the Trinity, the Holy Spirit, has been very influential and has emphasized Christian mysticism. What some Catholics now say is that contemporary spirituality and the needs of the world call for a greater emphasis on the first person of the Trinity, the Creator. They speak about the need to understand and embrace creation, life, and the delicate relationships that sustain it. While such a shift may seem subtle and need not exclude other approaches to the Trinitarian God, it can influence the way a believer looks at his or her religion and religious experience.

While a Jesus-centered theology would stress the human Redemption story, which, in turn, rests upon the anthropocentric Adam and Eve story, a Creator or creation-centered theology would stress the cosmic story, the creation of galaxies, of the solar system, of the planet, and the evolution of species, including humanity. This story incorporates the knowledge of modern science and sees relationship in complex webs of ecological support systems. Again, neither story need exclude the other, but depending on the story one chooses, different values and attitudes toward the body develop along the way. If the former stressed dualism, the later stresses process. If the former views God as transcendent, the latter sees God as part of all that is. If the former separates body and soul, the latter sees the two as one. Or, as Rohr has put it:

> *It has been widely assumed, for some strange reason, that our souls are in our bodies. And when our bodies die—according to this scenario—our souls go to heaven or hell or somewhere else. But it seems much closer to the truth to turn things around and say our bodies are part of a larger world-soul.*

> *Think of the body as incarnation. Whether we consider the smallest level, the cell, or the largest level, the cosmos, this truth stands out. And why wouldn't it be true of all the stages in between. All these parts are swirling around one another. . . . And each seems to think it is independent, but it's not.*[9]

For many Catholics creation-centered spirituality has unleashed enormous spiritual energy. In some ways the growth of a creation-centered outlook on life is highly compatible with Catholicism, a religion that emphasizes a sacramental approach to life. Sacraments are ordinary substances and actions that point believers toward the mystery of the divine. They are signs of God's love. They connect the ordinary with the extraordinary; they express relationships in acts of worship; they hint at the unity of all that is; and they express awe. The sacramental tradition beginning with Christian baptism and most frequently expressed in the shared breaking of bread and the drinking of wine in the Eucharistic celebration run deep in the Catholic faith. Finding God in nature and celebrating the connectedness of all of creation, then, as creation-centered spirituality does, is highly supportive of Catholic spirituality. It is not surprising that many Catholics have become leading figures in this spiritual-ecological field. One of the key insights that flows from a creation-centered view of things, is that the "original blessing," or creation itself, is the foundation truth and precedes the Fall and Original Sin by billions and billions of years. However, it has been sin, not blessing, that has so heavily influenced the Catholic outlook on human sexuality.

Consider this time line: First, reduce 15 billion years, an estimated age of the universe, down to one hundred years. With this contraction, *Homo sapiens*, the human species, appears only on the last day of the ninety-ninth year of that one-hundred-year period. The Neolithic Village Age, which included the domestication of plants and animals and goddess worship, begins at 11:20 P.M. on that last day and continues to 11:40 P.M. The age of classical religious culture of which we are a part begins at 11:40 P.M. and continues to this minute, 11:59 P.M. on the last day of the one-hundred-year span. Creation started a long time ago.

THOMAS BERRY

In the minds of most creation-centered spiritual thinkers, the leading figure during these past two decades has been a Passionist priest named Thomas Berry. A frail, driven man, he has just entered his eighth decade of life and sees himself as part of a larger effort to shake up humanity into ecological consciousness before the planet dies from human greed and shortsightedness. Berry lives with apparent peace of mind, but his demeanor conceals deep apprehensions. Since the 1988 publication of his book, *The Dream of the Earth,* Berry has been cited as the indisputable foundational figure, the Thomas Aquinas, of ecological theologians.[10] Environmentalists have long blamed biblical tradition—especially God's injunction to humanity in Genesis to "subdue the earth"—for providing cultural sanction for the Industrial Revolution and the plundering of nature. Berry is clearly among those who criticize Christianity for its preoccupation with "redemption out of this world through a personal Savior relationship that eclipses all concerns with cosmic order and process."[11] He has spoken about the need to put aside Scripture for a while to discover the sacredness in the natural order. Judaism and Islam, too, err in his eyes by overemphasizing humanity's relationship to a transcendent God. Mainline religions, he says, ignore humankind's primordial genetic attachment to the natural world. "The same atoms that formed the galaxies," Berry likes to say, "are in me." In short, God may be our father but Earth is truly our mother.

In his writings and talks, Berry insists on telling the creation story, the sacred story of the universe. He says it unites all religious stories. He sees it not only as a scientific story but a mystical tale.

Through the late 1970s and 1980s, Berry's ideas simmered at the edges of Catholic thought, even as they percolated more vigorously in the ranks of the environmental movement. But in the 1990s, the sometimes seemingly rebellious words of this Passionist priest, this self-proclaimed "geologian," have spread more rapidly in Catholic circles, whether in universities or at the social activist level. For many, Berry has become a kind of cult leader, a wise and mysterious guru. He is simple and unassuming. Virtually all the clothes he owns he wears or carries with him in a small suitcase when he travels.

Born in Greensboro, North Carolina, he was ordained a priest in 1942, spent ten years in monasteries, served as a chaplain in the North Atlantic Treaty Organization, taught Chinese and Indian history, studied Native American culture, and has served as president of the American Teilhard (de Chardin) Association. Today, he heads New York's Riverdale Center for Religious Research located along the Hudson River.

"Listen to these words carefully," Berry says. "The universe is a communion of subjects, not a collection of objects." He repeats his words slowly. "The universe is a communion of subjects, not a collection of objects." These two phrases,

Berry believes, unlock the secrets of proportion, relationship, humility, awe, prayer, Earth, sky, humanity, and sexuality. He also knows it takes time to digest, but says that if humanity would only become aware—really aware—of the sacredness of all relationships, it would understand the need and means to live in harmony and love. Failure to grasp this truth, however, could very well mean the failure to save the planet from ecological destruction.

He insists all ideas about God and God's relationship with humanity stem from nature. "Imagine," Berry says, "living on the moon and looking endlessly at the essentially flat and formless lunar landscape. If our planet's landscape were as barren as the moon's, our image of the divine would be just as barren. We derive our image of the divine from the natural order." He insists, "The environmental crisis is fundamentally a spiritual crisis." Berry maintains that humanity is at a crossroads of epochs. He speaks in biblical terms, using Exodus imagery: "We are now at a critical moment in evolutionary history. Either the human community will leave the desert to enter a new age, either it will live in harmony with the natural order, or both will perish in the desert."

"In biological terms, the planet Earth is at the end of the Cenozoic period. This is being terminated by the industrial economy that humans have imposed on the planet during these past two centuries. In this context, the major life-giving systems of the planet, air, water and soil are severely diminished in their life-giving capacities," Berry says. "To establish a viable situation for the earth community requires a transition from the Cenozoic to what might be termed the Ecozoic period of Earth history. [The problem is] we have ruined the Cenozoic mode of life expression before we have discovered our way into the Ecozoic. Strangely, we do not feel in an agonizing situation because we are only dimly aware of the order of magnitude of what is happening to the planet." Berry is one who feels the agony. He is fueled by it.

Berry lists twelve principles for understanding the universe and the role of humanity within it:

1. The universe, the solar system, and the planet Earth in themselves and in their evolutionary emergence constitute for the human community the primary revelation of that ultimate mystery whence all things emerge into being.
2. The universe is a unity, an interacting and genetically related community of beings bound together in an inseparable relationship in space and time. The unity of the planet Earth is especially clear; each being of the planet is profoundly implicated in the existence and functioning of every other being of the planet.
3. From its beginning the universe is a psychic as well as a physical reality.
4. The three basic laws of the universe at all levels of reality are differentiation, subjectivity, and communion. These laws identify the reality, the values, and the directions in which the universe is proceeding.
5. The universe has a violent as well as a harmonious aspect, but it is consistently creative in the larger arc of its development.
6. The human is that being in whom the universe activates, reflects upon, and celebrates itself in conscious self-awareness.
7. The Earth, within the solar system, is a self-emergent, self-propagating, self-nourishing, self-educating, self-governing, self-healing, self-fulfilling community. All particular life systems must integrate their functioning

within this larger complex of mutually dependent earth systems.

8. Genetic coding is the process through which the world of the living articulates itself in its being and its activities. The great wonder is the creative interaction of the multiple codings among themselves.
9. At the human level, genetic coding mandates a further transgenetic cultural coding by which specifically human qualities find expression. Cultural coding is carried on by educational processes.
10. The emergent process of the universe is irreversible and nonrepeatable in the existing world order. The movement from nonlife to life on the planet is a one-time event. So, too, the movement from life to the human form of consciousness. So, also, the transition from the earlier to the later forms of human culture.
11. The historical sequence of cultural periods can be identified as the tribalshamic period, the Neolithic village period, the classical civilization period, and scientific-technological period, and the emerging ecological period.
12. The main task of the immediate future is to assist in activating the intercommunion of all living and nonliving components of the earth community in what can be considered the emerging ecological period of earth development. Functionally, the great art in achieving the historical goal is the art of intimacy and distance, the capacity of beings to be totally present to each other while further affirming and enhancing the differences and identities of each.

Some Catholic moral theologians say they see in Berry's thought promising avenues for the development of their discipline.[12] One such theologian is Father Stephen Dunn from St. Michael's, Toronto School of Theology. Dunn looks out at Catholic moral theology and sees a troubled discipline. Most theologians, he says, have left the age-old classicist world although they have not all settled in a common new world. "Moral theology's intellectual categories are not yet at the point of consensus," he says, adding that what is needed is a new "intellectual matrix" that is comprehensive, religiously convincing, and culturally inclusive. Dunn says Berry's ideas might be providing such a matrix. Especially pleasing to Dunn is Berry's "macrophase perspective" in which the human is seen as "that being in whom the universe reflects on itself and celebrates itself in conscious self-awareness."

What can the moral theologian learn from Berry? Dunn lists these points: One, the community of all earth creatures is primary to ethical thought. Two, God's creation must be thought of as ongoing. Three, creation as a theological horizon must be more in evidence in ethical deliberation. Four, the religious dimension of life must be thought of as advocating participation in earth's time development processes. Natural law's "participation in the mind of God" becomes participation in the work of creation, a mysticism of earth participation, grounded in a deep ecological religious ethic. Five, Christ in the mystery of the Incarnation must be appreciated as participating in the evolution of the earth and the cosmos. Six, Christ in the mystery of Redemption must be appreciated in the totality of salvation history going back in time to the beginning of the universe and forward to the evolutionary future. Seven, revisioning becomes an essential task for ethics. And eight, the earth's urgencies become humanity's primary urgencies.

Berry, says Dunn, "has accomplished what Vatican II

aspired to achieve, transcending the dichotomous framework with which the Catholic community has been approaching the ethical and religious dimensions of reality. He therefore opens the door to an ethics that is participative, religious, and Christian."

MATTHEW FOX

No other writer has done more to popularize creation-centered spirituality than has Matthew Fox, the founding director of the Institute in Culture and Creation Spirituality at Holy Names College in Oakland, California. Like Berry, Fox maintains that the spiritual story begins with creation and cosmos. Cosmology, the story of the universe, Fox says, precedes anthropology, psychology, and all theology. The human story, he explains, is "the jewel" in the far larger story. Fox sees in creation-centered spirituality the reawakening of Christian awe and wonder as well as a more positive self-affirmation.[13] If all origins are sacred, he says, then human beings "are not here to bemoan our existence, to blame ourselves or others, or to wallow in our sinfulness. Rather, we are here to return blessing for blessing and to give our gift back to the larger community."[14]

Speaking at the College Theological Society's annual 1990 meeting at Loyola University in New Orleans, Fox defended his writings, saying they are an expression of "Trinitarian Christianity," although he added he thought it was time to de-emphasize what he called "Jesusolarity." Out of the new cosmic story comes a sense of awe, and out of awe and wonder comes new imagery of the divine. In his presentation, Fox said the following:

It is not just our manner of imaging our relationship with

> *divinity that is challenged by ecology. Rather, the very images of the Divinity to whom we relate also undergo change. Today, under the impetus of the paradigm shift from an anthropocentric and patriarchal theological model to a more curved and maternal one, there is occurring simultaneously a veritable explosion of images of God. New names for the divine one—that are often deeply ancient ones—are emerging from many places. For example: Godhead; Goddess; Isness; the Beloved; God as Mother; God as Caring Father, not Theistic Father; Great Spirit; Holy Spirit; Sophia; Cosmic Christ; Cosmic Wisdom, the Sacred; the Face behind the Face; Compassion; the "I am" in every creature; Beauty; Justice; Underground River; Life—all these invite us to rediscover the Divine all about us and within us.*[15]

Fox makes it clear he thinks Christians need to rediscover a sense of mysticism, buried in Christian tradition. With this mysticism comes passion, compassion, and awakened eros—and this is good, he says. "An awakened passion can lead to a renewal of compassion, a fuller, deeper living out of our interdependence with all creation."

In part because of his popularity and in part because of his provocative and iconoclastic style, Fox's ideas have been challenged by some in the church. He has been accused of neglecting the transcendent nature of God and of teaching a form of pantheism.[16] In 1988 the Vatican ordered him to stop teaching or speaking publicly for a year while they investigated his works, including his writings on creative ritual, feminism, and earth-based spiritualities. For years Fox had troubles with his Dominican superiors who asked that he leave California and return to Chicago to be in closer contact with the Dominican community. Finally, on April 15, 1994, Fox announced that he had left the Catholic Church and joined the Episcopal Church. "I don't have to deny my roots to know that I've grown beyond them," he explained a year after being dismissed from the Dominicans for refusing to return to Chicago. At the time he left the Catholic Church he said he planned to work to develop new worship rituals attractive to the young, adding that "to attempt to do innovative ritual within Roman Catholicism today is obviously not possible." Fox accused the pope of having "shut the windows" so as not to see "the suffering and pain among women, youth, native peoples, lesbians and gays and the earth creatures themselves."

Vatican Suspicions

Fox is only one of a list of Catholic Church figures who have gotten into trouble in recent years for allegedly deviating from the official church line on matters of human sexuality. In 1983, the Vatican began an investigation of Seattle Archbishop Raymond Hunthausen and found him guilty of assorted offenses, among them allowing contraceptive sterilization in hospitals and showing support for gay and lesbian Catholic groups. In 1985, Rome stripped Hunthausen of most of his episcopal authority, but in 1987 Hunthausen's powers were restored following strong protests by many U.S. Catholics and their bishops. Catholic theologians have been watched carefully. Father Charles Curran provoked a punishment. The Vatican's Congregation for the Doctrine of the Faith in 1986 revoked his license to teach theology at the Catholic University of America, Washington, D.C., because of his views on sexual and medical ethics, including artificial birth control and sterilization. Curran now teaches at Southern Methodist University.

Not only theologians have drawn adverse attention when

their work involves sexuality. Agnes Mary Mansour had been a Sister of Mercy for thirty years when, with the permission of Detroit's then Archbishop Edmund Szoka, she became director of the Michigan Department of Social Services in 1983. That department administered Medicaid funding for abortions. Although Mansour personally opposed abortion, she did not obstruct funding. At a meeting with the archbishop and a papal delegate only four months after she began the job, Mansour was told to resign the job or leave her order. She left the Mercy Sisters. Two other Mercy Sisters, Elizabeth Morancy and Arlene Violet, soon followed in Rhode Island where Morancy served in the legislature and Violet was attorney general.

Father Andre Guindon, a member of the Oblates of Mary Immaculate, was a professor of moral theology in St. Paul University, Ottawa, Canada, until his death from a heart attack in 1993. In his teachings and published works beginning in the mid-1970s, he tried to present sexual ethics in ways he viewed as compatible with traditional church teachings, ways that also make sense in the world today. His 1986 book, *The Sexual Creators: An Ethical Proposal for Concerned Christians,*[17] eventually came under scrutiny in Rome, and in 1992 it was severely criticized by the Congregation for the Doctrine of the Faith for the way it dealt with birth control, marriage, and homosexuality, among other issues. Guindon defended himself and explained that he had attempted to formulate a sexual morality that rested upon the opening words of the Christian Creed, specifically the phrase, "God, creator of heaven and earth." Guindon said that "any ethic which considers sexual activity as sullied a priori with a touch of evil postulates a dualism" that the church should not accept.

"This clashes directly with our faith in a Creator in whom no evil originates," he said. His efforts to construct a more positive view of sexuality won considerable support among Catholic theologians in Canada and the United States but no converts in Rome.

There have been numerous attempts in Catholic circles in the past two decades to place sexuality in a more positive light, even to see in sexual acts reflections of the divine. Catholic feminists have taken the lead in such writings. Hand in hand with this shift has been the depiction of God as mother or nurturer. Eroticism, rather than being viewed as a lapse from strict control of the body by the mind, is seen in this literature as a means of approaching God, as imagining divine love. To think that erotic experience can allow insights into divine truths is to turn traditional Catholic thinking on sex on its head—but this is precisely what a growing number of Catholics are doing in their writings and research. It is both an indication of deep and painful division within the church and a vibrancy that is likely to burst forth in some yet unknown direction in the years ahead.

Demetria Martinez, a Catholic novelist, is representative of this new genre of Catholic thought. She brings to her works a Latina earthiness and a longing for mystical love. Martinez has said that "acknowledging mysticism's roots in the erotic is one of feminism's key insights."

"Sensual enjoyment," she added, "might reveal more about the nature of the divine than abstract, doctrinal 'truths.' "[18]

She continues as follows:

> *This departs from Christianity's historical tendency to imagine the body (and by extension, women) as sinful. In the past twenty*

> *years a body of feminist literature has emerged identifying the erotic with not only what happens in bed but with the ability to understand the world through feeling. As such, the erotic is a source of power distinct from patriarchal definitions of power that pit reason against emotion, equating the latter with dark, mysterious forces (epitomized in the "feminine" archetype) that must be controlled, not honored. . . .*
>
> *To be present in one's body, attuned to emotions that heat and cool the blood, to honor gut feelings and the five senses—this way of awareness, also demands theological reflection. For not only is being grounded in the physical a way of experiencing the divine, but it is also a point of departure for spiritual healing. . . .*
>
> *We have the ingredients for an "erotic" religion, one that honors feeling and locates power in bodily wholeness (as in Jesus' healing miracles), but we have yet to assemble them in any meaningful way for women. Our tradition speaks of the "sacramental life," of Jesus as "man and God." But our theology and our stories (less so than our ritual) are impoverished to the degree that they abstract from detail—without which the erotic cannot exist.*
>
> *How did Mary feel during her pregnancy? What does it mean that the mother of God menstruated? Did Jesus enjoy eating? Did he feel sexual desire? The degree to which we flinch at these questions is a measure of how great the gulf is between faith and flesh. . . . When religion leaves the land, leaves ecstatic dance and prophetic chant, it becomes increasingly a matter of verbal exhortation, of moralistic rhetoric, where people are told what to feel and believe, because they no longer feel and believe it.*

While such writing may seem far from more traditional Catholic postulations about the divine, it does reflect new energies and a growing awareness that theological questions dealing with human sexuality need further examination and that many potential insights into Christian meaning await the exercise. Whether church authorities like it or not, Catholics writers are examining as never before what it means to believe in a religion that both honors creation and prays to a God who took on human flesh. Furthermore, with the development of the social sciences, Catholics and other believers are learning much more about what they think and how they feel about their religious beliefs and how these thoughts and feelings affect their lives. This is an unprecedented development in the history of religion. For centuries historians recorded what religion taught; now they are able to record how those teachings have or have not been received and integrated into peoples' lives.

ANDREW GREELEY

No one has studied and written more about the way sex relates to religion and shapes the lives of Catholics than has sociologist and novelist Father Andrew Greeley. His research in the early 1970s was the first to show that Catholics were overwhelmingly disregarding the 1968 birth control encyclical, *Humanae Vitae*, and that its publication had resulted in a serious eroding of episcopal church authority.

Greeley's values are contained in symbols, and symbols are contained in stories. So he writes Catholic stories, and his novels have sold in the millions. He speaks of the theology of story, saying that believers tell religious stories of themselves and others to help give meaning to their lives. He says these stories help predict the way people live out their lives. "The idea is that religion is, first of all, an experience of the holy, the sacred, the good, and then it's the image and the memory which recalls that experience, what we would call a symbol, and then it's the story we tell to others to explain the symbol and to recount our experience. That's religion," Greeley has said.[19]

The institutional church has not treated its people well, Greeley maintains. Church teachings on sexuality have not taken into account how Catholics engage in or look at their sexual experiences. He likes to note that the only time the hierarchy ever asked lay Catholics to contribute to a better understanding of sexuality—by allowing some to participate in the pontifical commission studying birth control—it entirely disregarded what they had to say. In his 1990 book, *The Catholic Myth,* he argues—and his research supports his position—that religion is more about imagination than it is about doctrine. Greeley writes: "Religion, I am convinced, is imaginative before it is propositional. It begins with experiences which renew hope, is encoded in images or symbols which become templates for action, is shared with others through stories which are told in communities and celebrated in rituals." The importance of this, says Greeley, is the need to grasp the insight that religious formation stems primarily from experience, what he terms the "popular tradition." Official teachings, or "the high tradition," are not nearly as important. This helps explain, he says, why so many disgruntled Catholics can criticize church authority, disregard its teachings on sexuality, and yet remain Catholic. Greeley says Catholics are remarkably faithful to their religious beliefs no matter how negative their experiences have been with the Catholic institution. Those beliefs, he says, work out of a deeper realm within the believer. Simply stated, he says, Catholics like being Catholic. They especially like the "sacramentality" of the church. By "sacramentality" he means the imaginative outlook that views creatures as metaphors for

God, as hints of what God is like. Greeley's research has shown that sacraments are at the top of Catholic lists of reasons why Catholics stay in the church.

In recent years, Greeley has aimed his sociological expertise at the way Catholics behave sexually. Through numerous studies and population samples, he finds strong linkage in married couples between erotic love and a healthy religious belief. "Falling in love is a delicious experience, obsessing, delightful, exhausting, exhilarating, frustrating, wonderful, terrifying," he has said.[20] "Yet, is the question of romantic love finally settled? May it not provide challenges to church teachers, to theologians and perhaps even to married people? Can romantic love last? Do some people live happily ever after? Is romantic love a subject about which the faithful ought to be consulted?"

Greeley certainly thinks so, noting that while neither the theological community nor the church's bishops would deny that lay experience contains valuable insights, few church leaders take the time to examine them. Romance, Greeley observes, "seems to result from a combination of religious and erotic behaviors that do not substitute for one another. Religious imagery, symbolism and behavior are intimately connected to romance: Half of those who think the spouse is godlike and who make love frequently"[21] (several times a week) report the strongest romantic feelings. "The greatest payoff in romance . . . comes from (or relates to) a mix of religion or religious images and frequent sex." In short, good sex is good for religion and good religion leads to healthy sex.

With these findings, he turns to the church theologians and bishops and poses six questions he feels they would benefit by answering:

1. Might not the romantic love depicted in those marriages most capable of sustaining it be the metaphor par excellence for the love of God for his people and of Jesus for his church?
2. Might not eros and erotic playfulness be an ultimate empirical correlate of marital indissolubility and hence a goal to be urged by religious teachers?
3. Might not the abandon of sexual inhibitions be one indicator of the disappearance of the protective barriers that represent sin in the world? As such, might not the goodness of such abandon be an appropriate matter for theological reflection and Christian education?
4. Does not the relationship between erotic play and religious imagery and devotion suggest that the biblical metaphor in which sexual love is taken to be a hint of divine love deserve to be taken more seriously and more concretely than most theologians and teaching authority pronouncements have thus far been willing to admit?
5. Should not theologians and teachers both reconsider their skepticism about romantic love and reflect on it as sacramental and, indeed, as Sacrament?
6. Should not the experience of romance and abandon in married love become a primary source of theological reflection both about marriage and sexuality.

One of Greeley's most provocative findings has been that Catholics enjoy sex more than most others—despite traditional negative teachings linking sin and sex. He research has found that despite the dark cloud that has hung over sexuality—what Greeley calls "the shadow of St. Augustine"—the sex lives of Catholics have generally not suffered. He attributes this to their tendency to pay more attention to Catholic "popular tradition" than to Catholic "high tradition." Some of Greeley's findings include the following:[22]

1. Sixty-eight percent of the Catholics as opposed to 56 percent of the others engage in sexual union at least once a week. Catholics are significantly more likely to have sex weekly or more often than all others combined and also more likely to have sex frequently than are Liberal and Fundamentalist Protestants.
2. Frequency of intercourse declines with age but less precipitously among Catholics than among others so that Catholics are one quarter again more likely than others to have sex at least once a week when they are fifty-five years or older (50 percent versus 40 percent).
3. Catholics—especially Catholic women—score significantly higher on the sexual playfulness scale. For example, Catholics are half again as likely (three out of ten as opposed to two out of ten) to say they have purchased erotic undergarments either often or sometimes. They are also significantly more likely to report showers or baths with their spouse.
4. On all three of these measures, the effect is strongest in endogamous Catholic marriages.

But are Catholics telling the truth about their sexual behavior? Greeley insists they are. The ones in the best position to answer that question are the spouses of Catholics who themselves are not Catholic, he says, and he has studied them as well. Here he found that Protestant men report more frequent intercourse with Catholic wives than wives who themselves are Protestant.

And why do Catholics enjoy sex so much? Greeley says

this is so because they bring a playfulness to their sex. And they do this because of the gracious images of God they carry within them, images fostered by their religion, images of benign human relationships—mother, spouse, friend, and lover—as metaphors of God.

Greeley has said the following:

> *The church's own metaphors suggest that the sexual bond is a story of human love, triumphant, defeated, and resurgent. The bonding love between God and humans is not the story of a single act or a group of single acts but rather a story of long and frequently reinforced relationship, one that is (from the human viewpoint at any rate) often marked by diminution and resurgence, decline and growth, near-death and rebirth, pleasure and pain and yet more pleasure. It is precisely this kind of image that has made the Catholic experience of sex . . . somewhat unique; and it is this imagery to which Catholics turn when they must make decisions about sex.*[23]

The stories contained in the profoundly Catholic images of "Spouse," "Lover," "Mother," and "Friend," are all stories of pleasure and passion that are sustained, Greeley has said, through a long process of bonding and not merely in certain isolated acts.

It would be wrong, however, to leave the impression that the discussion of carnal love, still in relative infancy, is about seeking pleasure and passion for its own sake. It is, instead, about integrating and understanding the body as sacred gift. It is about getting beyond mistrust and fear of the body, getting beyond excessive dualism and moving toward wholeness and health. Western culture, largely influenced by Christian theology over the centuries, has struggled to come to terms with the body, variously shrouding its expressions of physical intimacy with fear or, on the other hand, idolizing those expressions in ways that trivialize and demean. Missing has been the healthy balance between body as source of evil and body as source of self-gratification. Some say this is because Western culture has not taken body experience very seriously in doing theological reflecting; there has been little "body theology." And what is body theology? Most simply put, "it is doing theology in such a way that we take our body experiences seriously as occasions of revelation."[24] Reflecting on the Incarnation of Christ, it is to explore the mystery and meaning of a God who is at once fully spirit and fully flesh, a God who shares every aspect of what it is to be human. As appealing as it may be, however, it may not be possible to ever get completely beyond that dualistic thinking that separates spirit and flesh, casting one as good and the other as evil. James B. Nelson, professor of Christian Ethics at the United Theological Seminary of the Twin Cities, New Brighton, Minnesota, author of *Body Theology,* writes of a dualism "that splits us into the war of spirit versus body," and calls it an "enduring and fundamental problem."[25] He sees manifestations of this dualism in sexism, in homophobia and in often violent meanings of what he sees as our cultural masculinity—and not without even further serious widespread repercussions, which he lists as including social violence, racism, and ecological abuse. Integrating body and spirit and moving toward a healthier human sexuality is in Nelson's eyes to face "the most troubling and divisive question" facing churches today. Many other Christian ethicists, psychologists, and theologians would agree with him. They see it as a vital task aimed at reconditioning a religion and, indeed, a culture to look at human sexuality in a new and healthier light.

Writes Nelson, explaining the challenge:

> *Our sexuality, I believe, is a precious gift from God, critically important as part of a divine invitation. It is an invitation that we come together with each other and with God in relationships of intimacy and celebration, of faithfulness and tenderness, of love and justice. Our sexuality is a gift to be integrated fully and joyously into our spirituality. Our [sexual] orientations, whatever they may be, are part of that gift—to be received with thanksgiving and honored by each other.*[26]

Until recently, most Christian and Jewish writings about the body and sexuality were one-directional. They began with religion and moved to the body, not the other way around.[27] Exploring body theology is intended to reverse that direction and to help reflect on bodily experiences as a realm of the experience of God. Seen in this light, a Christian approach to sexuality is not primarily to codify rules to govern behavior as much as it is an opportunity to understand and celebrate God's infinite love and creation design. It is to recognize and honor and be thankful for a sacred and precious gift.

IX

Population

On the September, 1994, Cairo conference's opening day, women had already emerged as the new brokers of population and development issues. It did not auger well for the Vatican. Norway's prime minister, Gro Harlem Brundtland, gave a bold, hard-hitting speech, jumping fully into the religious debate that had so characterized months of preconference deliberations. Sending out a message aimed at the Vatican and Islamic fundamentalists, she said that religion should not be used to prevent women from having access to family-planning services. "Morality becomes hypocrisy if it means accepting mothers' suffering or dying as a consequence of unwanted pregnancies and illegal abortions. Decriminalizing abortion should be . . . a necessary means of protecting the lives of women," she said. The statement, which drew loud applause, seemed to indicate that women were not about to back down from their goal of having access to the full range of reproductive health services—regardless of who opposed them.[1]

The road to the International Conference on Population and Development in Cairo began in the 1950s when early voices and some governments first started to talk of the threat of rising populations, which, they said, were already straining some local resources and impeding development. A group of technical experts from seventy-four nations met in Rome in 1954 to discuss the issues. A similar conference was held in Belgrade in 1965. In the 1960s donor-funded, family-planning contraceptive programs were first launched in developing nations. By the mid-1990s more than half the women in the developing world were using some form of contraception. With these programs, however, came criticisms and controversy, not a small part of it coming from the Vatican. Some Third World nations saw imperialistic intent as well as violations of human rights in "population control" efforts. Out of this grew what was called the North-South divide, with the North (the richer, industrialized countries) pushing population control and the South (the poorer, less developed countries) seeking more development aid. This division reached its peak at the first U.N. World Population Conference, held in Bucharest, Romania, in 1974, a gathering that brought delegations from 136 countries. Out of hard negotiations emerged a document setting forth recommendations and principles eventually approved by all but one nation-state—the Vatican.

By 1984, some of the North-South division had curiously reversed itself. The second U.N. conference, this time held in Mexico City, drew delegates from 147 nations. Coping with painfully slow development issues, most nations of the

South by then acknowledged the need for family planning to stabilize population growth. The U.S. delegation, meanwhile, shaped by the anti-abortion Reagan administration and allied with the Vatican, declared population growth to be "a neutral phenomenon" as it related to development.[2] Following the conference, the U.S. "Mexico City policy," as it came to be known, significantly curbed financial aid to family-planning groups worldwide, arguing that these groups fostered or tolerated abortion. By 1992, the U.N. Population Fund could meet only a third of its requests for family-planning assistance.

There was little doubt among most international planners that something had to be done to curb the world's expanding population growth. By the mid-1990s the world population growth was at an all-time high. Some 94 million people—roughly the population of Mexico—were being added annually to the earth's population, then at 5.7 billion. More than 95 percent of these increases were occurring in the poorest nations where food supplies are at best modest. These increases were already taxing the earth's timber, topsoil, pure water, fish, and wildlife resources.

The population increases are sobering: It took 123 years for world population to increase from 1 billion to 2 billion. Succeeding increments of 1 billion took 33 years, 14 years, and 13 years. The transition from 5 billion to 6 billion people is expected to take only 11 years and be completed by 1998. Population experts say world population could reach 10 billion or more by the year 2050. Their best-case scenarios, including successful funding and implementation of family-planning programs, lower the figure to 7.8 billion. The difference—2.2 billion—equals the earth's entire population in 1950.[3]

For at least a half year leading up to the Cairo conference the Vatican was sending out strong signals it did not like the shape of the preliminary conference document worked out over some two years of conferences and discussions. The Vatican's firm opposition to birth control, officially restated in its 1968 encyclical, *Humanae Vitae,* has kept Rome out of step with most other international development and population organizations for years. It is difficult to overemphasize how important holding the line against artificial birth control has been for Pope John Paul II. During one trip to South Africa, for example, he condemned birth control forty times in ten days of public speeches. For the pope, the Cairo document seemed almost like a world rejection of his core belief, despite some difficult demographic information that the world was being forced to face. Consider that when *Humanae Vitae* was written more than a quarter century ago by Pope Paul VI, the world population was approximately 3.5 billion, or 2 billion fewer people than when delegates converged on Cairo. Nevertheless, Rome saw in the ideas presented in Cairo a greater problem, a spiritual problem. It saw in Cairo the threat of the international community's seeming continued abandonment of traditional sexual morality and, in an effort to curb population growth, the possible forsaking of human dignity by making persons means to planning ends instead of ends in themselves. But above all, Rome feared the conference would embrace abortion as an internationally accepted means in population control programs. No United Nations population gathering had ever done that before.

As the September 1994 Cairo conference edged closer, the Vatican, led by Pope John Paul II, raised the level of its worldwide assault against it. Catholic prelates throughout the world became increasingly vocal in condemning the proposed conference declaration. Speaking in virtual chorus, they revealed an intensity of concern that reflected the way the Vatican had approached the meeting for months. Pope John Paul had made it clear he believed the United Nations, by its approach to population control, was undermining human dignity and threatening the primary building block of society, the institution of the family. Hardly a day went by in the months leading up to the conference without some Catholic bishop speaking out against the Cairo conference.[4] In June 1994 the pope, meeting with the bishops of Ecuador, said that divorce, abortion, "antibirth campaigns," and cohabitation without marriage were some of "the evils affecting the institution of the family."[5] The next day the heads of the Latin American bishops' conferences condemned the proposed U.N. document, saying its proposals would especially hurt the poorest of people, especially indigenous Indians. They said it had "a racist aspect," and they repeated the pope's objections to proposals advocating a wider distribution of contraceptives and access to abortion and sterilization.

Later that week, Archbishop (later Cardinal) William H. Keeler, president of the U.S. bishops' conference, condemned the U.N. draft, saying it "is devoted less to population and development concerns and more to the advocacy of policies in conflict with fundamental moral values."[6] The same day, the Vatican newspaper, *L'Osservatore Romano,* published an article calling upon the state to protect the right of children to grow up in a traditional family environment. A commentary in the newspaper condemned the artificial insemination of women in lesbian relationships, saying the practice must be made illegal. In the article, Franciscan Father Gino Concetti, a moral theologian, said, "No baby wants to be known as the child of a 'single mother,' and even less of a 'lesbian mother.'"[7] On June 26, the pope, in a Sunday talk, said the true language of love goes beyond instinct. Because responsible sexuality involves a commitment between a man and a woman and is open to new children, he said, there is no moral basis for "free love, homosexuality and contraceptive birth control." He offered a prayer that Mary, as the "model of femininity," would help contemporary men and women avoid "making sex banal in the name of a false modernity," and he asked for prayers that representatives attending the conference would make decisions based on true human values.[8]

The Cairo conference was to draw together some fifteen thousand foreigners, including delegates from 180 nations where a cacophony of voices would vie to influence the final wording of the 113-page document aimed at setting the course for international population and development programs over the next two decades. Planners hoped to reach a consensus on the conference statement, but the strong antidocument offensive spearheaded by the Vatican was appearing to make that a more difficult task. Just days before the conference began, the pope, speaking at his summer residence, once again deplored the direction the Cairo conference appeared to be taking. He said that nothing less than "the future of the family and society is at stake" in the policies under consideration, praying that Mary would "open the eyes of humanity in this crucial passage of its history" and promote "wise and prudent" decisions. "I'm especially concerned about a certain tendency in the conference's preparatory document to view sexuality in an overly individualistic manner, without enough consideration of the important social implications for marriage and the family," the pope said, adding that it had long been recognized that the family, as the natural element and foundation of society, is more necessary than the state. He said it would be a serious mistake for the Cairo conference, in its concern over rapid population growth, to "be satisfied with accepting or even favoring a sexuality that is uprooted from ethical references." Instead, he said, experts should promote a "culture of responsible procreation."[9] The pope explained that despite contemporary moral failures in sexual behavior, these principles remain valid—not as a question of faith, but as an anthropological fact. The Vatican campaign captured headlines around the world, and conference organizers were forced to defend themselves, saying that Rome's fears were exaggerated and that Vatican officials were distorting the proposed document's contents. The controversy put the Clinton administration, a strong conference backer, on the defensive. It did not want to be seen as supporting abortion; nor did it want to be seen as backing off its "safe, legal and rare" abortion standard or its strong support for family-planning programs.

As Cairo got under way, Vice President Al Gore, the official head of the U.S. delegation, speaking the first day, indicated he was interested in reconciling differences over the document. He told delegates the United States did not advocate an international right to abortion but believed it was up to each country to decide. He was extending an olive branch to Rome, but it was not accepted. At a later news conference, Vatican spokesman Joaquin Navarro-Valls attempted to refute reports—"to correct the line of some papers"—that the Vatican had been involved in a "holy alliance" with Islamic countries to forge a strong anti-abortion conference lobby.[10] However from Day One, the Vatican appeared to be in a diplomatic bind. It almost eagerly led the charge against abortion rights advocates; yet it did not want to appear to be manipulating the conference. Nevertheless, months of Vatican attacks on the working paper had left a bitter feeling among many delegates. Navarro-Valls countered the criticism by insisting on what many thought beyond the realm of possibility—that the Vatican would compromise and in the end it would sign the document. Neither in Bucharest in 1974 nor in Mexico City in 1984 had the Vatican signed the final statement.

Bishop James McHugh of Trenton, New Jersey, another member of the Vatican delegation and the person responsible for founding the anti-abortion National Right to Life Committee in 1966, told a swarm of journalists early in the gathering that on the fundamental issues of abortion and contraception there was nothing to debate. He explained that his delegation wanted "to restore a sense of balance to the population debate," that is, less emphasis on contraception and abortion and more on development. But the Vatican strategy caused just the opposite to happen—the conference became riveted on human sexuality issues instead of other pressing development issues, and so other issues were shortchanged. The voices of environmentalists, of women from Third World countries, the sound of the growing debate between industrialized nations and developing countries—all were largely drowned out by the din of the abortion debate.

Going into the conference, delegates had already agreed on nearly 90 percent of the document. Disputed wording was bracketed. Finding agreement on the other 10 percent was to be no easy task. During the second day of the conference, delegates worked to come up with a new text for the most contentious passage in the entire proposed statement, paragraph 25 in Chapter 8. It was quickly referred to simply as "8.25." It began as follows:

> *All governments, intergovernmental organizations and relevant nongovernmental organizations are urged to deal openly and forthrightly with unsafe abortion as a major public health concern. . . . Unwanted pregnancies should be prevented through sexual health education and through expanded and improved family-planning services, including proper counseling to reduce the rate of abortion.*

A committee headed by Ambassador Nicolas Biegman of the Netherlands undertook the project. The task was to soften wording enough to please the Vatican and a handful of other nations without losing the support of those who liked the original language. He begged delegates to approve the compromise and get on with other matters. The new wording read, "In no case should abortion be promoted as a method of family planning." This was essentially the position the U.N. gathering had taken ten years earlier in Mexico City. Both the new and compromise texts went on to say that where abortion is legal, it should be safe. By nine that evening and after grudging acceptance by some nations, the Vatican said it could not budge, it could not accept the compromise, asking for more time. Only a handful of mostly smaller nations supported the Vatican's rejection. Those allied with the Vatican during the conference were several Catholic nations—Malta, Honduras, Guatemala, Nicaragua, and Argentina—but no Islamic states, with the exception of Morocco. Notably absent were the major Catholic countries such as Mexico, Brazil, and even the pope's post-Communist, native land, Poland.

Delegate bitterness grew as word got out the next morning that the Vatican had refused to compromise. Soon delegates' frustrations were giving way to outright anger. "When the Vatican said it could not accept the compromise, some simply booed; others yelled no in disbelief. It was shocking," said Jeannie Rosoff, a member of the U.S. delegation and president of the Alan Guttmacher Institute. "Protocol was broken, an indication of just how upset people were."[11]

The next day, an editorial appeared in one of the three conference newspapers, *ICPD Watch*, summing up many delegates' sentiments. "The Holy See," it stated, "would like to wish away abortion by insisting that it be kept out of the 'Program of Action' and out of society." A delegate at a women's caucus accused the Vatican of wanting to restrict national sovereignty. "How else could anyone object to a phrase that implies abortions—only if they are legal—should be safe." Following the Vatican's objection, conference leaders announced that further discussion on the abortion paragraph would be postponed for two days, until the end of the week. Also deferred was discussion of Chapter 7, which dealt with reproductive rights and family planning, another minefield. The morning after the controversial vote, Maher Mahran, Egyptian minister of state for population and family affairs, also accused the Vatican of trying to dictate to the world. "Does the Vatican rule the world?" he asked. "We respect the Vatican, we respect the pope, but we don't accept anyone to impose his ideas. If they are not going to negotiate, why did they come?"

Many delegates to the Cairo conference said that the Vatican's actions were not in keeping with its traditionally low-profile diplomacy. Pope John Paul's outspoken vocal opposition to the Cairo efforts was viewed as somewhat uncommon, and it caused some to ask why it should have an observer status at the United Nations when other religious groups do not, for example, Buddhists, Muslims, and Jews. The answer is that the Vatican, or the Holy See, is, in fact, an independent state. It entered the modern international stage thanks to the 108.7 acres of territory it was conceded by the Lateran Pacts of 1929. This was all that was left of the Papal States, acquired in the fifth century and finally relinquished when Italy was united in 1871. Even between 1871 and 1929, when the state came into being the Vatican continued to receive and send diplomatic representatives. A 1957 agreement between the Holy See and the United Nations reads: "the (Vatican) Secretariat of State wishes to make it clear that the said relations should be understood as being established between the United Nations and the Holy See."[12]

Conference organizers shifted ground. Rather than getting controversial phrases out of the way, they decided to get on with other matters, deferring the most controversial texts so that other areas of the document could receive more attention. In the days that followed, the Vatican got the following sentence out of brackets and into the final document: "In no case should abortion be promoted as a method of family planning." This was the position that had finally emerged from the Mexico City conference. It was a position with which most delegates in Cairo seemed comfortable but it had been dropped as some sought to make abortion rights part of the ordinary reproductive health package. Though the Vatican "won" the round on abortion, it was not yet satisfied with the way the final document handled the controversial abortion matter. This meant it could not sign on to Chapter 8, the chapter entitled "Health, Morbidity and Mortality." The Vatican explained its position:

> *The final document, as opposed to the earlier documents of the Bucharest and Mexico City conferences, recognizes abortion as a dimension of population policy and, indeed, of primary health care, even though it does stress that abortion should not be promoted as a means of family planning and urges nations to find alternatives to abortion.*

Adding to conference tensions was a conflict between church morality and women's suspicions. The Vatican saw its role as upholding traditional morality; women saw their roles largely as changing the status quo. This might not have mattered as much in the past, but at Cairo, more than at any previous U.N. gathering, the agenda was shaped by women's views and voices. Women had gained considerable influence in the field of reproductive health and demographics during the 1980s. For decades, when population planners spoke about the world's poorest women, they concentrated on how to keep them from having more babies. Providing sterilization and IUDs, handing out contraceptives, and imposing quotas on family size constituted the major population-control thrusts. In recent years effective women's voices have argued that these methods are often demeaning and sometimes coercive and that shifts have been needed. The new directions the women called for included more prenatal care, education for girls, and promotion of women's equality. The proponents of this change argued that birth rates in poor countries will decline only after the status, health, education, and economic opportunities for women have risen. The Cairo document draft, was, then, more of a "Southern," or development-oriented document and a shift from earlier contraceptive approaches. At first glance, it seemed as though this would please the Vatican. However, coupled with calls for women's freedoms came demands for reproductive health services and counseling as rights for all women, including teenagers. This troubled Vatican officials who spoke critically of a growing "contraceptive mentality."[13] Women activists, meanwhile, wanted access to legal abortion as a means of securing full reproductive health care. The Catholic Church preferred the "development" approach, arguing that long-term answers would be found in achieving a more just distribution of the world's resources, although curiously those bishops who became most associated with the causes of the poor in Third World nations, such as San Cristóbal (Mexico) Bishop Samuel Ruiz Garcia, have often gotten into trouble with Rome for their so-called revolutionary ties.

The grueling nine-day conference finally ended on an upbeat note as the Vatican, surprising many, announced it would endorse all but the two most contentious chapters of the sixteen-chapter document. Archbishop Renato Martino, the chief Vatican delegate, said, "The current 'Program of Action' opens out some new paths concerning the future population policy" so that "on this occasion the Holy See wishes, in some way, to associate itself with the consensus, even if in an incomplete or partial manner."[14] The two chapters the Holy See said it could not accept—Chapters 7 and 8—dealt with reproductive rights and safe abortion. Said Martino: "Nothing is to be understood to imply that the Holy See endorses abortion or has in any way changed its moral position concerning abortion or contraceptives or sterilization or the use of condoms in HIV-AIDS prevention programs." The announcement marked the first time the Vatican allowed itself to become officially associated with the major thrusts of a U.N. population document. The Vatican announcement drew loud applause. It had been widely suspected among delegates and nongovernment activists that the Holy See would not sign the consensus statement. Tim Wirth, the U.S. undersecretary of state for global affairs, speaking after the announcement, expressed delight. The 113-page declaration endorsed for the first time a new concept of population policy that goes beyond traditional family planning to such areas as reproductive health care, the empowerment of women to make their own family-planning choices, and equality of the sexes. Where it is not against the law, the declaration implies, health care should include abortion in conditions that are safe. As bewildered as were many Cairo delegates at Vatican heavy-handedness during the gathering, they were equally relieved at conference's end to find a sense of Vatican diplomacy restored.

The Vatican recalcitrance throughout the gathering obscured the fact that the Catholic Church had actually shifted its own approach to population control, beginning in the 1950s and 1960s, when early indications of the population explosion began to be reported. The Vatican moved from viewing any family planning as a moral evil to begrudgingly seeing it as a necessity, to actively supporting population control—provided it is done through "natural means," that is, through periodic abstinence. This is called the rhythm method, or Natural Family Planning (NFP). Advocates of NFP claim the method is about as effective as birth-control pills and cite a use-effectiveness rate of 94.8

percent. Critics say that what is not stated is that this rate is attained by a small segment of the population and that the pregnancy rate is in excess of 5 percent a year.[15] Women with variably spaced menstrual periods, indicating irregular and unpredictable ovulation, have substantially higher rates of unintended pregnancy. Critics of NFP say it is not practical for many couples in the Third World, who are often illiterate and poor and often separated from spouses for weeks at a time.

Oral contraception remains one of the most popular methods used in the United States. Advocates say the pill is highly effective. When the pill was introduced more than three decades ago, John Rock, the Harvard Catholic gynecologist who pioneered its development, was vitally concerned that the church review the facts and find the approach acceptable. In a nationally syndicated interview in 1983, Rock, then eighty-three, was referred to as the "father of the pill," and "a Catholic in love with his church." After the pill was launched and it was obvious that it was destined to have a major impact on fertility control, Rock wrote in his book entitled *The Time Has Come—A Catholic Doctor's Proposals to End the Battle Over Birth Control* (Knopf, 1963) that "American Catholics, from bishops down to rank and file, must ponder with utmost seriousness the relationship between excessive fertility and excruciating, ruinous poverty in the nations of Asia, Latin America and Africa, where two-thirds of the world's population live." At that time Luigi Mastroianni Jr., a young gynecologist, was working with John Rock. Now the director of the Division of Human Reproduction at the University of Pennsylvania Medical Center in Philadelphia, Mastroianni wrote the following a few years ago:

> *I witnessed firsthand the concern and caring of this extraordinary physician-scientist and accepted then, as I do now, the argument that the pill is but an extension of the systems that operate in nature to inhibit ovulation when there is stress and during pregnancy and lactation. Since its introduction, the pill has been modified many times, and the complications reported with the high dose of pills used initially have been virtually eliminated.*[16]

Catholic church critics, including some Catholic moral theologians, continue to decry church teaching on birth control, arguing that the intent is the same whether the means is "artificial" or "natural," and therefore, the church should not distinguish between the two. Further, they have argued that by opposing artificial birth control the church weakens its opposition to the greater evil, abortion. No other Catholic Church teaching is as disputed as its stand on birth control. Opposition to the teaching extends well within the church hierarchy despite heavy pressures by Rome to toe the line.

At a gathering of European bishops in Rome, for example, in 1991, German Bishop Norbert Werbs boldly suggested that the church manifest the mercy of Jesus by "lifting from the shoulders of parents the weight of the distinction between natural and artificial means of birth control."[17] He said he doubted whether this distinction is demanded by the gospel. Later, the head of the German bishops' conference, Karl Lehmann, asked whether it might be time for the church to rethink its position on birth control. He said the pope speaks a fundamental "no" to it but is not concerned with the consequences. The German bishops, however, he said, "see more clearly the concrete situation and the pain it causes people." The retired archbishop of Vienna, Franz König, a few years ago again insisted that "the question of world overpopulation cannot be simply ignored." He referred to the "irritating" distinction between birth control that is natural (approved) and artificial (condemned)—"as if even from the moral viewpoint what is important is the 'trick' of cheating nature." In the church, argued König, "too little is said of the fact that conscience is the final standard."[18] The auxiliary bishop of Vienna, Helmut Kratzl, also spoke of the church's need "to win back its credibility on questions of sexual morality."

At a 1988 Vatican conference on AIDS, a top church spokesman gave an example of the incredible lengths to which legalistic defenders of papal policy will go. Monsignor Carlo Caffara, dean of the Vatican's Institute on Marriage and Family Studies, said that if one spouse has AIDS, the couple must practice total abstinence. But if such abstinence might lead to adultery or grave harm to conjugal peace, the couple may licitly have unprotected sex and risk infection. In an open letter to the pope, theologian Father Bernard Häring, professor emeritus of Moral Theology at the Alphonsian Academy in Rome, spoke of the many good and intelligent Christians inside and outside the Catholic Church who find scandalous the thought-models, methods of argument, and imputations of guilt proposed by Caffara and others. These good and intelligent people, he said, are the basis of any hope that the Vatican will "rethink" the fateful matter of world overpopulation.[19]

Many of the delegates to the 1994 Cairo gathering were, in fact, Catholics, and many found themselves advocating positions, supportive of their governments, that opposed the teachings of their church. Further, some nongovernmental Catholic activists came to Cairo to lobby for document positions that conflicted with the Vatican. One of these was

Marquette University theologian Daniel C. Maguire, who addressed the session in his capacity as president of the Religious Consultation on Population, Reproductive Health and Ethics, a nongovernmental organization. He praised the conference document, saying a "remarkable consensus has been reached" on important development matters, including empowering women, offering hope to parents, formulating plans to eliminate poverty, and offering greater care to the earth. Sadly, he said, the Vatican's "idiosyncratic fixation" on contraception and abortion had "overshadowed" a "moral triumph."[20] That was not the way the Vatican, out of step with the international community on contraception and attempting to hold the line on abortion, had seen it in Egypt during those nine contentious days.

Sex and Authority

In the Catholic Church, the issues of sex and authority go hand in hand. This has long been the case, but never more so than during the past quarter century, ever since Pope Paul VI's encyclical *Humanae Vitae* reaffirmed the ban on artificial contraception. The pope thought the encyclical would settle festering moral questions; instead, it raised more. He thought the encyclical would shore up papal teaching authority; it had the opposite effect. Torn between following the advice of his pontifical commission, which supported changes in church teaching, and his desire to remain consistent with earlier papal declarations, Paul VI choose the later course. The need to assert church authority persuaded him. After all, he reasoned, how could the Holy Spirit have allowed the church to have been wrong for so many years on an issue of such importance? What would the faithful think if the church were to admit error? Catholic teaching can't just change. Or can it? Years ago the church changed its teachings on usury; later, on slavery. But these facts did not sway him. Despite clerical and lay counsel and the expectations of millions of Catholics that he would change church teachings, he reaffirmed the sinfulness of artificial contraception. Ironically, what Pope Paul could not have known at the time was how overwhelmingly his encyclical would be rejected by Catholics and how this rejection would dramatically damage church credibility and, in turn, Catholic belief and practice.

Critics of the Second Vatican Council like to blame post-conciliar Catholic erosion on the council's "excesses." However, studies do not support this view. Research conducted by the sociologist Father Andrew M. Greeley and supported by other surveys found that *Humanae Vitae* was the culprit. Greeley found that the encyclical so shook Catholics that, by itself, it would have reduced religious practice by almost one-half. That decline never fully occurred, and the reason it did not, Greeley found, was the favorable impact the Second Vatican Council was having on the lives of most Catholics. They liked the reforms and the call to greater participation in the church. In the end, the reduction in Catholic practice was held to about one-third. Eight years after *Humanae Vitae*, Greeley concluded that only about "one-sixth of American Catholics" continued to support the church's birth control ban and the "overwhelming majority of American Catholics" endorsed the council's changes.[1] "The encyclical and not the council is responsible for the deterioration of American Catholicism in the last decade," he wrote. "Had it not been for the council, the deterioration would have been worse."

Greeley's studies led him to conclude the following:

The Vatican Council was one of the most successful religious phenomena in human history. A dramatic and sudden change occurred in aspects of Catholic life which had not been touched for a millennium and a half. Within a decade, these changes had been accepted by the overwhelming majority of American Catholics, by virtually all the subpopulations within the American Catholic community. Furthermore, the council unleashed in the church positive forces which, if given half a chance, would have made for growth not decline.

The blighting of the success of the Vatican Council can be attributed to a failure in leadership, in particular, failure in the area of sexuality. Humanae Vitae *was as much a symptom as a cause. The concerns of the pope when he wrote the encyclical were surely valid—the importance of human life, the sanctity of marriage, the link between sexuality and procreation. There are undoubtedly life-hating forces in the world, and they may be even stronger now than they were ten years ago. But the mistake made by the encyclical, and still made by many Catholics, is summarized by the dictum that support for birth control inevitable leads to support for abortion. There is, however, no necessary logical or psychological link between the two. Our evidence would indicate that the overwhelming majority of American Catholics are quite capable of making the distinction between the two moral issues.*

Reflecting on the state of the church in light of his data, Greeley continued:

Married people concluded that the largely celibate ecclesial authority simply did not understand the problems that married people had to face, and ought not, therefore, to be taken seriously when it addressed itself to marriage problems. . . . Quite simply, the encyclical was a shattering blow to the ecclesiastical loyalty of many American Catholics. . . .

We are now in a situation of theological impasse. Humanae Vitae *is still the law of the Church; loyalty to it seems to be an absolute criterion for promotion to the hierarchy . . . but in the United States and in every other country where research has been done, the encyclical is ignored by the laity and most of the lower clergy.*

Those words were written two decades ago; by all available evidence, they stand today. It is not as if bishops have been unaware of the problem. But they, too, are caught in the bind between the hard-line papal stance on birth control and the practices of the overwhelming majority of Catholics. Sporadic episcopal efforts to draw attention to this crippling gulf have been slapped down by Rome. Early in Pope John Paul II's pontificate, at a 1980 synod of the world's bishops in Rome, Archbishop John Quinn of San Francisco, then president of the National Conference of Catholic Bishops, reported the figures from a study at Princeton University that concluded that 76.5 percent of married American Catholic women were using some form of birth regulation and that 94 percent of these women were using methods condemned by the church. Perhaps Quinn thought such alarming figures might trigger a discussion of the topic, but they fell flat at the Vatican. There simply would be no further discussion. Word spread that Quinn's lonely but brave remarks had hurt his chances for further ecclesial advancement. It has been a rare occasion since that a Catholic bishop has brought up the birth control issue in Rome. Although *Humanae Vitae* has never been proclaimed to be an infallible Catholic teaching, it has received the strongest of affirmations during the pontificate of Pope John Paul II. While on a trip to South Africa, the pope mentioned birth control no fewer than forty times. Reaffirming *Humanae Vitae* for Pope John Paul II has been a personal passion. There has been no room for discussion here.

Married Catholics couples have not been the only ones whose sexual experiences have caused them to ask questions about the use of church authority. Women in general have linked sexual issues with male celibacy in the church. The question often gets asked this way: Who is to have the final say over women's bodies? Celibate men, the women argue, simply cannot know what it means to be a woman and to become pregnant, sometimes against one's will and in an act of violence. However one finally comes to judge the morality of birth control and abortion, women know they bring to the discussion one thing men can never address: personal experience. Their perspective is different. Male celibates, these women say, cannot understand the situation as they do. What upsets Catholic women most, given the nature of authority in the church, is that they have absolutely no say in the formulation of official Catholic teachings on sexual morality. The temptation for many women is to walk away from church sex teachings altogether. Many, of course, have already taken that path. So sexuality and authority are linked. At the center of that linkage is the church's refusal to allow the ordination of women. That would be the door through which women would have to pass to have direct influence on the formulation of sexual teachings. And the door is closed. Moreover, Pope John Paul II said in May 1994 that the door would be closed forever and no one could discuss the matter further. The ordination issue eventually touches on all Catholic sexual morality. What growing numbers of Catholics are beginning to recognize is that, whether or not women priests would change church teachings, having them part of the decision-making process in matters pertaining to human sexuality would greatly enhance church credibility. On the other hand, their continued exclusion becomes a serious liability. Women's ordination, then, becomes one of the most important issues facing the Catholic Church in the twenty-first century. Yet on the surface there appears to be almost no understanding among the Catholic hierarchy as to the gravity of this matter and what it could mean for the future of Catholicism, especially in the Western world.

Many gays and lesbians also link sex and authority issues. Why, they ask, would a loving God create them as "intrinsically disordered," as the church claims they are. Why would a God of infinite compassion forbid them from ever experiencing sexual intimacy, as the church has decreed? Or could it be that the church got it wrong? Could it be bad theology? Or even prejudice? Even fear? Not a few gays and lesbians ask whether the prelates who speak out so strongly against them might be covering up their own sexual insecurities. Or their own sexual inclinations? Are some among them closeted gays, they ask?

If women in general have problems with church authority, Catholic feminists, including feminist men, have no doubt about their views on the issues. Most have rejected patriarchal organizations, seeing them as outmoded historical remnants. They do not take seriously pronouncements formulated solely by males. In effect, they have moved into a form of psychological schism from the Catholic hierarchy.

What is new is their refusal to "leave" the church. They see themselves as fully Catholic, participate in Catholic liturgies, say Catholic prayers, receive Catholic sacraments but on their own terms. In a way, they are not unlike parts of the broader Catholic community that see the Rome of recent years more as a nuisance than as a font of wisdom. Maintaining their Catholic identities and pondering the Vatican situation, they have developed a kind of "this too shall pass" mentality. "We are the church and they can't drive us out," is the thinking. In the end, millions of Catholics, depicted as "dissenters" or "cafeteria Catholics" by Rome, have labored to find ways to stay faithful to the church they love. They feel they cannot be anything but Catholic. It is in their culture, in their traditions. While the church's sexual teachings have managed to force many out, many others have made private accommodations. They see their Catholic heritage as too valuable to give up. They want their children to grow up Catholic, though the task of raising children in the faith is made more daunting by the church's sexual teachings.

Most Catholics deplore the deep divisions that characterize Catholicism at the end of the twentieth century. Church historians, however, recognize that divisions in the church are nothing new. Catholicism has always been made up of a diverse lot, often influenced by local customs, cultures, and historical accidents. Throughout history, a variety of differing theological interpretations, practices, and beliefs have been reconciled at ecumenical councils. Catholicism has always been something akin to a large family coming together at the table, each member with a slightly different view of the world. There is never full agreement, and occasionally there are sharp differences. But like family members, they eat the same food and part with a willingness—even an eagerness—to come back again. Nevertheless, divisions within the church since the Second Vatican Council have been especially pronounced. And most of these can be traced back to some aspect of human sexuality.

Hard-line conservative Catholics deplore the unwillingness of many of the faithful to accept the pope's teachings. They see the crisis as a sign of growing secularism within the church. They blame much of the crisis on "lax" U.S. bishops who fail to enforce Catholic orthodoxy. Indeed, many of these Catholics have reported to Rome what they consider to be breaches of orthodoxy in local dioceses. They have organized letter-writing campaigns to alert Rome to "problems." Curiously, despite the hierarchical structure of the church organization in which authority and teaching is to flow down with feedback flowing back up, U.S. conservatives have often bypassed their own bishops and have gotten more sympathetic hearings among conservative prelates in the Vatican. On the Far Right, an alliance has formed that has isolated and diminished the stature of many U.S. prelates. For their part, most U.S. bishops try to stay in the middle, between right and left, although more than fifteen years of Pope John Paul II–directed episcopal appointments have increasingly moved the U.S. bishops to the Right.

In the Catholic Church, unlike other American organizations, the primary right-left political spectrum is not shaped by social issues and the role of government in these issues. It is primarily shaped by how "conservative" or "liberal" a bishop is on those issues that deal with private morality, most often sexual morality. In the Catholic conversation most bishops tend to be progressive on the social issues, but what distinguishes them—and places them on the spectrum of church politics—is how they line up on such issues as treatment of gays and lesbians, divorce and remarriage, women's involvement in the local church, and birth control. Large numbers of U.S. bishops, even perhaps a sizable majority, are not pleased with how the Vatican is handling the birth control issue. To publicly say anything about it would constitute ecclesial suicide. There is a widespread sense among Catholics, including the U.S. hierarchy, that the best that can be done while Pope John Paul II remains pope is simply to ride things out. Change, it is hoped, will come later. In the mid-1990s, Catholicism is in a kind of gridlock. Everything on these issues that can be said seems to have been said. Much cannot be said. Catholics know their place and have generally found their niche. Nothing much will change until there is a new pope.

At the same time, those who await change, those most dissatisfied with the leadership of the John Paul II papacy, often joke that matters cannot get worse. And then find out they have. An example was the Vatican's October 1994 statement, or reaffirmation, that divorced Catholics in unsanctioned second marriages cannot receive the Eucharist. While this has long been official church teaching, the practice has often not been enforced. Indeed, most priests and bishops would say it cannot be enforced. So why make it an issue? They note that many Catholics in second marriages have found ways to accommodate to the church in good conscience. While officially those Catholics whose marriages have not been blessed by a priest are not permitted to receive the sacrament of the Eucharist, many do so. Although Rome may say the theology these Catholics employ is wrong, these divorced and remarried Catholics tend to see the sacraments as spiritual aids and not as barriers to participation in church life. The sacraments affirm and direct Catholic lives, with the Eucharist as the most important to most Catholics. The Vatican, however, felt required to remind divorced and remarried Catholics that the unity they were finding in the Eucharist was a "false" unity because their marriages had not been officially sanctioned by the church.

"If the divorced are remarried civilly, they find themselves in a situation that objectively contravenes God's law. Consequently, they cannot receive holy communion as long as this situation persists," the Vatican's Congregation for the Doctrine of the Faith said in a letter to the world's bishops. The document challenged "pastoral solutions," advanced in many countries in recent years. The statement, signed by Cardinal Joseph Ratzinger, was a response to a 1993 proposal by three German bishops—Karl Lehmann of Mainz, Oskar Saier of Freiburg, and Walter Kasper of Rottenburg-Stuttgart—who wanted an exception clause added to this long-standing church law. They suggested that some Catholics, who in good conscience contend their first marriage is invalid but who cannot obtain an annulment, could be allowed to receive the Sacrament. The three said the main question is whether the church should decide on the reception of Communion or whether Catholics in a second marriage not blessed by the church should be allowed to make the decision based on a well-formed conscience. The Vatican wanted nothing of such "pastoral" proposals. Divorced and remarried Catholics who did not obtain an annulment are prohibited from receiving Communion, Rome said, with one exception—if the couple in question refrains from having any sexual intimacy.

The Vatican document stated that to allow divorced and remarried Catholics to receive Communion would be to lead them into "error and confusion regarding the church's teaching about the indissolubility of marriage." However, Catholics in such unions can receive the Sacrament after obtaining "sacramental absolution" and abiding by what is commonly referred to as the "brother-sister solution." In Vatican language, the couple must "take on themselves the duty to live in complete continence, that is, by abstinence from the acts proper to married couples." The Vatican supported its stand in theological terms. "Receiving eucharistic communion contrary to the norms of ecclesial communion is therefore in itself a contradiction. Sacramental communion with Christ includes and presupposes the observance, even if at times difficult, of the order of ecclesial communion, and it cannot be right and fruitful if a member of the faithful, wishing to approach Christ directly, does not respect this order."

Critics of the Vatican statement noted that the early Christian Church viewed marriage as a civil contract and made no declarations about the validity of marriage and its relationship to sacrament. Gradually, around the period of the fall of the Roman Empire in 476 the church increased its involvement in the legal aspect of marriage.

The number of Catholics involved is significant. It is estimated that there are between 6 and 8 million divorced and remarried U.S. Catholics. The church does not allow divorce but grants "annulments," a practice that many bishops and theologians see as only further eroding church credibility. A Catholic can receive an "annulment" if it can be found that for some reason the marriage was not valid from the start. Catholics wanting annulments then set out to find such reasons, including maturity of intention at the time or an attitude of a spouse. While frequently there are solid grounds for granting annulments, the practice often becomes a legal game, an effort aimed more at fulfilling canonical requirements than healing old wounds and restoring the petitioner to spiritual health. Between 45,000 and 50,000 Catholic annulments have been granted in the United States annually from the late 1980s to the early 1990s, representing a small fraction of the number of Catholics who get divorced each year.

Another example of Rome's clampdown on matters pertaining to sexual conduct, alienating Catholics along the way, occurred in January 1995 when Bishop Jacques Gaillot of Évreux, France, while visiting the Vatican, was told he had only twenty-four hours to clear out of his diocese. He was to be removed by Rome as bishop. The Vatican said its decision was made because Gaillot had failed to act in unity with the rest of the church hierarchy. It was later learned that the French bishops, while aware of Vatican dissatisfaction, had not been informed of Gaillot's pending removal. Bishops are the heads of their dioceses. Many Catholics, including some ecclesial theologians, saw in Rome's action an unprecedented use of papal authority. French Catholics viewed Gaillot as a good prelate, but a maverick of sorts, a bishop who spoke his own mind. For years he had questioned the church's teaching on birth control and on celibacy for priests and its condemnation of condoms in AIDS prevention programs. He also was an outspoken advocate for the homeless and the poor of France. In the weeks that followed his removal, widespread demonstrations erupted throughout France. The Vatican action was condemned in many French newspapers; Vatican officials and French bishops reported receiving thousands of letters complaining of the decision. Later the French bishops, wanting to make a public gesture on behalf of Gaillot, promised to continue to pay his salary and social welfare taxes and help him resettle in Paris. He moved into a building occupied by homeless squatters.

Karol Wojtyla

To understand the mind of Pope John Paul II it is helpful to know a bit about his life.[2] Karol was nine years old when, on April 13, 1929, his mother, Emilia, died. He grew up as an only child—close to no woman—in his one-parent family with his disciplinarian father, a junior officer in the Polish army. His brother, Edmund, a medical doctor, was fourteen years older and away from home. Edmund died two years later in a scarlet fever epidemic. At age twenty, Wojtyla witnessed the collapse of his hopes, personally and nationally. His university was closed, its professors hauled away to concentration camps, and Poland was occupied by German forces. His response was to write a play (now lost) on the Book of Job.[3] His Job suffered atrociously, and the play ends with a resurrection vision. At age thirty, Wojtyla had been a priest for just three years. The "liberation" brought to Poland by the Russian army resulted in a Communist government dominated by the Soviet Union. The poet-actor-priest led a spiritual resistance movement. At age forty, Wojtyla was a moral philosophy professor in the Catholic University of Lublin and auxiliary bishop of Kraków since 1958. He taught a form of theology based on Thomas Aquinas and the dignity of the human person, claiming that artificial contraception degrades women by turning them into sex objects. At age fifty Wojtyla, now a cardinal, defended religious liberty stoutly, more as a right the church claims

311

against atheist regimes than one it concedes to fellow Christians or nonbelievers. Meanwhile, he found the Second Vatican Council's statements about the omnipresence of grace in the world to be wildly optimistic. He was already suspicious of liberal theologians, accusing them of emptying the churches of the West with their secularizing theology. They showed insufficient subordination to papal teaching authority. Nothing in his Polish experience had prepared him for the concept of "loyal opposition" found in Western democracies. At age sixty, Wojtyla was now pope and there was early euphoria in the church. His election was a triple surprise: the first non-Italian since 1523, the first Slav ever, the youngest pope since Pius IX in 1846. His return to his homeland in June 1979 was seen as a triumph, illustrating the reality of spiritual power. The Polish government had all the physical power needed to keep him out, but it could not do so without a revolution. He told his fellow Poles that his election was "providential"—God's way of letting the Slav voice be heard in the church, compensation for many years of torment and suffering. And at age seventy, Wojtyla had survived an assassination attempt, and he told visiting prelates that the Lady of Fatima had personally spared his life so he could lead the church into the twenty-first century. He had seen the Berlin Wall come down and the Soviet Union dissolve. In Prague he rejoiced with a fellow intellectual, President Václav Havel, that a free Central Europe had been restored.

If his message to the nations had won some sort of hearing, especially east of the river Elbe, his message to the church was not always so gratefully received. With Marxist nations on the retreat and dissolving, the external threat to Christianity had waned. Nevertheless, threats inside the church remained. Perhaps the most serious in the pope's eyes were wayward theologians who were too heavily influenced by modern society and culture.

Veritatis Splendor

By the 1990s, Catholics were aware of Pope John Paul II's deeply conservative nature. They knew his childhood had deprived him of close nurturing associations with women. They knew he looked at the church through the prisms of his Polish experience and of the threats Nazi totalitarianism and Marxist communism had posed. They knew he felt he had to be vigilant, to strike out against the evil forces of the world. They knew he brought to his pontificate decades of personal suffering. All this they knew had helped shape the many volumes of his writings through the years. Nevertheless, many Catholics were still caught off guard by Pope John Paul II's tenth encyclical, dated August 6, 1993, when it was released to the press on October 5 of that same year.

Veritatis Splendor ("The Splendor of Truth") represents the final linkage between the moral absolutes of church sexual teachings and the teaching authority of the church. In his encyclical, Pope John Paul II said he alone, as pope, as supreme instructor, knew and had the right to express moral absolutes. Others, including Catholic theologians influenced by the modern world, did not. The encyclical called for a restoration of rules of behavior in moral theology. But the rules would belong to the pope. Pope John Paul saw a crisis in the world that was reflected in the church. There is a difference between right and wrong, between acts that are commendable and acts that are contemptuous, he said. The church must express its uncompromising stand as a beacon of light in a dark world. "Modern tendencies" and "certain currents of thought" are creeping in and undermining sound doctrine, he said, adding that this was leading to confusion and even to a crisis in the church. *Veritatis Splendor*, addressed to the bishops of the Roman Catholic Church, was not aimed at Catholics untrained in moral theology. It never reached a wide audience. But it astonished many Catholics by its claims.

In *Veritatis Splendor*, Pope John Paul II again said that contraception under any circumstances is "intrinsically evil" and therefore can never be justified. The encyclical deals in moral absolutes in which no concern for intentions, circumstances, or consequences plays a part. It further implies that persons with secular approaches to morality cannot be moral in the true sense of the word.

To understand the significance of what the pope said, it helps to go back to the Second Vatican Council when the world's bishops tackled similar questions. In 1964–65, as the final drafts of the council document *Gaudium et Spes* took shape, the problem was how to move from general principles to "questions of special urgency," for example, marriage, culture, war and peace.[4] In the past one might have expected the usual Catholic triad of Scripture, tradition, and natural law to serve as support. Not so. The transition to practical moral problems, the bishops said, is to be accomplished "in the light of the gospel and of human experience." This was a most significant development. As *National Catholic Reporter* Vatican affairs writer Peter Hebblethwaite reflected:

> *This was truly a remarkable change of approach. It shifted the emphasis from "nature" to the "person," from "acts-in-them-*

selves" to "acts-in-a-personal-context," from abstract "goods" to be protected and promoted come what may to what is "good-for-the-person."

Now, in every case, Veritatis Splendor *chooses and restores the first limb of these alternatives. But this is not just another way of shedding tears over the sabotage of Vatican II. It concerns "the problem of the 'sources of morality,'" which is what* Veritatis Splendor *is really about.*

Catholic moral theology is a practical discipline. It grew out of the need of confessors [priests] to assess the degree of guilt. Sinners in the box [confessional] were not usually inquiring about the nature of sin; on the contrary they were there precisely to confess what they thought were sins. So they recounted their acts—what they had done. The confessor, however, could not take the recital at face value: He needed to know something about the "intention" or aim of the act and something of its circumstances and results. By discreet questioning he elicited the relationship between acts-ends-circumstances, and so behaving "rather as a healer than a judge" (as Trent said) was able to steer the penitent toward a more mature moral judgment, a more authentic repentance and a firmer purpose of amendment.

Now Veritatis Splendor *breaks with this wise tradition. . . . The encyclical seeks to isolate certain "acts" and declare them to be "intrinsically evil," such that no appeal to intentions, circumstances or results can modify that judgment. But in most cases, knowing the act-in-itself, we suspend moral judgment until we know a little more about the context.*

Let the act-in-itself be one of sexual intercourse. Unless we know whether it was between husband and wife, wife and someone else's husband, husband and a prostitute, wife and a priest, we cannot judge whether the act is holy or how sinful it may be. This is basic to confessional practice, and also to its theology.[5]

Reactions to the encyclical were mixed, as have been reactions to Pope John Paul's pontificate. Conservatives were elated, progressives depressed. One of the most personal reflections recorded at the time came from Redemptorist theologian Father Bernard Häring, in his eighties and probably the best-known moral theologian in the Catholic Church. He spoke with frankness about the loss of heart he felt after reading the encyclical:[6]

> Veritatis Splendor *contains many beautiful things. But almost all real splendor is lost when it becomes evident that the whole document is directed above all towards one goal: to endorse total assent and submission to all utterances of the pope—and above all on one crucial point: that the use of any artificial means for regulating birth is intrinsically evil and sinful, without exception, even in circumstances where contraception would be a lesser evil. The pope is confident that he has a binding duty to proclaim his teachings with no calculation whatsoever about the foreseeable practical consequences for the people concerned and for the whole church. He would consider such considerations unlawful and dangerous because they take into account a weighing of values. Whatever the risk, whatever the danger, he believes that his insights brook no dissent but can be met only with obedience. . . .*
>
> *There is here a striking difference between our pope today and John Paul I, who, before his election, had for many years been an outstanding teacher of moral theology. As Albino Luciani, he had suggested a change of doctrine; then when Paul VI in his encyclical* Humanae Vitae *reiterated the ban on contraception, he decided to keep silent. Soon after his election as pope, however, he left no doubt that he would propose a review of the teaching, with emphasis on a consultative approach.*
>
> *As a moral theologian, John Paul I shared fully the conviction of*

> *the vast majority of moral theologians of the past and of the present that it is unlawful and possibly a great injustice to impose on people heavy burdens in the name of God unless it is fully clear that this really is God's will.*
>
> *John Paul II's mentality is different. His starting point is a high sense of duty, combined with absolute trust in his own competence, with the special assistance of the Holy Spirit. And this absolute trust in his own powers is coupled with a profound distrust toward all theologians (particularly moral theologians) who might not be in total sympathy with him.*

Pope John Paul II's eleventh encyclical, *Evangelium Vitae*, released March 30, 1995, constituted a practical follow-up to *Veritatis Splendor*. *Evangelium Vitae*, "The Gospel of Life," set out a moral vision aimed at overcoming what the pope referred to as the modern "culture of death." The encyclical portrays a consistent ethic of life, representing an implicit endorsement of Chicago Cardinal Joseph Bernardin's own "consistent ethic of life." At the heart of the encyclical is an urgent plea to reverse world trends toward social acceptance and legalization of abortion and euthanasia. In some of the strongest language ever used in an encyclical, the pope writes that "by the authority which Christ conferred upon Peter and his successors and in communion with the bishops of the Catholic church, I confirm that the direct and voluntary killing of an innocent human being is always gravely immoral."[7] This means no one can morally permit "the killing of an innocent human being, whether a fetus or an embryo, an infant or an adult, an old person, or one suffering from an incurable disease, or a person who is dying," the pope says.

"Nor can any authority legitimately recommend or permit

such an action," he adds. The pope then invokes the same authority to condemn all direct abortion as "a grave moral disorder, since it is the deliberate killing of an innocent human being." By the same logic that applies to abortion, he says, "the use of human embryos or fetuses as an object of experimentation constitutes a crime against their dignity as human beings." The encyclical includes in the "culture of death" contraception, sterilization, reproductive technologies that replace sexual intercourse, and the destruction of and experimentation on preimplanted embryos. These condemnations are not new. The strength of a papal condemnation of capital punishment, however, is new.

In the encyclical, the pope attributes threatening trends toward the devaluing of human life in part to "a profound crisis of culture," which he says has led many to lose their moral bearings.[8] He roundly condemns "powerful cultural, economic and political currents" today that have unleashed "a war of the powerful against the weak. . . a kind of 'conspiracy against life.'" At 194 pages in the English version, the 1995 encyclical was the longest of the eleven that had by then been issued by Pope John Paul.

Evangelium Vitae carried forward several key themes developed in Pope John Paul's 1993 encyclical on the foundations of morality, *Veritatis Splendor.* As he did in the 1993 document, the pope argues in *Evangelium Vitae* that the problem today is not just the continuing existence of evil and sin, but widespread cultural relativism and individualism in which any sense of sin is severely distorted or even lost. The encyclical's strength rests in its forcing of greater awareness concerning the sacredness of life and the many assaults modern society is making upon life. Many Catholics and others, recognizing the growing ways life is being attacked today, gratefully received the pontiff's words. The encyclical's weakness, however, continues to stem from the way it approaches and separates good and evil. In stark contrast to evil in the world comes the church with absolute truth and goodness. Such a thoroughgoing opposition between the church and the world, or the gospel and culture, has not been the typical Catholic approach.[9] Some Protestant approaches have seen the world primarily in terms of the opposition between grace and sin, but the Catholic tradition has not traditionally seen sin as destroying the human and its basic goodness but only infecting it. The Catholic position has seen the divine as mediated in and through the human. Catholic theology has held that the glory of God is the human person come alive. The human person is an image of God precisely because, like God, she or he has intellect, free will, and the power of self-determination. The Catholic tradition has insisted on the basic goodness of the human and of human reason. The church in its history has supported and encouraged human truth, beauty, and goodness.

Furthermore, history shows that at times the church can learn from the world—for example, the condemnations of slavery and torture and the support of political rights and the role of women. The pope's strong oppositional approach allows one to put one's own position under the good or the positive aspect of life while assigning those who disagree to the negative camp of the culture of death. This tends, however, to create a triumphalism of the church as identified with the forces of good and life and fails to recognize the church's own failures in promoting life. However tempting the good-evil imagery, it fails on the historical evidence (the trail of theocracies, including Catholic-inspired theocracies, has often been bloody and repressive) and tends to preclude efforts to enter into meaningful dialogue with those outside the church whose moral vision might differ from Catholic teaching.

Pope John Paul II paints the life-death dichotomy with absolute clarity. He speaks "truth" to the world. However, claiming to alone know and speak absolute "truth" creates its own heavy burdens. Such a presumed monopoly on truth, besides making dialogue with the wider human family more difficult, also means that Catholic teachings on faith or morals, as in the case of *Humanae Vitae,* may not easily be reversed, not without taking a toll on church credibility.

Both *Veritatis Splendor* and *Evangelium Vitae* vigorously affirm a single theological pathway as true for all time for the doing of Catholic moral theology. In Pope John Paul II's vision the only pathway for determining complete "truth" has been granted by God to the church. This means that the pope's absolute moral message concerning the fabric of "the Gospel of Life" now includes the sole identifiable means of arriving at it—the papacy itself. Pope John Paul II's basic thesis about a failure to respect the sacredness and dignity of human life in our contemporary society is clearly needed. It is also shared by many people today. And many would recognize the tendency among some today to reduce morality only to the question of freedom. Such an emphasis easily leads to an ethical relativism, and ethical relativism bankrupts morality and humanity by denying any possibility of human community and working together. This the pope both recognizes and fears.

However, the life-death, good-evil oppositional approach concerning abortion, for example, covers over the lack of certitude that the Catholic tradition has always recognized with regard to the theoretical understanding of when individual human life begins. For the greater part of its existence the Catholic Church held for delayed animation according to which the human soul was infused sometime after conception. Pope John Paul II alludes to this tradition without explicitly recalling it. The more recent Catholic position has maintained that in practice one must act as if the human person is present from the moment of conception. This is a prudential judgment, however, and lacks absolute certitude. Further, modern biology does not recognize conception as occurring in a moment but rather as a process taking hours or days. Some in good faith and with some reason on their side could disagree with the pope's judgment.

Catholics have much respect for the pope and the papacy. He is meant to be the sign of unity in the church. However, Pope John Paul II, in his growing insistence on uniformity in sexual morality and in his willingness, even eagerness, to press his moral vision as singularly truthful, has increased divisiveness within Catholicism. Hope for change among many Catholics now comes with an eye on a future pope and a move toward a more healing atmosphere within the church. It stems from the hope of a return to openness and moderation, acceptance of varied opinions and theologies, a return to a catholicity of ideas in church discussions.

Many Western Catholics, steeped in participatory democracy, including a commitment to freedom of speech, have viewed Pope John Paul II's pontificate as anachronistic, unable to connect with their lives. For these Catholics authority is earned and exemplified; it cannot be dictated. They admire the pope's courage to speak forthrightly, to offer the world a clear and needed vision of right from wrong. However these same Catholics are less willing to concede that the pope alone has the full vision or that offering honest criticism should lead to condemnation by Rome. Punative actions offend a Western commitment to open inquiry and deny the freedom of speech and a commitment to human rights. The core of the problem within the church has to do with the sometimes conflicting visions of how truth is obtained and proclaimed.

Pope John Paul II sees truth as revealed to the church, in the final analysis, through the pope alone; other Catholics may share this vision, but they do not share it entirely. They also see truth as a discernment process not limited to the church but one that involves the entire human family. The Vatican perspective sees truth as abstract and absolute throughout time; others also see it as being revealed and developed through the ongoing efforts of the human family. The problem for many Catholics with Rome's approach is that it leads to a church and to a world of insiders and outsiders. Some have access to the "truth" and others do not. Inevitably, those who "have the truth" attack those who do not. Within the church so-called dissenters become the greatest and most threatening enemies because they are watering down the faith or, worse yet, proclaiming heresy. In fact, this is where Catholicism finds itself in the later years of Pope John Paul II's pontificate. Self-proclaimed truth squads, sometimes bypassing local U.S. bishops, have reported to Vatican officials and have gotten sympathetic hearings.[10] The Vatican has appointed commissions to investigate U.S. seminaries to assure theological orthodoxy. Similarly, it pressured the leaders of U.S. Catholic universities to assure that what it sees as "dissenting" Catholic voices not be allowed to teach theology. The result of this coercion, in the eyes of some, has been significant, including "a serious loss in theological credibility."[11] In the mid-1990s, many U.S. Catholics who depend on Catholic institutions for their livelihood dare not speak publicly if they disagree with the Vatican. Their jobs could be on the line. All of this stems from a clampdown by Rome, an effort to enforce greater orthodoxy, as Rome defines it. Whatever the intentions, the results have been to send shivers down the spine of the church. What saddens Catholics, looking back nearly twenty centuries to the life and times of Jesus, the compassionate healer, the liberator, is to find themselves operating in an organization that seems at times to conduct itself in a manner far from the spirit in which Jesus taught.

It was in the early 1980s that U.S. Catholics first began to talk about the changing atmosphere in the church. They spoke of the growth of "the chill factor." Most would say things have only gotten colder since that time. During Pope John Paul II's pontificate, the Vatican has criminalized dissent; has taken control of nominations of all theologians, including moral theologians, who teach in church-related institutions of higher learning; has taken control of the nominations of all bishops and other church officeholders; has demanded that educators express a new confession of faith, including assent to noninfallible (that is, fallible) papal teaching and a particular oath of fidelity toward the supreme pontiff; and has investigated the "trustworthiness" of Catholic bishops, removing those found wanting in Rome's eyes. Such a centralization of authority and papal power is unprecedented in modern Catholic history and probably in church history. Vatican critics point out that in virtually every instance basic Catholic doctrine has not been the issue. The issue has been sexual morality or issues pertaining to sex and gender.

Church Models

Competing for ascendance as Catholicism enters the twenty-first century are two competing models of church.[12] One sees itself as primarily vertical in nature; the other sees itself as primarily horizontal in nature. The former model envisions a God "up in heaven" who sends down graces through a series of chosen mediators, the pope, bishops, priests. The other envisions a God who is among the people and shares their experiences. While this is an oversimplification, most Catholics consciously or unconsciously work out of one of the two metaphors of church. Catholic ecclesiology recognizes aspects of both models. Especially since the Second Vatican Council, Catholics have been moving toward the horizontal model of community. Vatican II offered as the primary definition of the church the "People of God." In this model, God is not "above"; God is within the church, present to it in Word and Spirit. Jesus did not leave the world in his Resurrection; Jesus in Resurrection became the Christ dwelling "until the end of the world" with those who in faith and hope accept the redeeming truth that unending life comes from the Cross. But this has not been the model of church for the pontificate of Pope John Paul II. He sees himself as intermediary between the "God above" and the church "below."

Theologian Häring writes the following:[13]

> *The pope is aware that the vast majority of married people are unable to fall into full agreement with the absolute ban on contraception, that they resist the emphasis with which it is inculcated and cannot follow the arguments by which it is justified. Most moral theologians, probably, are of the same mind. The papal response to this public opinion in the church is not new but is now*

delivered with a new emphasis: The church is not democratic; it is hierarchical.

Let us ask our pope: Are you sure your confidence in your supreme human, professional and religious competence in matters of moral theology, and particularly sexual ethics, is truly justified? As to contraception, there is no word on the subject anywhere in divine revelation. This is a matter of what we call the natural law written deep in the hearts of men and women, and therefore we must and can find a fruitful approach that is appropriate. Because natural law is "open to the eyes of reason," we should reason together gently and patiently as we consider the case "on either side" (Rom. 2:12, 16).

The hierarchical constitution of the church cannot in the least contradict or disallow this approach in any matter that concerns the law written in our hearts and calling for a response from our consciences. Away with all distrust in our church! Away with all attitudes, mentalities and structures that promote it! We should let the pope know that we are wounded by the many signs of his rooted distrust and discouraged by the manifold structures of distrust.

Perhaps not surprisingly, the way the Vatican has tightened its grip of authority has given rise to broader questions concerning church governance and structure. It is not a case of disgruntled Catholics wanting to reject church authority. Catholics recognize the need for institutions and acknowledge the need for authority structures to govern those institutions. What upsets many Catholics is the kind of authority operating in the church. Catholics want healthy authority and too often what they find, many say, is unhealthy authority. They see authority that fails to trust; authority that attempts to control; authority that demeans;

authority that refuses to empower and liberate; authority that puts law above the spirit of compassion found in the Gospels. Catholics who question authority, or as they see it, unhealthy authority, do not see themselves doing it to tear down the church but to restore it to health.

In the Catholic Church, authority questions eventually get traced back to the final authority figure, the Roman pontiff. It is a sign of the times that some Catholics have begun to ask questions about the papacy and the Catholic teaching of papal infallibility. Essays have appeared in Catholic publications as the subject has been broached gently but honestly. Bernard Cooke is a Catholic theologian who teaches at Incarnate Word College in San Antonio, Texas. Writing recently, he gave light to the private thoughts of many Catholics as they consider the papacy in modern world. Cooke wrote that the "time may have come to ask bluntly, but not antagonistically, some very basic questions about the nature and role of the papacy in the life of the church."[14] Noting that "these questions are not entirely new," he went on to say, "There has been a mounting chorus of responsible voices within the church, from a wide range of people, suggesting that the prevalent attitude of many Catholics toward the papacy and some recent statements emanating from the Vatican are an over-reading of the true authority and power of the Holy See."

Questions about the papacy and the proper limits of papal teaching authority surfaced immediately before and after the publication of the encyclical *Humanae Vitae* in 1968, but they date back as far back as the First Vatican Council, when papal infallibility was initially declared in 1870. The First Vatican Council was a monumental council. It was during this gathering of Catholic bishops that they declared the doctrine of papal infallibility. Literally it means not being able to err. In theological terms it means the Holy Spirit protects the church from error when it solemnly defines a matter of faith or morals. The doctrine is widely misunderstood both inside and outside the church. Infallibility, as defined by Vatican I, states that the pope possesses "the infallibility with which the divine Redeemer willed his church to be endowed in defining the doctrine concerning faith and morals." It does not mean everything the pope has to say about faith and morals is true or without error. When does the pope speak infallibly? According to the doctrine, when he specifically speaks *ex cathedra* (from the chair of Peter) on a matter of doctrine or morality. While this doctrine has never been officially used in relation to any teaching on sexual morality, it has in recent decades entered into church discussions concerning papal intentions on statements dealing with these matters. It, so to speak, raised the ante and created an atmosphere in which dissent from official teachings became more difficult. One of the most penetrating examinations of the question of infallibility appeared in the 1970 book *Infallible? An Enquiry* by the Swiss theologian Father Hans Küng, republished as *Infallible? An Unresolved Enquiry* in 1995.[15] In the book, Küng questioned papal infallibility as an authentic church doctrine. He was later stripped of his position as Catholic theologian at the University of Tübingen, Germany, in 1979, a little more than a year after John Paul II became pope. Küng remains, however, at Tübingen as professor of ecumenical theology and director of the Institute of Ecumenical Research.

Central to any infallibility inquiry are these questions: Does the pope's claim to unquestioned authority constitute a basis for the legitimacy of the claim, or is there in the unformulated belief of the Christian community some kind of underlying presumption of this ultimate papal prerogative?[16] There are other questions: To what extent is the kind of power and authority claimed and exercised by the papacy consonant with the kind of power and authority claimed and exercised by Jesus of Nazareth? Is there a place in the church for monarchical authority when Jesus himself repudiated political power and when Jesus and the earliest Christian generations needed to radically reinterpret the concept of Messiah, rejecting the implication of kingship that had been central to Jewish expectations and replacing it with the prophetic character of Jesus' ministry.

Bernard Cooke has written the following on this aspect of papal authority:

> *The real issue is monarchical power, whether the monarchy in question be worldly or spiritual. It has proved to be a blessing that the papacy has perforce ceased to be an earthly monarchy. But there remains the question of a spiritual monarchy. At least at first blush, monarchical understanding of the church and of the papacy's role contrasts fundamentally with Jesus of Nazareth. One is faced with clear cognitive dissonance. In the gospel scene of Jesus' temptation in the desert, one finds a distillation of the forces that work with or against God's reign. Jesus is asked to prove his messiahship by tempting God and employing means of "salvation" other than God's. The culminating temptation comes when Satan offers Jesus ultimate economic and political power, "all the kingdoms of the earth," as the path to saving humankind. Jesus' refusal to bow to this worship of earthly power puts him squarely at odds with our ordinary understanding and esteem of power. . . .*
>
> *The gospels describe Jesus explicitly and without qualification rejecting the political model for the reign of God. Careful study of*

the New Testament writings suggests that Jesus did not use any model for thinking about the church because he did not envisage a future church as a structured religious community. He did not foresee or plan for any ordained officials. Much less did he himself establish the initial form of any institutional structures or rituals. What he did was to initiate a work of salvation whose nature would lead to certain structures evolving in the course of history. Jesus "instituted the church" by living as he lived, by dying as he did, and by passing into that realized state of humanness that he shares with those who accept it. Jesus exercised power and continues still to exercise that power, the power of God's Spirit of truth and love. For the papacy, then, as for all structured elements of the church, that raises a critical question: Can we Catholics still maintain that aspects of the church's life such as the papacy are really de jure divino, *that is, initiated and empowered by God?. . .*

The question must be posed to all Christian institutions, including the papacy: Is the power they exercise the power of God's Spirit or some other forms of power that are not congruent with the action of that Spirit? Or to pose the question more specifically: Is the political model that has for centuries grounded our understanding of the papacy really applicable to the Christian community? And if it is not, how are we, in a way that is faithful to the person and ongoing mission of Jesus, to think about the role of the bishop of Rome?[17]

These are tough questions and not easily dealt with, especially not in the current climate in the Catholic Church. But they reflect the serious thinking of educated and active Catholics, including church theologians. No doubt, there are many in the church who see such questions as heretical, as completely unwarranted. This, too, exemplifies the way the church has become divided in recent decades. One's attitude toward the way the pope has dealt with women and the sexual issues is a fair indicator where a Catholic is likely to fall along the divide.

U.S. Catholic Snapshot

Repeated U.S. surveys on Catholic attitudes regarding morality show them growing increasingly independent of the Vatican. Such surveys have confirmed Rome's worst fears, causing it to speak out with ever greater vehemence on moral matters. From the Vatican's perspective, U.S. Catholics live in a state of virtual apostasy. The polls show that Rome's thunderous condemnations, however, have failed to win many converts to its viewpoints. So the cycle of internal dysfunction continues.

One Gallup survey asked questions of U.S. Catholics in 1987 and repeated those questions in 1993 in order to measure change in attitudes.[18] In almost every instance the move was toward a more independent stance, a move away from Rome. For example, between 1987 and 1993 polls found a significant increase in Catholics saying, "You can be a good Catholic without obeying the church's teaching regarding abortion." The percentage of women saying you can be a good Catholic without obeying the church's teaching on abortion jumped from 34 percent in 1987 to 56 percent in 1993, while the percentage jump for men was from 45 percent in 1987 to 55 percent in 1993. Women appeared to show a substantial change over the six-year period in attitudes on moral issues affecting them. "On any of the issues that seem to touch on sexuality, women took a much more radical stand than they did the last time" the poll was conducted, said Ruth Wallace, professor of sociology at George Washington University and one of the developers of the survey. "They were more progressive, more questioning of the authority of the church." Asked if church teaching on abortion had strengthened or weakened church commitment, 36 percent of the women interviewed said it had strengthened it and 25 percent said it had weakened it. Six years earlier, 46 percent said church teaching on abortion had strengthened their commitment to the church and 19 percent said church teaching on abortion had weakened their commitment to the church.

Asked in 1993 if the church's position against the ordination of women had strengthened or weakened their commitment to the church, 13 percent of women said it had strengthened their commitment and 27 percent said it had weakened their commitment. Six years earlier, 23 percent had said it had strengthened commitment and 22 percent had said it had weakened it. The poll showed that only a minority of lay Catholics think that only bishops should determine the morality of key questions of Catholic practice. Only one out of four Catholics thinks that only the bishops should have the authority to decide about remarriage without annulment.

An examination of attitudes of young Catholics does not give much hope that this independent-mindedness among U.S. Catholics will soon disappear. The poll found older Catholics being the most conforming to official church teachings and the youngest surveyed the least conforming. For example, among Catholics fifty-five-years old and older, 34 percent said the individual should have the final say on the morality of sex outside of marriage. Among eighteen- to thirty-four-year-olds, the figure was 51 percent. The poll also found that Catholics had been greatly disillusioned by reports of sex abuse by clergy. Fifty percent of those surveyed said such reports had weakened their commitment to the church. According to William D'Antonio, sociologist at Catholic University in Washington, D.C., the "consistency" and the "direction of the findings" indicate that a "new voice" is emerging in the church, one expressing a "strong sense of the personal autonomy, pluralism and democracy that permeate the larger American society." He added that the argument that "voices of dissent come only from the marginal Catholics is strongly refuted by these data."

Change in Catholic attitudes has been a constant in church history. Traditionally, change enters the church from the bottom up. While church councils have gathered through the centuries to proclaim teachings, the teachings themselves have been influenced by Catholic practice and belief. Many Catholics would argue there is little reason to think the situation is any different today.

Credibility

The most common criticism made of the Catholic Church's sexual teachings—and perhaps the most damning—is that they are simply not credible. No matter how hard the Vatican tries to convince Catholics, the Vatican's case somehow rarely seems to persuade the faithful. It is not so much that U.S. Catholics are renegades or that they see themselves as lacking room for further moral discernment. Most are searching for guidance. They want to find ways to be faithful to the church, and most recognize the need for authority. Most reflective, discerning, and open-minded Catholics, however, cannot accept Catholic sexual morality as pronounced in strict absolutes. Many end up walking away. Given all the painfully obvious evils in the world today, they ask why the church insists on speaking out most vociferously about sexual sins. They ask why all sins of the flesh are considered to be of a "serious matter," meaning the "type of action that is calculated to provoke the mature and sensitive person to a radical existential break with the God of salvation."[19] They ask how it is possible that all sins of masturbation are of such a serious nature. Might not loneliness, prolonged absence from one's spouse, and frustrated relationships mitigate the objective sinfulness of the act? They ignore a theology that fails to make distinctions in the gravity of sins. They ask how sexual intercourse with the use of a condom is always "an intrinsically evil" act. They ask how the use of a condom to prevent the spread of the AIDS virus, even within marriage, can be as morally wrong as passing the virus to another. They ask how artificial birth control can be regarded as evil in all cases and natural family planning can be viewed as good if the intention not to conceive a child is the same in each instance. They ask how a compassionate church can teach that gays and lesbians can never under any circumstances express sexual intimacy. They ask how the church can teach a host of sexual absolutes that never take into consideration circumstances. Can artificial insemination, even with a husband's sperm in order to have a child, be gravely wrong? The list could go on. "It just doesn't make any sense," is the common response. Many Catholics raised in the faith hang on, disregarding the teachings. The young, more frequently, simply don't want to be bothered.

XI

❖ ❖ ❖

Theology and the Future

Catholicism's current divisions run deep and most originate in theology. They do not appear insurmountable, but will require years of painstaking efforts—and an atmosphere of honesty and openness within the church—to be worked out. The Catholic renewal of the Second Vatican Council, followed by strong reactions to that renewal, most notably during the pontificate of Pope John Paul II, have ripped Catholicism from centuries of safe moorings. The church, meanwhile, is being propelled into a modern age radically unlike anything it has ever experienced. Changing circumstances continue to place great pressures upon the church. Catholics, meanwhile, find themselves pained and troubled. Many ask deeply penetrating questions about their church: How should authority be wielded? What is the nature of the priesthood? What shape should the institutional church take? How can it truly become inclusive? What, indeed, should its twenty-first century mission be? Is Catholicism primarily about upholding defined "truth," and if so, how does that truth continue to be defined? Or is Catholicism primarily about proclaiming the good news of the Gospels by working for peace and justice in the world? The most hopeful response to these last questions is that "either/or" answers are not required, that inclusive "both/and" visions can come about. Most Catholics recognize aspects of their faith life in both truth and justice. Why the conflict? Some theologians trace the modern struggle to the inadequate way any person perceives and portrays God today.

> *Where he is seen as lawgiver or as lover, as liberator or a judge, as narrator or as artist, human perspectives of God may with more or less inadequacy portray something of him, but none in isolation is at all capable of comprehending the height or depth or breadth or richness of divine reality.*[1]

Much remains unclear. Theology is not a precise science; mystery will always be involved. Yet, looking back over a quarter century or more of Catholic experience, undeniably the issues of human sexuality have been the most contentious within the church and appear related to the way God is envisioned and spoken of by the Catholic faithful. From imagination and language rise meaning and purpose. The church has much work to do in these areas. The lessons of the past quarter century also seem to indicate that significant Catholic integration and healing cannot occur—either for the institution as a whole or for millions of Catholics at a personal level—until accommodations between conflicting visions have been made.

Catholics today feel these divisions. They suffer from these divisions. Hardly a Catholic parish or Catholic family has been spared the pain. However, as Catholics acknowledge the hurt, only a relatively few are able to explain how or why it has come about. To do so requires some understanding of the theological landscape, even more precisely the landscape of moral theology, in which these struggles are being played out. Libraries are filled with books on Catholic moral theology. It is an active and vital field of study, especially since the Second Vatican Council. Virtually any portrayal of moral theology involves vast simplification. Yet tendencies are pronounced and can serve as an outline to further understanding.

The conflicting forces of Catholic moral theology involve the drive toward totality on the one hand and the recognition of diversity on the other. Catholic moral theology since the days of Thomas Aquinas has proclaimed a living, unified, intelligible vision in which moral evaluation occurs. In this scheme the morality of sexual acts is seen in the light of a preexisting law called natural law. It governs all, is intelligible to all, but is proclaimed by the church. During this century and especially in the wake of the Second Vatican Council, Catholic theologians began also to consider history, sociology, and anthropology, having acquired the theoretical ability to stand outside history and see it as history, rather than being immersed in it. These capabilities allowed greater awareness of circumstances and, if not allowing complete objectivity, moved the analysis to particulars demanding their own analysis. Circumstance entered theological discourse as did the need to understand the persons as well as the acts before coming to moral judgment. Just as there has been a strong counterreaction to the renewals of the council, so too has there been a strong counterreaction to the recognition of diversity. Pope John Paul II, both in *Veritatis Splendor* and in *Evanglium Vitae,* vigorously attempted to reestablish a total moral vision. He has condemned any recognition of moral diversity, saying it leads to moral relativism. This fear and tendency may be well founded, but the Catholic theologians who have been developing moral theology maintain that recognizing diversity does not necessarily require the abandoning of certain moral principles. Again, the healthy future may rest in living with and accepting those tensions that arise while recognizing value in both approaches. Balance appears required. It is when one attempts to eliminate or dominate the other that unbearable conflict results.

Today, within Catholicism theologians approach moral theology in two ways. While a minority of theologians would adamantly maintain one approach excludes the other, most appear to be working for some integration of both. Unfortunately, given the climate of today's church and the explosive nature of the work, moral theology is finding itself with increasingly fewer committed students. The two models, or approaches to moral theology, have been labeled the classicist model and the historical consciousness model. The Vatican and other conservative moral theologians work out of the classicist model, which goes back centuries. It sees as a threat the historical consciousness model, which dates back to the Enlightenment but has been developed widely in the Catholic Church in this century.[2] In Catholic theological circles, the general movement has been away from classicism and toward historical consciousness. This disturbs Rome. It has been a source of great irritation. From Pope John Paul II's perspective, the newer approach threatens eternal truths and he is all that stands in the way of disaster.

Briefly, a sketch of the two approaches to moral theology are as follows: Classicism understands reality in terms of the eternal, the immutable, and the unchanging; historical consciousness gives more importance to the particular, the contingent, the historical, and the individual. Historical consciousness, meanwhile, can be contrasted with the other extreme of sheer existentialism that sees the present moment in isolation from the before and the after. Historical consciousness recognizes the need for both continuity and discontinuity. The Catholic tradition recognizes historicity in its rejection of revelation as coming from "the Scripture alone." Scripture is understood and communicated in the light of the Catholic experience, in the light of cultural realities. Catholicism's teachings, therefore, have developed and evolved, and this "creative fidelity" is consistent with the historical consciousness worldview.

The classicist worldview is associated with the deductive methodology that deduces its conclusions from its premises, the eternal verities. Historical consciousness, on the other hand, recognizes the need for a more inductive approach. The need to maintain both continuity and discontinuity argues against a solely one-sided inductive approach. One problem posed by the inductive approach is that it can never achieve the same degree of certitude for its conclusions as can the deductive methodology. The manuals of Catholic moral theology until the Second Vatican Council in the mid-1960s exclusively employed the deductive, or legal, model as primary. According to this model, the function of human conscience is to obey divine law, or to live in accord with natural law. The classicism model gives more significance to nature and acts than it does to persons. This, then, has led to a sexual ethics that teaches absolutes such as the grave evil of masturbation, artificial contraception, sterilization, artificial insemination, and homosexual acts. Such actions contravene natural law. The church teaches that all sexual activity has a twofold purpose—procreation and love union—and that every sexual act must respect that twofold purpose. The sex act itself must be open to procreation and expressive love. Such an understanding forms the basis for the teachings that masturbation, contraception, and artificial insemination, even with the husband's sperm, are always wrong. They are not natural. They go against the divine plan. There is no room for compromise on the subject.

Pope John Paul II has shown great reluctance to embrace historical consciousness as a model for moral theology. By temperament and training he is a philosopher who studied, taught, and wrote in the more classicist philosophical model. Indeed, *Veritatis Spendor* depicts historical consciousness as subversive and a threat to church unity.[3] Many loyal Catholics face a dilemma: an inability to subscribe to many of the traditional moral teachings as "absolutes" involving serious sin or involving "intrinsically evil" acts. The church's teaching against artificial contraception is the most widely cited example. Yet theological discussions that point to alternative moral means of making moral judgments are almost entirely outlawed in Catholic seminaries and even in some Catholic colleges and universities. The current atmosphere within the church does not allow for much diversity of opinion. In April 1995, for example, a theology professor who signed an open letter to Pope John Paul II calling for further discussion of women's ordination was dismissed from her teaching post at St. Meinrad Seminary in St. Meinrad,

Indiana. The seminary, which trains priests for Catholic dioceses around the world, fired Sister Carmel McEnroy for her "public dissent" from church teaching. The move followed a March visit to the seminary by a committee of U.S. Catholic bishops headed by Archbishop Elden F. Curtiss of Omaha, Nebraska. McEnroy's name had appeared with hundreds of others under a published statement titled "An Open Letter to Pope John Paul II," challenging the pope's May 1994 declaration that the question of women's ordination is "definitively" closed.[4]

Missing for many Catholics has been an open atmosphere in which the discussion of human sexuality and gender-related issues is possible. Missing has been an alternative to the "legalistic" moral theology that judges acts instead of the total functioning of the person. Missing in recent years has been acceptance of theological efforts that take into consideration contemporary scientific discussions or the experiences of people. Meanwhile, the Vatican has attempted to marginalize the work of those moral theologians who have incorporated the historical consciousness model. But their writings will not go away. Catholic history is full of examples of teachers who, rejected during their lifetimes, were elevated as models of wisdom after their deaths. It is unlikely that historical consciousness as an approach to moral theology is in danger of disappearing. To the contrary, it remains mainstream in many U.S. schools of theology, including some Catholic institutions of higher learning. While classicism is the approach to theology preferred by Rome, its supporters outside Vatican walls are outnumbered.

There is substantial thought among Catholics that the church renewal begun during the Second Vatican Council, including council documents that in part used inductive reasoning to assess the church and give direction to it, will take more time to work itself out. The full fruits of renewal, this reasoning goes, will not be seen until well into the twenty-first century. Vatican II supporters see *Humanae Vitae* and Pope John Paul II's "restoration" efforts, including *Veritatis Splendor* and *Evangelium Vitae,* as having slowed—but not having ended—church theological renewal. They see the strongly conservative John Paul II pontificate as a reaction to the council, a regrouping period before the church continues with its renewal journey. That efforts to return the church to old thinking and theologies have not had widespread success, these Catholics say, is a good sign Catholic renewal will continue in the years ahead. Adding to the momentum of change are other factors as well. The classicist theology is Western and European in its origins. It grew almost entirely out of Western culture. The Roman Catholic Church has been largely shaped by Western culture as well. The church, however, has grown enormously in the twentieth century, and much of this growth has been in Africa, Asia, and Latin America. These cultures will almost certainly help shape the church in the coming century. The experiences of African, Asian, and Latin American Catholics will vie to find their places. It was only in the 1960s that for the first time the church's demographic balance shifted away from a Eurocentric to a global church. As this has happened, Third World theologies have grown within the church. Liberation theology, whose roots come from Latin America, has spread to other parts of the church. Liberation theology uses inductive methods of assessment even as it maintains a scriptural base. During the twentieth century the Catholic Church has truly become catholic, its influence felt throughout the globe. But such growth cannot happen without local cultures eventually finding their ways into the larger body of the church. In a way, this revolutionary process parallels the revolution going on within the Catholic Church in the West as educated women begin to study and write church theologies. The Catholic Church is ripe for enormous change in the twenty-first century.

Many church observers, realizing that the dispute in Catholicism is primarily of a theological nature, with moral theology and issues of authority closely linked, see the gradual shift to new theological methods as inevitably moving to changes in church authority and even structure. The Vatican, fearing the same, is doing what it can to return to theologies that grew out of the works of Thomas Aquinas (1225–74) and gained hold at the Council of Trent in the mid-sixteenth century.

Pope John Paul II, by issuing *Veritatis Splendor* in 1993 and *Evangelium Vitae* in 1995, and through them insisting on the sole validity of the deductive, legalistic, classicist approach to theology, is attempting not only to set the church's course on sexual morality but also to shape its authority structure well beyond his pontificate. Here again sexual ethics and authority get linked. Not a few church theologians see these encyclicals as further efforts to undo the work of the Second Vatican Council, which called upon the church to develop new approaches to theology. Consider the following admonition given by Vatican II in this regard from the *Pastoral Constitution on the Church in the Modern World*:[5]

> *The church safeguards the deposit of God's Word, from which religious and moral principles are drawn. But it does not always have a ready answer to individual questions, and it wishes to com-*

bine the light of revelation with the experience of everyone in order to illuminate the road on which humanity has recently set out.

The council then went on as follows:[6]

For recent studies and findings of science, history, and philosophy raise new questions which influence life and demand new theological investigations.

Furthermore, while adhering to the methods and requirements proper to theology, theologians are invited to seek continually for more suitable ways of communicating doctrine to the people of their times.

May the faithful, therefore, live in very close union with the wise men and women of their time. Let them strive to understand perfectly their way of thinking and feeling, as expressed in their culture. Let them blend modern science and its theories and the understanding of the most recent discoveries with Christian morality and doctrine. Thus their religious practice and morality can keep pace with their scientific knowledge and with an ever advancing technology. Thus, too, they will be able to test and interpret all things in a truly Christian spirit.

Following the council, many moral theologians set out to collaborate with modern sciences to gather empirical data that would help them formulate theologies based on a better understanding of human sexuality. Those efforts are the ones viewed with suspicion, even condemned, by the Vatican in recent years.

COLLEGIALITY

The Second Vatican Council stressed the idea of collegiality—meaning that all the bishops share in church decision making. When the bishops met in Rome in the mid-1960s large numbers of them were convinced that the monarchical model of church was an accident of history and in need of modification. Further, the bishops decided that shared decision making would be more in keeping with emerging democratic trends. Conservatives resisted, but reformers won the day. It was decided that collegiality of the bishops would be the means to these desired ends and that regular synods, or meetings, of the world's bishops, would collectively administer the church. This entailed decentralizing church authority, stripping the Roman Curia of much of the power it had accrued.

The Roman Curia is a group of various Vatican bureaus that assist the pope in the day-to-day running of the church. It is made up of sacred congregations, the most important being the Congregation for the Doctrine of the Faith, responsible for safeguarding Catholic doctrine on faith and morals. There is a Catholic saying that "popes come and go but the curia remains." It speaks to the power and obstinate nature of the curia. The Roman Curia has the reputation of holding the reins of power in the church and not wanting to give them up. Since the Second Vatican Council, the Roman Curia has been reluctant to implement collegiality. It has downplayed the importance of national bishops's conferences that came out of the council as counterforces to the curia. Periodic synods, or gatherings of the world's bishops, to help administer the church, have also been deemphasized by the curia and by Pope John Paul II. While they have occurred every few years during his pontificate, they have become largely advisory in nature, with the Roman Curia writing the final drafts, which are then redrafted and issued by the pope. This is not the kind of collegiality the Second Vatican Council seemed to have had in mind.

According to the Vatican II document *Dogmatic Constitution on the Church,* authority is given not just to Peter and his successors but to the whole college of the Apostles and to those who succeed to the apostolic commission: "Together with its head, the Roman Pontiff, and never without its head, the episcopal order is the subject of supreme and full power over the universal Church." This collegial union is especially apparent in an ecumenical council, but it is also manifested "in the mutual relations of the individual bishops with particular churches and with the universal Church. . . . In and from such individual churches there comes into being the one and only Catholic Church. For this reason each individual bishop represents his own church, but all of them together in union with the Pope represents the entire church joined in the bond of peace, love, and unity." Catholic theologians see the church as fully existing "in each legitimate local congregation,"[7] as was the case in the New Testament, and also in the communion of all these local congregations. This means the local bishops are not mere delegates of the pope, but have the authority to run their local churches. The centralization of authority that has occurred during Pope John Paul II's pontificate, many church observers say, has thwarted the implementation of collegiality as the council intended. This centralization of authority in Rome has not come without a sense of resentment among many of the bishops. Nor without building pressures for change in the years ahead. With the Roman Curia writing and issuing church documents without meaningful consultation or input from local bishops or lay Catholics, tensions have increased within the church.

Privately many U.S. bishops say that the Vatican has gone too far in centralizing authority and they feel powerless to change matters. Yet the profound sense of loyalty to Rome that they feel makes it difficult, or impossible, for them to object in public. Such objections, they contend, could be misconstrued as a lack of loyalty. Above all, they say they fear showing discord within the ranks of the episcopacy.

New Approaches

If the outcome of the conflict in the field of moral theology appears uncertain, it seems there is less disputing trends among the faithful. Beginning with their massive rejection of *Humanae Vitae*, the birth control encyclical, U.S. Catholics have increasingly disregarded Rome's exhortations, especially when they do not match with lessons of their own experiences. Initially this placed U.S. Catholic confessors and counselors in awkward positions, caught between official church teachings and private belief and practice. Over the years both confessors and lay Catholics have made their accommodations. Repeated surveys of U.S. Catholic beliefs and practices have shown the gap widening between what the official church teaches on many sexual matters and what many practicing Catholics in good conscience believe. This has led to an increase in a traditional Catholic distinction, one that arises when a Catholic faces a priest seeking moral counsel on a sexual matter and possible absolution for sin, between the "moral" and the "pastoral" solution. The former has its place in natural law, but the later finds its way into the heart of the counseling priest. The former upholds the universal norm; the latter, the particular circumstance of the penitent. The former recognizes the law, the official teaching; the latter, the compassionate exception to the law. Some have suggested that what is basically at issue here is the tension that exists between the challenge and the comfort of God's call.[8] Others see in these distinctions a duplicity that cries out to change the methods and guidelines of Catholic moral theology. Catholic confessors who operate out of traditional classicist moral theology represent a small minority in the U.S. clergy. Catholic conservatives see this as tragic development; Catholic progressives see it as a hopeful sign.

U.S. Catholics, meanwhile, have been settling questions of conscience with less direction from priests in the form of the sacrament of reconciliation, traditionally the sacrament of penance. A generation ago, many Catholics would participate in the sacrament monthly or more. Today, large numbers of Catholics almost ignore it all together or involve themselves in it when some form of collective reconciliation takes place in a local parish. This might involve a prayer service, an examination of conscience, and individual absolution by several priests. General absolutions have also occurred in which a priest or bishop holds a prayer service and offers his absolution to all in attendance. This practice, however, has been condemned by Rome. Whether the relatively recent disregard by Catholics for the sacrament of reconciliation stems from disagreement with the church on its sexual teachings or is the result of other trends is not entirely clear. The church's sexual teachings, beginning with its reaffirmation of church condemnation of birth control, has led to a decay of Catholic credibility in Catholic institutions, studies have shown.[9]

Today, Catholicism continues to undergo enormous change even as church leaders cling to sacred traditions. New ways of examining theology and moral questions have entered the faith of Catholics even as some church leaders stress the need to hold to traditional ways. While it is sometimes difficult to get a handle on these changes at any one point, it is less difficult to trace these changes to their sources. One of the most striking reasons for current change in the Catholic Church stems from the emphasis the Second Vatican Council gave to sacred Scripture and the call to Catholics to make Scripture an essential part of their lives. Catholics appear to have taken the call seriously. Scripture reading groups have come to life throughout the church. There are far too many to be led by priests, the traditional interpreter to Catholics of the sacred texts. As Catholics have rediscovered Scripture, they have also developed new methods and windows through which to look when assessing Catholic sexual teachings. Scripture and church law are not necessarily in conflict; however some, rightly or wrongly, have often found them to be. Traditional Catholic morality on sexual matters, based in natural law theology, works out of absolute right and wrong. New Testament Scripture sees Jesus condemning legal codes, replacing them with basic admonitions to love and to forgive. Curiously, Pope John Paul II is a living example of scriptural renaissance within the church. His writings are heavily based in Scripture and Scripture stories. His 1995 encyclical, *Evangelium Vitae,* while traditional in perspective, was a meditation on Scripture passages.

Especially since the Second Vatican Council, the Catholic Church has become far more Scripture oriented than at virtually any other time in its history. Catholicism today is only beginning to understand and feel the effects of this revolution within the church. Christian love is now generally recognized as the necessary starting and ending points of all moral reflections. This has had a significant impact on moral theology. Christian love is seen as an intimate participation in the life of God, who is love (1 John 4:8,16). Christian love is seen as a sacred gift from God that is mediated by Christ and activated by the Spirit.[10] Christian love is seen as the story of the experience of God in community as the beginning point of reconciliation of body and spirit, self and others, and humanity and God.[11]

Since the Second Vatican Council, the Catholic Church has witnessed other new trends that have helped shape its sexual ethics. Perhaps the most important has been the revolutionary introduction of psychology as a means toward a better understanding of the natural order. Modern psychologists such as Erich Fromm and Rollo May insist, for example, that a person's capacity to love depends on his or her personal maturity. In one way or another, this insight has found its way into a host of Catholic texts on the meaning and development of sexuality. What does love require, a Catholic theologian asks, answering his own question: It requires "self-knowledge, effort, conviction, courage, generosity, respect, a sense of responsibility, sensitivity, patience and a fundamental acceptance of oneself with all of one's strengths and limitations."[12] The point is that modern psychology often agrees with the basic Christian principle that people are called to love others as self. Further, healthy expressions of human sexuality cannot be divorced from this basic command. The problem of an unhealthy sexuality arises when people have not resolved the inevitable crises of human growth and have not attained sufficient human maturity for Christian love. In this light, healthy human sexuality is seen as a growth process. It is seen as in need of nurturing, but within the context of values central to Christian life. In the mid-1970s, a number of U.S. moral theologians, commissioned by the Catholic Theological Society of America, were called upon to develop new guidelines for sexual ethics. To determine the morality of sexual behavior, they suggested answering certain questions. They asked: Does sexual behavior realize values conducive to growth and integration? Is it self-liberating? Other-enriching? Honest? Faithful? Socially responsible? Life-serving? Joyous? Finally, are all these values enlightened and permeated by the core principle of Christian conduct, the gospel of love? If so, they answered, the actions are likely wholesome and moral.[13]

It is a rare person who does not seek moral guidance. Most people recognize the need in some form for help or assurance on sexual matters. Two Catholic counselors who have been offering such counsel are Fran Ferder, a member of the Franciscan Sisters of Perpetual Adoration, and Father John Heagle. The two are codirectors of the Therapy and Renewal Associates, a ministerial counseling and consultation service for the Archdiocese of Seattle. They counsel and assist Catholics on sexual questions. They talk about working toward a new and comprehensive Catholic theology of human sexuality, saying its formation will require a number of "shifts" from old ways of thinking to new ones. They list some of these shifts as follows: A shift from a static to a developmental view of psychosexuality; from an emphasis on procreation to one on generativity; from a focus on genitality to a wider understanding of human sexuality; from suspicion of sexual energy to its celebration; from sex education to sexual formation; from dualism (for example, evil body, good spirit) to integration as a framework for understanding psychosexuality; from sexual sin as illicit pleasure to sexual sin as a violation of a person; from patriarchy to partnership as the philosophical mind-set for determining sexual ethics; and from sexual abstinence to reverence in relationships as the hallmark of sexual holiness. They maintain healthy psychosexuality is obtained only through a lifelong growth process.

They write the following:

> *The unfolding of our bodily energies, the emergence of self-awareness, the development of our ability to know and name our feelings—all these play a vital part in the process. . . . If the journey is blunted, wounded, or traumatized in some way, our capacity for human closeness will not be fully realized. Psychosexual development is another phrase for our pathway to love.*[14]

They are only two among many who, influenced by psychology, are bringing new insights into the sexual discussion within the church. A vision of sexuality as part of a lifelong growth process, as part of what it means to be Christian, they say, affirms its sacredness and the centrality of Christian love. Such thoughts are gaining popularity within the church while challenging it to approach the human sexuality discussion with new openness. It is a challenge that will not go away. Catholic tradition is evolutionary. What is new is not meant to replace the old. Rather it is meant to transform it. Essentials do not change; accidentals do. Their call, then, is for continual discernment. It is for the development of a reasoned faith and a reasoned morality.

At the end of the twentieth century and another millennium of church history, Catholicism is fractured and hurting. Sexual teachings, not basic doctrine, is the cause of most of the alienation and pain. A generation after the council, the church remains very much in a transformational process. Change continues to occur as Catholics react to new social and cultural realities, as they imagine new ways of being Catholic. Movement is certain even though the path is not always clear. Resistance to change is seen as yet another sign of the birthing process. Meanwhile, the entrance for the first time into the Catholic theological conversation of the thoughts, voices, and writings of untold numbers of educated Catholic women assures that new visions of church, already being born, will not go away, and will have greater sway in the decades ahead. That this is an often painful and confusing time for Catholicism makes it no less vital. Indeed, these are signs of energy and life.

Catholics are caught between the old and the new. It is not necessarily a comfortable experience, but it is at times also exciting, full of energy and expectation. The story of sexuality and Catholicism, especially in the last third of the twentieth century, is one of enormous change among Catholics in attitudes, values, practices, and theologies—if not in official teachings. Looking back at the Second Vatican Council, it may well be that the transformation it helped initiate is still closer to the beginning of the process than it is to the end. Catholics know well that none of this comes easily, but they are both comforted and emboldened by the belief that the Spirit is alive in the world and in their church.

So in this story faith receives the last word. It shapes meaning and needs to cast light on any evolving Catholic understanding of the nature and role of sexuality. Belief in human dignity as a sacred gift requires profound reverence and respect for the creation process, including all aspects of human relationships. Catholicism is echoing this refrain with growing purpose and assurance, a sign that, despite the turmoil, it is headed in the right direction.

Notes

Chapter I *(Sexuality and the Christian Tradition)*

[1] Richard McBrien, *Catholicism,* rev. ed. (HarperSanFrancisco, 1994), p. 3. The book contains a solid overall view of the Catholic faith, its doctrines, theologies, and the church's relations with the modern world.

[2] Anthony Kosnick et al., *Human Sexuality, New Directions in American Catholic Thought,* (New York: Paulist Press, 1977), p. 7ff. The book reassesses Catholic sexual morality and was the work of a commission of the Catholic Theological Society of America. The report represents a comprehensive reevaluation of Catholic sexual morality. After its completion and publication, it was criticized by many U.S. bishops and as well as by the Vatican.

[3] Ibid., pp. 7–8.

[4] McBrien, *Catholicism,* p. 898.

[5] Kosnick et al., *Human Sexuality,* p. 22.

[6] Uta Ranke-Heinemann, *Eunuchs for the Kingdom of Heaven: Women, Sexuality and the Catholic Church* (New York: Penguin Books, 1990), p. 9.

[7] Margaret A. Farley, "Sexual Ethics," in *Sexuality and the Sacred,* ed. James B. Nelson and Sandra P. Longfellow (Louisville, Kentucky: Westminster/John Knox Press), p. 58.

[8] Ibid.

[9] Ranke-Heinemann, *Eunuchs,* p. 61.

[10] Ibid.

[11] Ibid., p. 77.

[12] Kosnick et al., *Human Sexuality*, p. 39

[13] Ibid., p. 43.

[14] Ibid., p. 41.

[15] *Religion and Sexual Health*, ed. Ronald M. Green (Boston: Kluwer Academic Publishers, 1992); "Sexual Ethics in the Roman Catholic Tradition," by Charles Curran, pp. 17–21; and *Abortion and Catholicism, the American Debate*, ed. Patricia Beattie Jung and Thomas A. Shannon (New York: Crossroad, 1988); "Public Dissent in the Church," by Charles Curran, p. 310.

[16] Kosnick et al., *Human Sexuality*, p. 43.

[17] *Eunuchs*, p. 156.

[18] Farley, "Sexual Ethics," p. 63.

[19] *Human Sexuality*, p. 44.

[20] Henry Davis, *Moral and Pastoral Theology* (London: Sheed & Ward, 1936), p. 177f.

[21] It is technically correct to refer to many of the Catholics cited in this book as Roman Catholics in the United States. However, they are commonly referred to as "U.S. Catholics," and will be described as such in future references.

[22] Kosnik et al., *Human Sexuality*, p. 45.

[23] In more recent years, encyclicals have taken their names from words used in the opening line of the document.

[24] Kosnik et al., *Human Sexuality*, p. 45.

[25] Ibid., p. 46.

[26] Ibid.

[27] Ibid.

[28] Curran, "Sexual Ethics," p. 17.

CHAPTER II *(Church Reform)*

[1] Peter Hebblethwaite, *Pope John XXIII, Shepherd of the Modern World* (Garden City, New York: Doubleday, 1985). This is the best biography of Pope John XXIII, written sympathetically. The story of his election begins on p. 270.

[2] Ibid., Pope John XXIII, *Journey of a Soul* (New York: McGraw-Hill Book Company), p. 325.

[3] Lisa Sowle Cahill, "Current Teaching in Sexual Ethics," in *Readings in Moral Theology*, No. 8, ed. Charles E. Curran and Richard McCormick (New York: Paulist), p. 525.

[4] *The Modern Catholic Encyclopedia* (Collegeville, Minnesota: The Liturgical Press, A Michael Glazier Book), p. 425.

[5] Robert Blair Kaiser, *The Politics of Sex and Religion* (Kansas City, Mo.: Leaven Press, 1985), p. 60. The story of the discussion and politics involved in

efforts by some Catholics to change the church's stand on birth control during the 1960s is captured in this book, from which much of this account is taken.

[6] Ibid., p. 5.

[7] Ibid., p. 23.

[8] Ibid., p. 17.

[9] Peter Hebblethwaite, *The Year of Three Popes* (San Francisco: Collins Pub., 1978), p.vii.

[10] Kaiser, *The Politics of Sex and Religion,* p. 55.

[11] Robert McClory, *Turning Point* (New York: Crossroad), p. 63. The book offers a concise look at the development of the papal commission deliberations as seen through the eyes of a lay participant, Patty Crowley.

[12] Kaiser, *The Politics of Sex and Religion,* p, 93.

[13] Ibid.

[14] McClory, *The Turning Point,* p. 75.

[15] Ibid., p. 115.

[16] Tad Szulc, *Pope John Paul II, The Biography* (New York: Scribner, 1995), p. 255.

[17] Kaiser, *The Politics of Sex and Religion,* p. 180.

[18] Richard McBrien, *Catholicism* (HarperSanFrancisco, 1994), p. 982. The book provides a summary of the commission documents as well as the general pros and cons in the birth control debate.

[19] *National Catholic Reporter,* April 15, 1967.

CHAPTER III *(Birth Control)*

[1] Andrew M. Greeley, "Contraception: A Baby among Church's Sins," *National Catholic Reporter,* Oct. 15, 1993.

[2] J. T. Noonan Jr., *Contraception* (Cambridge, Mass.: Harvard University Press, 1986), pp. 400–17.

[3] Ibid.

[4] Pope Paul VI, *Humanae Vitae* (Rome: July 29, 1968), no. 11.

[5] Ibid., no. 12.

[6] Ibid., no. 16.

[7] Anthony Kosnik et al., *Human Sexuality, New Directions in American Catholic Thought* (New York: Paulist Press, 1977), p. 48.

[8] Ibid., p. 49.

[9] Andrew M. Greeley, "Looking Back on the Encyclical after 25 Years," *National Catholic Reporter,* Oct. 15, 1993.

[10] Robert Blair Kaiser, *The Politics of Sex and Religion* (Kansas City: Leaven Press, 1985), p. 211 ff. The story of Bishop James P. Shannon's reaction to *Humanae Vitae* is also documented in an unpublished history of the *National Catholic Reporter*

by Dr. Michael R. Real, "The *National Catholic Reporter:* Its Struggle for Influence and Survival."

[11] Ibid., p. 199.

[12] Ibid., p. 207.

[13] Peter Hebblethwaite, "Encyclical Insists Intercourse Is a Language of Love," *National Catholic Reporter,* July 16, 1993.

[14] Ibid.

[15] Kaiser, *Politics of Sex,* p. 194 ff. A good summary of dissenting voices.

[16] Charles Curran, "Encyclical Left Church Credibility Stillborn," *National Catholic Reporter,* July 16, 1993.

[17] *Readings in Moral Theology, No. 8,* "Statement by Catholic Theologians, Washington, D.C., July 30, 1968" (New York: Paulist Press, 1993), p. 135.

[18] Robert McClory, *Turning Point* (New York: Crossroad, 1995), p. 142.

[19] Bernard Häring, *My Witness for the Church* (New York: Paulist Press, 1992), pp. 80–81.

[20] Ibid.

[21] *Humanae Vitae,* no. 6.

CHAPTER IV *(Abortion)*

[1] Laurence H. Tribe, Abortion: *The Clash of Absolutes* (New York: W. W. Norton & Company, 1992), pp. 4-5. The litigant in the suit was Norma McCorvey, who, more than a decade later, admitted she had not been raped and had made up the story, having gotten "into trouble" in the more usual way.

[2] George Gallup, *The People's Religion: American Faith in the 90s* (Macmillan, 1989), pp. 176-79.

[3] Charles Curran, "Public Dissent in the Church," in *Abortion and Catholicism: The American Debate,* ed. Patricia Beattie Jung and Thomas A. Shannon (New York: Crossroad, 1988), pp. 301–19. This essay is a personal account of the hierarchy's moves against one moral theologian and is useful in understanding the issues involved.

[4] *Catechism of the Catholic Church* (Libreria Editrice Vaticana, 1994), United States Catholic Conference, Washington, D.C., p. 547.

[5] John T. Noonan Jr., *The Morality of Abortion: Legal and Historical Perspectives* (Cambridge, Mass., Harvard Univerity Press, 1970), p. 3.

[6] Ibid., p. 5.

[7] Ibid., p. 6.

[8] Ibid., p. 7.

[9] Ibid.

[10] Ibid., p. 9

[11] Ibid., p. 14
[12] Ibid., p. 17
[13] Ibid., p. 18.
[14] Augustine of Hippo, *On Exodus,* 21. 80.
[15] Noonan, *The Morality of Abortion,* p. 19.
[16] Ibid., p. 20.
[17] Ibid., p. 23.
[18] Ibid., p. 33.
[19] Ibid., p. 36.
[20] *Collectanea de prop. fide 1,* No. 282 (Rome, 1907), p. 92, as cited by Jane Hurst in "The History of Abortion in the Catholic Church: The Untold Story," a series published by Catholics For A Free Choice, Washingon, D.C.
[21] Noonan, *The Morality of Abortion,* p. 45.
[22] Ibid.
[23] Ibid.
[24] Jane Hurst in "The History of Abortion in the Catholic Church: The Untold Story," p. 21.
[25] *Catechism of the Catholic Church,* p. 548.
[26] Carol A. Tauer, "The Traditional Probablism and the Moral Status of the Early Embryo," in *Abortion and Catholicism: The American Debate,* ed. Patricia Beattie Jung and Thomas A Shannon (New York: Crossroad, 1988), p. 55.
[27] Ibid., p. 56.
[28] Ibid., p. 57.
[29] Thomas A. Shannon and Allan B. Wolter, "Reflections on the Moral Status of the Re-Embryo," *Theological Studies,* Vol. 51 (1990), p. 610.
[30] Ibid.
[31] Timothy A. Byrnes and Mary C. Segers, eds. *The Catholic Church and the Politics of Abortion: A View from the States* (Boulder, San Francisco: Westview Press 1992), p. 155.
[32] Ibid., p. 153.
[33] Ibid., p. 7.
[34] Noonan, *The Morality of Abortion,* p. 45.
[35] Byrnes and Segers, *The Catholic Church and the Politics of Abortion,* p. 152.
[36] *Abortion and Catholicism,* p. 11
[37] Ibid., p. 16.
[38] Timothy A. Byrnes, "How 'Seamless' a Garment? The Catholic Bishops and the Politics of Abortion," *Journal of Church and State,* vol. 33, Winter 1991. This is an insightful article that explains how the bishops handled abortion as a political issue in the 1970s and 1980s, and the consequences of those efforts.
[39] Ibid.

[40] *Origins,* Catholic News Service Documentary Service, Washington, D.C., Statement of Archbishop Joseph Bernardin, September 2, 1976.

[41] Byrnes, "How Seamless a Garment?" p. 22.

[42] *Origins,* September 20, 1984.

[43] Byrnes, "How Seamless a Garment?" p. 26.

[44] Ibid., p. 27.

[45] Ibid., p. 28.

[46] Garry Wills, "Mario Cuomo's Trouble with Abortion," *The New York Review of Books,* June 28, 1990, p. 9.

[47] Archbishop John R. Roach and Cardinal Terence Cooke, "Testimony in Support of the Hatch Amendment," in *Abortion and Catholicism: The American Debate,* ed. Patricia Beattie Jung and Thomas A Shannon (New York: Crossroad, 1988), p. 29.

[48] Byrnes and Segers, *The Catholic Church and the Politics of Abortion,* p. 156.

[49] Ibid., p. 157.

[50] Ibid., p. 7.

[51] Ibid., p. 141.

[52] Ibid.

[53] Ibid., p. 142.

[54] Mario Cuomo, "Religions Belief and Public Morality," in *Abortion and Catholicism: The American Debate,* ed. Patricia Beattie Jung and Thomas A. Shannon (New York: Crossroad, 1988), p. 202.

[55] Byrnes and Segers, *The Catholic Church and the Politics of Abortion,* p. 163.

[56] *Origins,* "USCC Presidential Candidate's Questionnaire," Oct. 29, 1992.

[57] Jim Davidson, "Generational Differences among Catholics Emerge," *National Catholic Reporter,* Oct. 8, 1993.

[58] Byrnes and Segers, *The Catholic Church and the Politics of Abortion,* p. 165.

[59] Cardinal Joseph Bernardin, "The Consistent Ethic: What Sort of Framework?" in *Abortion and Catholicism: The American Debate,* ed. Patricia Beattie Jung and Thomas A Shannon (New York: Crossroad, 1988), pp. 260–67.

CHAPTER V *(Homosexuality)*

[1] Robert Goss, *Jesus Acted Up: A Gay Manifesto* (HarperSanFrancisco, 1993), pp. 32-34.

[2] *Catechism of the Catholic Church* (Libreria Editrice Vaticana), 1994, pp. 2357-58.

[3] Anthony Kosnick et al., *Human Sexuality: New Directions in American Catholic Thought* (New York: Paulist Press, 1977), p. 188.

[4] Ibid.

[5] Jeannine Gramick, ed., *Homosexuality and the Catholic Church* (Mt. Rainier, Maryland: New Ways Ministry), p. 162.

[6] Robert Nugent and Jeannine Gramick, *Building Bridges* (Mystic, Conn., Twenty-Third Publications, 1992), p. 195. The chapter entitled "Postscript" contains a concise history of Nugent's and Gramick's work and birth of New Ways Ministry.

[7] Nugent and Gramick, *Building Bridges,* 139–145. Contains a discussion of the letter.

[8] Jeannine Gramick and Pat Furey (Pen name of Robert Nugent), eds., *The Vatican and Homosexuality* (New York: Crossroad, 1988), p. xiv.

[9] John J. McNeill, *The Church and the Homosexual* (Boston: Beacon Press, 1976, 1993), p. xiii.

[10] Ibid.

[11] Kosnick et. al. , *Human Sexuality,* p. 214.

[12] Gramick and Furley, *The Vatican and Homosexuality,* p. xiv.

[13] Ibid., p 48.

[14] Ibid., p. xv.

[15] Ibid.

[16] Ibid., p. xvii.

[17] Ibid. p. 1 ff.

[18] McNeill, *The Church and the Homosexual,* p. xiii.

[19] Ibid., p. xiv.

[20] Ibid., p. xv.

[21] Jeannine Gramick and Robert Nugent, eds., *Voices of Hope: Positive Catholic Writings about Gay and Lesbian Issues, 1973–1995* (New York: Center for Homophobia Education, 1995). Full text contained in appendix.

[22] Ibid. The book contains a series of statements reacting to the Vatican document.

[23] Ibid.

[24] Ibid.

[25] *National Catholic Reporter,* July 31, 1992, "Groups Threaten to Retaliate by 'Outing' Gay U.S. Bishops."

[26] Ed Jeannine Gramick and Robert Nugent, eds., *Voices of Hope: Positive Catholic Writings about Gay and Lesbian Issues, 1973–1995.* Detroit Auxiliary Bishop Thomas Gumbleton has been one of the United States' most outspoken bishops on gay and lesbian issues. Statements of support are contained in this book.

[27] "Bishops Buck Criticism, Attend Gay Symposium in Chicago," *National Catholic Reporter,* April 10, 1992.

[28] "AIDS: Its Victims Are This Century's Lepers," *National Catholic Reporter,* July 6, 1984.

[29] *National Catholic Reporter*, May 16, 1986 (news brief).

[30] "Diocesan Ministries Gear Up for AIDS Epidemic," *National Catholic Reporter*, Dec. 12, 1986.

[31] "Dilemma for Religious Orders; To Test or Not to Test for AIDS," *National Catholic Reporter*, Sept. 2, 1988.

[32] "Vatican Paper: Promoting Condom No Answer to AIDS," *National Catholic Reporter*, March 18, 1988.

CHAPTER VI *(Celibacy)*

[1] Jo Ann McNamara, *A New Song: Celibate Women in the First Three Christian Centuries* (New York: Harrington Park Press, 1985).

[2] "Psychiatrist: How Possible is Celibacy Today?," *National Catholic Reporter*, March 19, 1993.

[3] Raymond J. Gunzel, *Celibacy: Renewing the Gift, Releasing the Power* (Kansas City, Missouri: Sheed & Ward, 1988), pp. vi, vii.

[4] The 1990 study is based on information that comes from the following book: Dean R. Hoge, *The Future of Catholic Leadership: Responses to the Priest Shortage* (Kansas City: Sheed & Ward, 1987), p.126. "As a rough estimate the number of young Catholic men who would be seriously interested in the priesthood under conditions of optional celibacy would increase four-fold or more from the present level."

[5] "Fewer Priests, More Catholics," *National Catholic Reporter*, Nov. 5, 1993.

[6] Ibid.

[7] Ibid.

[8] Ibid.

[9] "Weakland Willing to Propose Married Priests," Ibid., Jan. 18, 1991.

[10] "Bishops Paralyzed over Heavily Gay Priesthood," Ibid., Nov. 10, 1989.

[11] "Gays in the Clergy," *Newsweek*, Feb. 23, 1987.

[12] Robert J. Schreiter, *The Schillebeeckx Reader* (New York: Crossroad, 1984), p. 234.

[13] Uta Ranke-Heinemann, *Eunuchs for the Kingdom of Heaven: Women, Sexuality and the Catholic Church* (Penguin, 1990), p. 106.

[14] Heinz-J. Vogels, *Celibacy: Gift or Law* (Kansas City, Missouri: Sheed & Ward, 1993), p. 99.

[15] Philip Hughes, *A History of the Church* (New York: Sheed & Ward, 1949) vol. 11, p. 191.

[16] Uta Ranke-Heinemann, *Eunuchs*, p. 108.

[17] Ibid., p. 100.

[18] Ibid., p. 28.

[19] Ibid., p. 110.

[20] Ibid., p. 114.

[21] Peter Hebblethwaite, *Paul VI, The First Modern Pope* (New York: Paulist Press, 1993), p. 441.

[22] Ibid., p. 442.

[23] Ibid., p. 495.

[24] Vogels, *Celibacy,* p. 9.

[25] "Clergy Sex-abuse 'Survivors' Break Silence," *National Catholic Reporter,* Oct. 30, 1992.

[26] Ibid.

[27] Ibid.

[28] "Sex and Power Issues Expand Clergy-Lay Rift," *National Catholic Reporter,* Nov. 13, 1992.

[29] Ibid.

[30] Ibid.

[31] "Meeting Was Grace-filled: 'We Both Sought Reconciliation,'" Ibid., Jan. 13, 1995.

[32] "As Nation Discusses Pedophilia, Even Pope Admits It's a Problem," Ibid., July 2, 1993.

[33] Eugene Kennedy, "The See-No-Evil Problem, Hear-No-Evil Problem, Speak-No-Evil Problem Problem," Ibid., March 19, 1993.

[34] "Pope Defends Celibacy as 'Gift to Church,'" Ibid., Nov. 19, 1992.

CHAPTER VII *(Women and the Church)*

[1] "Teresa Kane Stance Wins Support, But Not in Rome," *National Catholic Reporter,* Oct. 19, 1979.

[2] "'Fight Sexism, Paternalism in Church'—Kane," Ibid., Sept. 5, 1980.

[3] *Catechism of the Catholic Church* (Libreria Editrice Vaticana, 1994), United States Catholic Conference, p. 394.

[4] "Dear U.S. Bishops, You Insult Our Intelligence," *National Catholic Reporter,* May 18, 1990.

[5] Anne E. Carr, *Transforming Grace: Christian Tradition and Women's Experience* (HarperSanFrancisco, 1988).

[6] "'Proceed with Caution,' 1,000 Women Support Road to Ordination," *National Catholic Reporter,* Dec. 12, 1975.

[7] Dennis Michael Ferrara, "Representation or Self-Enfacement? The Axiom *In Persona Christi* in St. Thomas and the Magisterium," *Theological Studies,* June, 1994, p. 195.

[8] Jame R. Roberts, "Women Priests: Reflections on Papal Teaching and

Church Response," *Religious Studies,* Langara College, Vancouver, British Columbia, Sept., 1994. p. 4.

[9] Ibid., p. 5.

[10] Ibid., p. 6.

[11] Ibid.

[12] Ibid., p. 12.

[13] Ibid.

[14] Ari L. Goldman, *The New York Times,* June 19, 1992.

[15] "Women React in Anger and Pain," *National Catholic Reporter,* June 17, 1994.

[16] "Obedient Bishops Anticipate Women's Anger," Ibid., June 17, 1994.

[17] Ibid.

[18] Ibid.

[19] Ibid.

[20] "Experts: Not Much Definite About 'Definitive,'" Ibid.

[21] Ibid.

[22] Rosemary Radford Ruether, "Pope's Letter Ups Ante on Ordaining Women," *National Catholic Reporter,* July 1, 1994.

[23] Carr, *Transforming Grace,* p 11.

[24] Ibid., p. 12.

[25] Ibid., p. 7.

[26] Uta Ranke-Heinemann, *Eunuchs for the Kingdom of Heaven: Women, Sexuality and the Catholic Church* (NewYork: Penguin Books, 1990), p. 21.

[27] Carr, *Transforming Grace,* p. 7.

[28] Ranke-Heinemann, *Eunuchs,* p. 183 ff.

[29] Elisabeth Schussler Fiorenza, *Discipleship of Equals: A Critical Feminist Ekklesia-logy of Liberation* (New York: Crossroad, 1993), p. 62.

[30] Ibid., p. 51.

[31] Ibid., p. 275.

[32] Carr, *Transforming Grace,* p. 21.

[33] Miriam Therese Winter, *Defecting in Place: Women Claiming Responsibility for Their Own Spiritual Lives* (New York: Crossroad, 1994), p. 241.

[34] Ibid., p. 242.

[35] Sallie McFague, *The Body of God: An Ecological Theology* (Minneapolis: Fortress Press, 1993).

[36] "Thinking of Universe as the Body of God," *National Catholic Reporter,* Mar. 25, 1994.

[37] Ibid., July 1, 1994.

[38] *Catechism of the Catholic Church* (Libreria Editrice Vaticana: 1994) p.7.

[39] "Some Want a Showdown on Language Issue," *National Catholic Reporter,* Nov. 18, 1994; and "Catholics Want Solidarity With Their Bishops," *National*

Catholic Reporter, Nov. 11, 1994.

[40] Winter, *Defecting in Place*, p. 101.

[41] Ibid., p. 112.

[42] Benedictine Sister Joan Chittister, *National Catholic Reporter*, July 5, 1991.

[43] *Origins*, Oct. 6, 1988, John Paul II, Mulieres Dignatatem, "On the Dignity and Vocation of Women."

[44] Ibid.

[45] "Women's Pastoral Called into Question in Rome," *National Catholic Reporter*, June 7, 1991.

[46] Ibid., June 7, 1991.

[47] "Bishops' Pastoral on Women: Good, Bad or Irrelevant," Ibid., Apr. 24, 1992.

[48] "Pope's Easter Letter to Priests Stresses Women," Ibid. Apr. 21, 1995.

[49] Ibid.

[50] Ibid.

[51] "Jesuits Set 21st Century Justice Course," Ibid., Apr. 7, 1995.

Chapter VIII *(Carnal Love)*

[1] Richard Rohr, *Quest for the Grail* (New York: Crossroad, 1994), p.166. The story was originally told at a Rohr-directed retreat. This book is an edited transcription of the retreat, put to words by Michael J. Farrell.

[2] Thomas Aquinas, *Summa Theologiae* ll-ll, q. 152. a. 1.

[3] Richard McBrien, *Catholicism* (HarperSanFrancisco, 1994), p. 560.

[4] Rohr, *Quest for the Grail*, p. 162.

[5] Carl Koch, *Creating a Christian Lifestyle* (Winona, Minn.: Saint Mary's Press, 1988), p. 252.

[6] Michael Barnes, *An Ecology of the Spirit: Religious Reflection and Environmental Consciousness* (New York: University Press of America, 1994), p. 169.

[7] Uta Ranke-Heinemann, *Eunuchs for the Kingdom of Heaven: Women, Sexuality and the Catholic Church* (New York: Penguin Books, 1991), p. 198.

[8] *Catechism of the Catholic Church* (Libreria Editrice Vaticana, 1994), 2352.

[9] Rohr, *Quest for the Grail*, p. 162.

[10] Thomas Berry, *The Dream of the Earth* (San Francisco: Sierra Club Books, 1988).

[11] "A New Story of Creation, It's the Season for a Theology of Ecology," *Newsweek*, June 5, 1989.

[12] Anne Lonergan and Caroline Richard, eds., *Thomas Berry and the New Cosmology* (Mystic, Connecticut: Twenty-Third Publications, 1990), p. 73.

[13] Matthew Fox, *Creation Spirituality* (HarperSanFrancisco, 1991), p. 27.

[14] Ibid., p. 37

[15] Barnes, *An Ecology of Spirit*, p. 66.

[16] Ibid., p. 75 ff., J. Patout Burns, professor in the Department of Religion at the University of Florida, in a speech, rebutted Fox's main theological premises.

[17] Andre Guindon, *The Sexual Creators: An Ethical Proposal for Concerned Christians* (Lanham, New York, London: University Press of America, 1986).

[18] Demetria Martinez, "Eroticism: Reconnecting Faith and Flesh for God's Sake and Ours Also," *National Catholic Reporter*, Mar. 22, 1991.

[19] "The Resilient Father Andrew Greeley," Ibid., April 30, 1982.

[20] Ibid., Jan. 25, 1991; and in Andrew Greeley, *Sex and the Catholic Experience* (Allen, Texas: Thomas More, 1994), p. 75.

[21] Ibid., p. 79.

[22] Ibid., p. 26.

[23] Ibid., p. 161

[24] James B. Nelson, *Body Theology* (Louisville, Kentucky: Westminster/John Knox Press, 1992), p. 9.

[25] Ibid.

[26] Jeffrey S. Siker, ed., *Homosexuality in the Church, Both Sides of the Debate* (Louisville, Kentucky: Westminster/John Knox Press, 1994).

[27] Siker, *Homosexuality in the Church.*

CHAPTER IX *(Population)*

[1] "Vatican OKs Most of U.N. Document after Cairo Tactics Stir Bitterness," *National Catholic Reporter*, Sept. 23, 1994.

[2] "Family Planners' Accord: Urgency, Vatican-Catholics; First-Third World Viewpoints Diverge," Ibid., Aug. 17, 1984.

[3] Ibid.

[4] "Vatican Attacks Set Stage for Cairo Meeting," Ibid., Sept. 9, 1994.

[5] "Vatican Builds to Showdown at Cairo Meeting," Ibid., July 15, 1994.

[6] Ibid.

[7] Ibid.

[8] Ibid.

[9] Ibid.

[10] "Rome Chides Gore, Approaches Libya, Iran," Ibid., Sept. 9, 1994.

[11] "Vatican OKs Most of U. N. Document after Cairo Tactics Stir Bitterness," Ibid., Sept. 23, 1994.

[12] "Vatican's Vaunted Diplomacy a No-Show," Ibid., Oct. 7, 1994.

[13] "Vatican Attacks Set Stage for Cairo Meeting," Ibid., Sept. 9, 1994.

[14] "Vatican OKs Most of U. N. Document after Cairo Tactics Stir Bitterness,"

Ibid., Sept. 23, 1994.

[15] Repartee section, Ibid., July 31, 1992.

[16] Ibid.

[17] "Rome's Birth-Control Conceptions Flunk Real-World Test," *National Catholic Reporter*, Sept. 4, 1992.

[18] Ibid.

[19] Ibid.

[20] "Vatican OKs Most of U.N. Document after Cairo Tactics Stir Bitterness," Ibid., Sept. 23, 1994.

CHAPTER X *(Sex and Authority)*

[1] Andrew Greeley, William C. McCready, and Kathleen McCourt, *Catholic Schools in a Declining Church* (Kansas City, Missouri: Sheed &Ward, 1976), p. 313.

[2] Peter Hebblethwaite, "Pope Soldiers On, Carries Weight of Seven Decades," *National Catholic Reporter*, Oct. 22, 1993.

[3] Ibid.

[4] "Vatican's Vaunted Diplomacy a No-Show," Ibid., Oct. 7, 1994.

[5] "Veritatis Splendor: Forward Into the Past," Ibid.

[6] Bernard Häring, "Encyclical's One Aim: Assent and Submission," Ibid., Nov. 5, 1993.

[7] "Pope's 'Culture of Death' Assessment Gets Agreement, With Reservations," Ibid., Apr. 14, 1995.

[8] Ibid.

[9] Charles Curran, "Encyclical is Positive, Problematic," Ibid., Apr. 14, 1995.

[10] Lisa Sowle Cahill, "Catholic Sexual Teaching: Context, Function, and Authority," in *Vatican Authority and American Catholic Dissent, The Curran Case And Its Consequences*, ed. William W. May (New York: Crossroad, 1987), p. 199. In this essay the author outlines current conflicts in Catholic moral theology and the ecclesial and social context in which these conflicts have occurred. p. 187 ff.

[11] William May, *Vatican Authority and American Catholic Dissent* (New York: Crossroads Publishers, 1987), p. 9.

[12] Bernard Cooke, "Renewal of Papacy Will Transform Church," *National Catholic Reporter*, Feb. 24, 1995; "Papal Pomp Contrasts with Simplicity of Jesus," Mar. 3, 1995; "God-with-Us Calls for New Type of Papacy," Mar. 10, 1995. In a three-part series, Bernard Cooke examines the modern papacy. Also, "Jesuits Set 21st Century Justice Course," Ibid., Apr. 7, 1995.

[13] Bernard Häring, "Encyclical's One Aim: Assent and Submission," Ibid., Nov. 5, 1993.

[14] Ibid., Feb. 24, Mar. 3, Mar. 10, 1995.

[15] Hans Küng, *Infallible? An Unresolved Enquiry* (New York: Continuum Books, 1995).

[16] *National Catholic Reporter*, Feb. 24, Mar. 3, Mar. 10, 1995.

[17] Ibid.

[18] "U.S. Catholicism: Trends in the '90s," Ibid., Oct. 8, 1993.

[19] Richard A McCormick, "Commentary on the Declaration on Certain Questions Concerning Sexual Ethics," in *Readings in Moral Theology No. 8, Dialogue about Catholic Sexual Teaching,* ed. Charles E. Curran and Richard A. McCormick (New York: Paulist Press, 1993), p. 570.

CHAPTER XI *(Theology and the Future)*

[1] John Mahoney, *The Making of Moral Theology,* (Oxford: Clarendon Press, 1989), p. 341.

[2] Charles E. Curran in "Official Catholic Social and Sexual Teachings: A Methodological Comparison," *Readings in Moral Theology No. 8, Dialogue about Catholic Sexual Teachings,* ed. Charles E. Curran and Richard A. McCormick (New York: Paulist Press, 1993), p. 536.

[3] Ibid.

[4] "Sr. McEnroy Dismissed from St. Meinrad," *National Catholic Reporter,* May 5, 1995.

[5] "Pastoral Consitution on the Church in the Modern World," no. 33, in *The Documents of Vatican II,* ed. Walter Abbott and Joseph Gallagher (New York: Associated Press, 1966).

[6] Ibid., no. 62.

[7] Richard P. McBrien, *Catholicism* (HarperSanFrancisco, 1994), p. 670.

[8] John Mahoney, *The Making of Moral Theology, A Study of the Roman Catholic Tradition* (Oxford, Clarendon Paperbacks, 1989), p. 329.

[9] Andrew Greeley, *Catholic Schools in a Declining Church* (Kansas City: Sheed & Ward, 1976), p. 129.

[10] McBrien, *Catholicism,* p. 938.

[11] Lisa Sowle, "Sexuality and Christian Ethics: How to Proceed," in *Sexuality and the Sacred, Sources for Theological Reflection,* ed. James B. Nelson and Sandra P. Longfellow (Louisville, Kentucky: Westminster/John Knox Press, 1994), p. 26.

[12] McBrien, *Catholicism,* p. 938.

[13] Anthony Kosnik et al., *Human Sexuality, New Directions in American Catholic Thought* (New York: Paulist Press), p. 95.

[14] Fran Ferder and John Heagle, *Your Sexual Self: Pathway to Authentic Intimacy* (Notre Dame, Indiana: Ave Maria Press, 1992), p. 131 ff.

Index